Personal Taxation 2007/08

NVQ Accounting Unit 19
AAT Diploma Pathway Unit 19

for June and December 2008 examinations

Aubrey Penning

Bob Thomas

osborne
BOOKS

Published by Osborne Books Limited
Unit 1B Everoak Estate
Bromyard Road
Worcester WR2 5HP
Tel 01905 748071
Email books@osbornebooks.co.uk
Website www.osbornebooks.co.uk

Design by Richard Holt
Cover image from Getty Images

Printed by CPI Antony Rowe Limited, Chippenham

British Library Cataloguing in Publication Data
A catalogue record for this book is available from the British Library

ISBN 978 1905777 129

Contents

Please note that the seven chapters and subsequent sections of the book each have a self-contained numbering system, rather than the traditional form of pagination which runs through the book.

Acknowledgments

The author wishes to thank the following for their help with the editing and production of the book: Mike Fardon, Mike Gilbert, Rosemarie Griffiths and Claire McCarthy.

The publisher is indebted to the Association of Accounting Technicians for its generous help and advice to its authors and editors during the preparation of this text, and for permission to reproduce extracts from the relevant Accounting Standards.

The publisher would also like to thank HM Revenue & Customs for its help, advice and kind permission to reproduce tax forms obtained from www.hmrc.gov.uk

Author and Technical Editor

Aubrey Penning, the author, co-ordinates the AAT courses at Worcester College of Technology, and teaches a range of units including Units 8 and 9 and the two taxation Units. He has over twenty years experience of teaching accountancy on a variety of courses in Worcester and Gwent. He is a Certified Accountant, and before his move into full-time teaching he worked for the health service, a housing association and a chemical supplier. Aubrey is co-author of *Managing Performance & Resources Tutorial* and *Cash Management & Credit Control* from Osborne Books.

Bob Thomas, the Technical Editor of this book, has been involved with the Education and Training activities of the AAT since 1986, including the development and piloting of the current scheme. He is an external verifier, a simulation writer, a moderator and a contributor at workshops, training days, conferences and master classes. He is a member of the Learning and Development Board and Chairman of the Assessment Panel.

Introduction

Personal Taxation 2007/08 has been written to provide a study resource for students taking courses based on NVQ Level 4 and Diploma Pathway Unit 19 'Preparing Personal Taxation Computations'.

Exams, Finance Acts and tax years

Forthcoming examinations for Unit 19 assessed by the AAT will be based on the following Finance Act and tax year:

Examinations in June and December 2008   Finance Act 2007   Tax Year 2007/08

This book has been designed to include guidance and exercises based on this tax year, and is therefore suitable for study towards either of the two examination sittings stated above. Those wishing to sit the examination in December 2007 should use the previous version of this book, *Personal Taxation 2006/07* (ISBN 978 1 905777 09 9), which uses data based on the tax year 2006/07. Please call 01905 748071 for details.

using the book

The text includes chapters that are designed to be progressive, so that issues covered in earlier chapters are referred to and applied in later chapters. The authors believe that this approach will lead to readers building up a solid understanding as they progress through the book. Note that the pagination of each chapter is self-contained, eg Chapter 1 contains pages 1.0 to 1.21.

At the end of each chapter there are student activities to reinforce the work studied. The solutions to some of these activities are contained in this book, while some are contained in the *Personal Taxation Tutor Pack* that is available to colleges and independent studiers.

examination practice papers

In addition to the five chapters on income tax and two chapters on capital gains tax, there are 8 'half-papers' in examination style for practice use. Four of these reflect the possible content of Section One of an AAT examination, and four are based on Section Two content. The Section One half-papers can be tackled after Chapters 1 to 5 have been studied, while the others require familiarity with the content of all the chapters.

There are also two full practice papers, together with the updated specimen paper that is published with kind permission of the AAT. The half-papers can also be linked together to provide additional practice of sitting a full paper. Recent examination papers, answers and examiners' comments are available on the AAT website.

Osborne Tutor Packs

The answers to selected Chapter Activities and all the Examination tasks in this text are set out in a separate *Personal Taxation 2007/08 Tutor Pack*, available to tutors and to students who have the permission of their tutors to have access to the answers. Please contact the Osborne Books Sales Office on 01905 748071 or visit the website for details of how to obtain the Tutor Pack.

INCOME TAX

Personal allowance

£5,225

Tax rates

	starting rate	basic rate	higher rate
General Income	10%	22%	40%
Savings Income	10%	20%	40%
Dividend Income	10%	10%	32.5%

Tax bands

	£
Starting rate	0 – 2,230
Basic rate	2,231 – 34,600
Higher rate	over 34,600

Company Car Benefit

% of List Price*	g/km
15%	140 (or less)
16%	145
17%	150

. . . and so on to a maximum of 35%

*add 3% for diesel (to a maximum of 35%)

Company Car Fuel Benefit

Percentage for car (see company car benefit above) x £14,400

Authorised Mileage Rates

Cars and vans	First 10,000 miles in tax year	40p per mile
	Additional mileage	25p per mile
Motor cycles		24p per mile
Bicycles		20p per mile

CAPITAL GAINS TAX

Annual Exempt Amount
£9,200

CGT rates

	starting rate	basic rate	higher rate
Gains	10%	20%	40%

Taper Relief – Non-Business Assets

Number of complete years	% chargeable
0	100
1	100
2	100
3	95
4	90
5	85
6	80
7	75
8	70
9	65
10 or more	60

Retail Price Index
Please see next page.

retail price index (for indexation allowance)

Note: the index figures with a grey background will not be needed.

	Jan	Feb	Mar	Apr	May	Jun	Jul	Aug	Sept	Oct	Nov	Dec
2001	171.1	172.0	172.2	173.1	174.2	174.4	173.3	174.0	174.6	174.3	173.6	173.4
2000	166.6	167.5	168.4	170.1	170.7	171.1	170.5	170.5	171.7	171.6	172.1	172.2
1999	163.4	163.7	164.1	165.2	165.6	165.6	165.1	165.5	166.2	166.5	166.7	167.3
1998	159.5	160.3	160.8	162.6	163.5	163.4	163.0	163.7	164.4	164.5	164.4	164.4
1997	154.4	155.0	155.4	156.3	156.9	157.5	157.5	158.5	159.3	159.5	159.6	160.0
1996	150.2	150.9	151.5	152.6	152.9	153.0	152.4	153.1	153.8	153.8	153.9	154.4
1995	146.0	146.9	147.5	149.0	149.6	149.8	149.1	149.9	150.6	149.8	149.8	150.7
1994	141.3	142.1	142.5	144.2	144.7	144.7	144.0	144.7	145.0	145.2	145.3	146.0
1993	137.9	138.8	139.3	140.6	141.1	141.0	140.7	141.3	141.9	141.8	141.6	141.9
1992	135.6	136.3	136.7	138.8	139.3	139.3	138.8	138.9	139.4	139.9	139.7	139.2
1991	130.2	130.9	131.4	133.1	133.5	134.1	133.8	134.1	134.6	135.1	135.6	135.7
1990	119.50	120.20	121.40	125.10	126.20	126.70	126.80	128.10	129.30	130.30	130.00	129.90
1989	111.00	111.80	112.30	114.30	115.00	115.40	115.50	115.80	116.60	117.50	118.50	118.80
1988	103.30	103.70	104.10	105.80	106.20	106.60	106.70	107.90	108.40	109.50	110.00	110.30
1987	100.00	100.40	100.60	101.80	101.90	101.90	101.80	102.10	102.40	102.90	103.40	103.30
1986	96.25	96.60	96.73	97.67	97.85	97.79	97.52	97.82	98.30	98.45	99.29	99.62
1985	91.20	91.94	92.80	94.78	95.21	95.41	95.23	95.49	95.44	95.59	95.92	96.05
1984	86.84	87.20	87.48	88.64	88.97	89.20	89.10	89.94	90.11	90.67	90.95	90.87
1983	82.61	82.97	83.12	84.28	84.64	84.84	85.30	85.68	86.06	86.36	86.67	86.89
1982	78.73	78.76	79.44	81.04	81.62	81.85	81.88	81.90	81.85	82.26	82.66	82.51

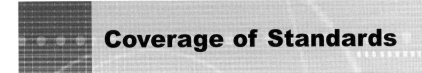

Coverage of Standards

UNIT 19: PREPARING PERSONAL TAXATION COMPUTATIONS

This unit is about preparing tax computations and returns for individuals. It is concerned with the Income Tax and Capital Gains tax liability of employed individuals, and also of self-employed individuals excluding any calculation of their business income. There are four elements in this unit.

The **first element** requires you to calculate income from employment, including benefits in kind.

In the **second element** you must calculate property and investment income and show that you apply deductions and reliefs and claim loss set-offs.

The **third element** is concerned with preparing Income Tax computations, based on your calculations of the client's earned and unearned income.

The **fourth element** requires you to prepare Capital Gains Tax computations. As well as calculating chargeable gains and losses, you need to show that you apply reliefs and exemptions correctly.

Throughout the unit you must show that you take account of current tax law and HM Revenue & Customs practice and make submissions within statutory timescales. You also need to show that you consult with HM Revenue & Customs in an open and constructive manner, give timely and constructive advice to clients and maintain client confidentiality.

Please note that the Performance Criteria quoted throughout the book still refer to the Inland Revenue which is now HM Revenue & Customs.

Element 19.1
Calculate income from employment

Performance Criteria

		chapter
A	Prepare accurate computations of emoluments, including benefits in kind	4
B	List allowable expenses and deductions	4
C	Record relevant details of income from employment accurately and legibly in the tax return	4
D	Make computations and submissions in accordance with current tax law and take account of current Inland Revenue practice	4
E	Consult with Inland Revenue staff in an open and constructive manner	1
F	Give timely and constructive advice to clients on the recording of information relevant to tax returns	1,4
G	Maintain client confidentiality at all times	1

Element 19.2:
Calculate property and investment income

Performance Criteria

		chapter
A	Prepare schedules of dividends and interest received on shares and securities	3
B	Prepare schedules of property income and determine profits and losses	2
C	Prepare schedules of investment income from other sources	3
D	Apply deductions and reliefs and claim loss set-offs	2
E	Record relevant details of property and investment income accurately and legibly in the tax return	2,3
F	Make computations and submissions in accordance with current tax law and take account of current Inland Revenue practice	2,3
G	Consult with Inland Revenue staff in an open and constructive manner	1
H	Give timely and constructive advice to clients on the recording of information relevant to tax returns	1,2,3
I	Maintain client confidentiality at all times	1

Element 19.3:
Prepare Income Tax computations

Performance Criteria

		chapter
A	List general income, savings income and dividend income and check for completeness	5
B	Calculate and deduct charges and personal allowances	5
C	Calculate Income Tax payable	5
D	Record income and payments legibly and accurately in the tax return	5
E	Make computations and submissions in accordance with current tax law and take account of current Inland Revenue practice	5
F	Consult with Inland Revenue staff in an open and constructive manner	1
G	Give timely and constructive advice to clients on the recording of information relevant to tax returns	1
H	Maintain client confidentiality at all times	1

Element 19.4:
Prepare Capital Gains Tax computations

Performance Criteria

		chapter
A	Identify and value disposed-of chargeable personal assets	6,7
B	Identify shares disposed of by individuals	7
C	Calculate chargeable gains and allowable losses	6,7
D	Apply reliefs and exemptions correctly	6,7
E	Calculate Capital Gains Tax payable	6,7
F	Record relevant details of gains and the Capital Gains Tax payable legibly and accurately in the tax return	7
G	Make computations and submissions in accordance with current tax law and take account of current Inland Revenue practice	6,7
H	Consult with Inland Revenue staff in an open and constructive manner	1
I	Give timely and constructive advice to clients on the recording of information relevant to tax returns	1,7
J	Maintain client confidentiality at all times	1

1 Introduction to income tax

In this chapter we provide a brief review of the UK tax system and an introduction to the income tax computation.

The chapter explains:

- how income is divided up for tax purposes
- how income tax is calculated
- how an individual's tax return works
- exempt income
- when an individual has to pay income tax
- the duties and responsibilities of a tax practitioner

PERFORMANCE CRITERIA COVERED

This chapter introduces the background to personal taxation, and covers some of the underpinning knowledge that is common to all four elements in Unit 19. In addition it covers the following performance criteria that are also common to each of these elements:

- consult with Inland Revenue staff in an open and constructive manner
- give timely and constructive advice to clients on the recording of information relevant to tax returns
- maintain client confidentiality at all times

A REVIEW OF THE UK TAX SYSTEM

When the word 'tax' is mentioned most people probably think of income tax (if they can bear to think of tax at all). Income tax is only one of the forms of taxation that is used to collect money for use by the UK government, but it does impact on a large proportion of the UK population.

In the first part of this book we will be examining how income tax works, and how we can calculate how much income tax individuals should pay. In the second part of the book we will be looking at how capital gains tax can affect individuals if they dispose of certain personal assets. We will also learn how to complete the tax returns for these taxes.

In the unit 'Preparing Personal Taxation Computations' we deal only with income tax and capital gains tax, and therefore we will be ignoring other taxes such as value added tax, corporation tax, and inheritance tax. National insurance contributions are also outside the scope of this unit.

We will now look at some of the background to the way that the tax system works, before going on to see how the numerical tax calculations work.

HM Revenue & Customs

Income tax and capital gains tax are both administered by the new government department, formed by the amalgamation of the Inland Revenue and HM Customs & Excise. HM Revenue & Customs contains the following three parts:

- **taxpayer service offices** are the main offices that the taxpayer deals with, and handle much of the basic income tax assessment and collection functions
- **taxpayer district offices** deal with more complex income tax issues
- **tax enquiry centres** deal with enquiries and provide forms and leaflets to taxpayers

These three functions are located in offices throughout the UK. In smaller centres some functions may be combined into one office, while in larger towns and cities they may be located separately.

the law governing tax

The authority to impose taxes comes from two sources. The first is legislation passed by parliament, known as 'statute law'. You may have heard of the 'Finance Acts'. These are generally published each year and give details of any changes to taxes. These changes will have been proposed by the Chancellor of the Exchequer (usually in 'the budget') and passed by Parliament. In this book we will be using information from the Finance Act 2007, which relates to the tax year 2007/08. We will see exactly what is meant by tax years later in this chapter.

There are also other statute laws that were designed to create frameworks for the way that certain taxes work that continue to be relevant.

The second source of tax law is called 'case law', and arises from decisions taken in court cases. Taxation can be very complicated, and sometimes disagreements between HM Revenue & Customs and taxpayers result in court cases. The final outcome of such cases can then become 'case law' and influence future interpretation of statute law.

Although there is a substantial amount of both statute law and case law that governs the UK tax system, this book will try to keep references to specific law to a minimum. While it will be important to know the rules that apply to certain situations, you will not be required to quote from the legislation in your examination.

information available from HM Revenue & Customs

In addition to the tax law outlined above, there are interpretations and explanations of various issues that are published by HM Revenue & Customs. The main ones are as follows:

- extra-statutory concessions are issued by HM Revenue & Customs when they agree to impose a less strict interpretation of the law than would otherwise apply in particular circumstances
- HM Revenue & Customs statements of practice are public announcements of how the HMRC interpret specific rules
- Guides and Help Sheets are issued to help taxpayers complete the necessary return forms and calculate their tax

A large array of publications and forms can be downloaded from the HM Revenue & Customs website at www.hmrc.gov.uk. It also provides data on rates and allowances for a range of tax years. You will find it useful to have a look at what is available on this site when you have an opportunity. It will also mean that you can obtain copies of tax returns to practice on when you reach that part of your personal tax studies. The HM Revenue & Customs website can also be accessed via a link from the Osborne Books Limited website at www.osbornebooks.co.uk

AN INTRODUCTION TO INCOME TAX COMPUTATION

An outline of an income tax computation is as follows:

	£
Income – both earnings and income from savings	X
Less: Personal allowance	(X)
Taxable Income	X
Tax payable on taxable income	X

A very simple income tax computation could be as follows:

	£
Income	6,000
Less: Personal Allowance	5,225
Taxable income	775
Tax payable at 10%	77

Later in this chapter we will deal with income tax computations in more detail, but first we will consider some of the issues that might arise in computing income tax.

HOW INCOME IS DIVIDED UP FOR TAX PURPOSES

The income that an individual generates is divided into categories, depending on what sort of income it is and where it comes from. These categories were previously called '**schedules**'. The categories are now simply named after the type of income that they include. This is done so that:

- the correct rules on how to work out the income are used (since these vary with the categories), and
- the correct rates of tax are used (since they can also depend on the type of income).

the main categories of income

'Property Income'	Rental income from land and property.
'Trading Income'	Profits of trades and professions (the self-employed and those in partnership).
'Savings & Investment Income'	UK Interest and UK Dividends.
'Employment, pension and Social Security Income'	Income from employment etc. Income tax is deducted from employment income under the system known as Pay-As-You-Earn (PAYE).

This list and descriptions have been simplified to include only the types of income that you need to know about. It does not include, for example, the categories that relate to overseas income.

tax years

For income tax purposes time is divided into 'tax years' (sometimes called 'fiscal years'). Individuals' income and income tax is worked out separately for each tax year. The tax year runs from 6 April in one calendar year to 5 April in the next calendar year. The tax year running from 6/4/07 to 5/4/08 would be described as the tax year 2007/08.

basis of assessment

As mentioned earlier, the income under each category will have different rules that determine how the income is worked out for tax purposes. The most important of these rules is known as the 'basis of assessment', and this simply considers whether the income assessable is the actual income *receivable* or the income *received* in the tax year itself. Later in the book we will look in more detail at the rules that govern each type of income. Here is a list of the main assessment rules for each category of income, with some comments about coverage in this book.

Property Income	**Rental income (after deducting allowable expenses), for the tax year, calculated on an *accruals* basis.** We will look in more detail at rental income in Chapter 2.
Trading Income	**Profits on an *accruals* basis (after deducting allowable expenses) for the accounting year that ends in the tax year.** In this unit we only need to be aware that profits of the self-employed are included in the income tax calculations of individuals. The calculation of the profit for trading income is dealt with in the Business Taxation unit.
Savings and Investment Income	**Gross interest *received* in the tax year.** **Amounts of dividends *received* in the tax year, plus the related tax credits.** We will look in more detail at interest received and dividends in Chapter 3.

Employment, pension and Social Security Income	Amounts *received* in the tax year from employment etc, plus the value of any benefits, less any allowable deductions.
	We will examine employment income in detail in Chapter 4.

HOW INCOME TAX IS CALCULATED

As already stated, income tax is usually worked out by using an 'income tax computation' for a specific tax year. This is a calculation that simply brings together the amounts of income from the various categories that apply to the individual and shows the workings for the tax that is payable. It is important that you are able to calculate an individual's income tax, so you will need to learn the basic computation structure and practice plenty of examples. The computation can be understood quite easily if we think of it as divided into three main parts.

1 The first part collects together and adds up the income from the different categories that are relevant. It is also a good idea to note in the computation any tax that has already been paid or deducted from each of these income sources, so that we can account for it later on. In complicated situations it will be necessary to calculate the income under each of the categories separately before the main computation is attempted.

2 The second part of the computation is where personal allowances are deducted from the total income from the first section. Every individual has a personal allowance for each tax year. This represents the tax-free portion of their income for that year. The final figure that results from this section is known as the 'taxable income'.

3 The third part of the computation is where the taxable income from the previous part is used to calculate the amount of income tax. This is carried out using 'tax bands' and the percentage income tax rates that apply to each band. The total tax from this calculation is then compared with the amount already paid to arrive at the amount still owing to HM Revenue & Customs (or to the taxpayer).

Throughout this book we will use the allowances and tax bands relating to 2007/08. Whatever tax year is used, the principles and process are the same.

Full details of allowances and tax bands can be found at the beginning of this book. The majority of this data will also be provided in your examination.

personal allowance

The basic personal allowance is £5,225 for 2007/08. This is the amount that an individual's income can amount to in the tax year before they start paying income tax. It is always deducted from total income in the computation before the tax is calculated. There are different allowances for those aged 65 and over.

tax bands

The tax bands apply to an individual's taxable income – their total income for the year after the personal allowance has been deducted. The tax is calculated by multiplying the percentage shown by the income that falls into each band. This is done by starting with the lowest band and working up as far as necessary. Although the tax rates have been the same for a few years, the bands vary slightly from year to year. The 2007/08 rates and bands are shown here:

Tax Bands for tax year 2007/08 – General Income	
Rate	*Taxable Income*
10%	up to £2,230
22%	over £2,230, up to £34,600 (ie the next £32,370)
40%	over £34,600

Note that there are other tax rates for savings and investment income (interest and dividends) – we will look at these later in the book.

This diagram shows how it works:

So, for example, if an individual had taxable genera
their personal allowance) of £10,000 in 2007/08, th

£ 2,230 x 10%	=	£223.00	(using up th
£ 7,770 x 22%	=	£1,709.40	(using part o
Total income tax		£1,932.40	

Remember that 'income' can include not only earnings from a job but also other forms of income.

The total income tax relating to a tax year is often referred to as the 'Income Tax Liability'. We will now use a Case Study to show the full process for a simple tax computation.

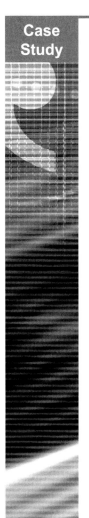

Case Study

SHELLEY BEECH:
BASIC INCOME TAX COMPUTATION

Shelley Beech works as an employee for a recruitment company. In 2007/08 she received £35,000 in income from this job, before her employer deducted £6,283 in income tax through PAYE.

She also received rent from the house that she had originally been left by her grandfather. The taxable amount of rent for 2007/08 has already been worked out as £9,500, but she hasn't paid any income tax on this yet.

Shelley is entitled to the basic personal allowance of £5,225 for the tax year 2007/08.

required

Using an income tax computation, calculate the total income tax that Shelley is liable to pay for the tax year 2007/08, and how much of this amount has not yet been paid.

solution

Following the format discussed earlier, we can produce an income tax computation as follows:

Shelley Beech – Income Tax Computation for 2007/08

	£	£
		Tax Paid
Employment Income	35,000	6,283
Property Income (rent)	9,500	-
Total Income	44,500	6,283
Less Personal Allowance	5,225	
Taxable Income	39,275	

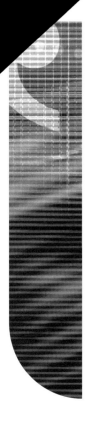

Income Tax Calculation:

£2,230 x 10%		223.00
£32,370 x 22%		7,121.40
£4,675 x 40%		1,870.00
£39,275	Total Income tax	9,214.40
	Less already paid	6,283.00
	Income tax to pay	2,931.40

To understand the above computation, you should note the following:

- The tax deducted at source is noted in the column on the right. The total of this column is then used in the final calculation to work out how much of the total tax is still unpaid.

- In this Case Study the taxable income of £39,275 is more than the £34,600 that forms the upper point of the 22% tax band. This means that the entire 22% band is used (£34,600 - £2,230 = £32,370), as well as some of the 40% band.

- The amount of taxable income to be taxed at 40% is calculated by deducting the amounts charged at other rates from the taxable income (£39,275 - £2,230 - £32,370 = £4,675). It is equal to the amount by which the taxable income exceeds £34,600.

HOW AN INDIVIDUAL'S TAX RETURN WORKS

The Tax Return is a document used by HM Revenue & Customs to collect information about an individual's income and capital gains. It is not sent out to every taxpayer – those who have uncomplicated income may never receive the form. This is because the mechanisms of Pay-As-You-Earn and other deductions of tax at source can often deal with these situations.

The types of situation that we are going to be studying are ones where the tax position is a little more complicated. These individuals may have income from several sources (perhaps including self-employed income, and/or income from rent), and may involve paying tax at the higher rate. Because HM Revenue & Customs will need to know all these individual's income details, a tax return must be completed. The current tax return operates under the 'self-assessment' system, whereby an individual declares his/her income and gains, and has the option of calculating his/her own tax. The tax return form therefore has the purposes of both itemising the income, and recording the amount of tax due.

structure of the tax return

Because different individuals have different circumstances, the standard tax return is divided into two parts.

The first part is sent to every recipient of the standard tax return, and is therefore common to all these returns. It requests general information, as well as details of:

- income from UK savings and investments
- income from pensions and social security benefits
- reliefs claimed for various expenditure
- specific allowances claimed
- the income tax due

The second part of the tax return consists of a series of supplementary pages that are only sent to relevant taxpayers. The main supplementary pages are for:

- employment income
- self-employment income
- partnership income
- income from land & property
- capital gains (profits made on selling assets)

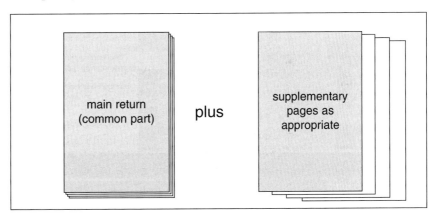

Each part of the tax return is divided into short sections that start with a question that can be answered 'yes' or 'no'. If the answer is 'yes' then the section needs further completion, whereas if it is 'no' then you can move on to the next section. For example in the common part of the tax return, a question asks 'Did you receive any income from UK savings and investments?' A positive response means that details of such income will then need to be given in that section, but those without such income can move on. This approach means that the form is not as difficult to complete as many people imagine.

An online version of the tax return can also be completed and submitted electronically as an alternative to the traditional paper-based version. Whether the tax return is submitted online or in paper-based form makes a difference to when it must be submitted by.

timing of the tax return

Around the end of the tax year (April 2008 for the tax year 2007/08) the following will happen. Relevant taxpayers will either be sent a paper tax return to complete, or a reminder that they need to submit an online return (if that's the way they have submitted previously).

With effect from the tax year 2007/08 onwards, the latest submission dates are as follows:

- Paper-based returns need to be submitted by 31 October following the end of the tax year. Provided they are correctly completed HMRC will then calculate the tax if the taxpayer (or agent) hasn't already done so. For the tax year 2007/08 the final date for paper returns is therefore 31 October 2008.

- Online submissions need to be made by 31 January following the end of the tax year. This provides an incentive to submit online since taxpayers have a deadline 3 months later than for the paper-based forms. Another advantage of submitting online is that the computer software automatically calculates the tax as the data is inserted. The online deadline for the tax year 2007/08 is therefore 31 January 2009.

An example of a tax return is reproduced in the appendix to this book. The return forms are also available from the HM Revenue & Customs website. As we progress through this book we will examine in detail how the various parts of the return should be completed.

SIMPLIFIED TAX RETURN

Some of the individuals who have traditionally received self-assessment tax returns as just described, actually have fairly straightforward tax affairs. For these individuals a simplified tax return is available. This return is only four pages long and is designed so that an automated data capture system can be used.

The simplified return is generally suitable for the following types of individuals who may also have modest income from property or savings:

- employees (other than company directors)
- self-employed (with turnover less than £15,000 p.a.)
- pensioners

EXEMPT INCOME

Exempt income is outside the scope of income tax. Exempt income will not have had tax deducted from it at source, and it should not appear anywhere in the income tax computation. You should make sure that you are familiar with the following abbreviated list of exempt income, since it is possible that items from it could be included in an examination task to test your ability to select the right income to include in a tax computation.

- Prizes are generally exempt from income tax. These include:
  - Premium Bond prizes
  - Lottery prizes
  - betting winnings (unless a professional gambler)

- Income from PEPs, TESSAs, and ISAs are all specifically exempt. These are all forms of investment that have been designed by the government to encourage saving and investment by exempting the income from tax.

We will look at savings and investment income in detail in Chapter 3.

We will now use a further Case Study to see how some of the issues covered in this chapter can be dealt with all together.

Case Study

MARK DOWNE:
INCOME FROM VARIOUS SOURCES

Mark Downe is a self-employed market trader. His profits (adjusted for income tax purposes) for the last two accounting periods were as follows:

Year ended 30/6/07	£24,000
Year ended 30/6/08	£25,000

He also has income from a house that he rents out to students. The following profits from this have been calculated on an accruals basis and adjusted for tax purposes.

6/4/2006 – 5/4/2007	£10,500
6/4/2007 – 5/4/2008	£13,000
6/4/2008 – 5/4/2009	£14,000

Mark won £12,000 on the National Lottery on 15th June 2007.

He was also employed as a part time barman from 1/7/2007 to 30/6/2008. He was paid on the last day of each month that he worked, and his monthly gross pay during this time was £500. He paid £990 under PAYE in 2007/08, and £330 in 2008/09.

Mark invested in a 'cash ISA' in 2007/08. This generated interest of £120 in that tax year.

required

1 Using an income tax computation, calculate Mark's income tax liability for 2007/08.

2 Specify which supplementary pages he will need to complete in his tax return for 2007/08, and state the latest date that the paper-based form should be returned to HM Revenue & Customs.

solution

This is more complicated than the last one, since we are given a lot more information about the taxpayer's income, some of which relates to a different tax year, and some of which is not taxable at all.

The income that should go into the tax computation for 2007/08 comprises:

- the profits from his self-employment for the accounting period ending in the tax year 2007/08, ie the profits for the year to 30/6/07: £24,000

- the rental income for the period 6/4/2007 to 5/4/2008: £13,000

- the part time bar work earnings received between 1/7/2007 and 5/4/2008, ie 9 months x £500 = £4,500

The lottery winnings and the interest from the ISA are both exempt.

We can now complete the income tax computation as follows:

1   **Mark Downe – Income Tax Computation for 2007/08**

	£	£
		Tax Paid
Trading Income	24,000	-
Employment Income	4,500	990
Property Income (rent)	13,000	-
Total Income	41,500	990
Less Personal Allowance	5,225	
Taxable Income	36,275	

Income Tax Calculation

£2,230 x 10%		223.00
£32,370 x 22%		7,121.40
£1,675 x 40%		670.00
£36,275	Income Tax Liability	8,014.40
	Less already paid	990.00
	Income tax to pay	7,024.40

2 Mark will need the supplementary tax return pages for employment, self-employment, and rental income, in addition to the common pages. He must complete the form for 2007/08 and return it to HM Revenue & Customs by 31 October 2008 at the latest.

WHEN TO PAY INCOME TAX

Some income tax is paid when the income that it relates to is generated. For example under the Pay-As-You-Earn system income tax is deducted from employment income by the employer, and paid over to HM Revenue & Customs on the taxpayer's behalf. In a similar way many forms of savings income have tax deducted at source by (for example) a bank or building society.

For other types of income there is no system set up to automatically deduct income tax. Rental income and income from self-employment are two examples of income where this is usually the case.

As we saw in the previous Case Studies, an income tax computation can be used to calculate both the total income tax liability and the part of this amount that has yet to be paid. It is this outstanding balance of income tax that will need to be paid to HM Revenue & Customs according to the following rules.

- The **final** date for payment of the income tax that relates to a tax year is the 31st January **following the end of that tax year.**

- For some taxpayers there may also be payments on account that must be made before the final date. These are due as follows:

  - The first payment on account is due on the **31st January within the tax year.**

  - The second payment on account is due on the **31st July following the end of the tax year.**

So for the tax year 2007/08 the payment dates would be:

31 January 2008 for the first payment on account,

31 July 2008 for the second payment on account, and

31 January 2009 for the final payment.

For the tax year 2008/09 the payment dates would be:

31 January 2009 for the first payment on account,

31 July 2009 for the second payment on account, and

31 January 2010 for the final payment.

Notice that when payments on account are required, two payments will be due on each 31st January. For example, on 31 January 2009 there would be due both

- the final payment for the tax year 2007/08, and

- the first payment on account for the tax year 2008/09.

Later in the book we will see how the payments on account are calculated, and which taxpayers need to make these early payments.

We saw earlier that the 31 January following the tax year was also the final date for submitting an online tax return, so we can build up the following calendar of key dates for the tax years that we are concerned with.

Sample Income Tax Timetable		
	Re Tax Year 2007/08	*Re Tax Year 2008/09*
31 Jan 08	First payment on account of income tax	
April 2008	2007/08 Tax Return Issued (or online reminder)	
31 July 08	Second payment on account of income tax	

31 Oct 08	Return to be filed if paper-based.	
31 Jan 09	Return to be filed if online submission used.	
	Payment of final amount of income tax for 2007/08	First payment on account of income tax for 2008/09
April 2009		Tax Return Issued (or online reminder)
31 July 09		Second payment on account of income tax
31 Oct 09		Return to be filed if paper-based.
31 Jan 10		Return to be filed if online submission used.
		Payment of final amount of income tax

THE DUTIES AND RESPONSIBILITIES OF A TAX PRACTITIONER

A **tax practitioner** is someone who helps clients on a professional basis with their tax affairs. The practitioner has responsibilities both:

* to the client, and
* to HM Revenue & Customs.

The AAT has published 'Guidelines on Professional Ethics' that deal with these and other issues. These apply to AAT students and members. The document can be downloaded from the website at www.aat.org.uk

With regard to **confidentiality** in general, the guidelines state that confidentiality should always be observed unless either

* authority has been given to disclose the information (by the client), or
* there is a legal, regulatory or professional duty to disclose information

The guidelines include the following regarding taxation services:

'A member providing professional tax services has a duty to put forward the best position in favour of a client or an employee. However the service must be carried out with professional competence, must not in any way impair integrity or objectivity, and must be consistent with the law.'

The guidelines also state that:

'A member should not be associated with any return or communication in which there is reason to believe that it:

(i)   contains a false or misleading statement;

(ii) contains statements or information furnished recklessly or without any real knowledge of whether they are true or false; or

(iii) omits or obscures information required to be submitted and such omission or obscurity would mislead the tax authorities.'

Dealing with professional ethics can be a difficult and complex area, and we have only outlined some main points. If you find yourself in a position where you are uncertain how you should proceed because of an ethical problem then you should first approach your supervisor or manager. If you are still unable to resolve the problem then further professional or legal advice may need to be obtained.

If you are studying for the AAT Diploma you will study this topic in more depth in the 'professional ethics' unit, covered by Osborne Books' *Professional Ethics.*

It will also be important to know what records will need to be kept regarding the client's income and tax affairs, and to ensure that such records are kept secure. The records must be sufficient to substantiate the information provided to HM Revenue & Customs. This would include documentation such as invoices, receipts, and working papers. These records must be kept as follows:

- In general records must be retained for approximately 1 year plus 10 months from the end of the tax year to which they relate. For example documents relating to 2007/08 must be retained until 31st January 2010. This is one year after the latest filing date for that year's online tax return.

- For those in business or clients who let property, the time is extended to approximately 5 years plus 10 months from the end of the tax year. If there is a formal HM Revenue & Customs enquiry into a taxpayer's affairs then the records need to be kept at least until the end of the enquiry.

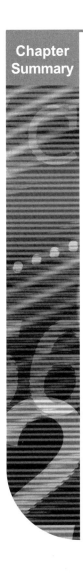

Chapter Summary

- Income tax in the UK is administered by HM Revenue & Customs. It is responsible for publishing documents and forms to gather information about how much tax is owed, and collecting the tax on behalf of the government. It is governed by statute law and case law.

- Income is divided into categories so that appropriate rules can be applied to calculate the amount of each different form of income.

- Income tax is calculated separately for each tax year, that runs from 6 April to the following 5 April. An income tax computation is used to calculate the tax by totalling the income from various sources, and subtracting allowances. The income tax is then calculated by reference to the tax bands and rates that relate to the tax year.

- Tax returns are used to collect information about individuals' income and tax each year. They consist of a common section plus supplementary pages that depend on the taxpayer's circumstances.

- Some specific forms of income are exempt from income tax and should not be included on the tax return.

- Income tax that has not been paid by deduction must be paid to HM Revenue & Customs by the 31 January following the end of the tax year. For some taxpayers there is also a requirement to make payments on account before this date.

- Tax practitioners have responsibilities to their clients (including confidentiality) and to HM Revenue & Customs. They must also ensure that all necessary records are kept for the required period of time.

Key Terms		
statute law	legislation that is passed by parliament – an example of statute law relating to taxation is the Finance Act 2007
case law	the result of decisions taken in court cases that have an impact on the interpretation of law
tax year	each tax year runs from 6 April to the following 5 April – tax years are also known as fiscal years
basis of assessment	the rule that decides what income from a particular source is taxable for a tax year – eg the basis of assessment for trading income is normally the adjusted profits of the accounting period that ends in the tax year
income tax computation	the format used to calculate income tax – it collates income from various sources, subtracts personal allowances, and calculates tax on the resultant taxable income
personal allowance	the amount that an individual's income can amount to before tax is charged – in 2007/08 the basic personal allowance is £5,225
taxable income	an individual's income after subtracting the personal allowance – it is the amount that is used to calculate the tax liability
tax bands	income tax is charged at various percentage rates according to the type of income and the tax bands – for example the 10% tax band for general income in 2007/08 relates to taxable income up to £2,230
tax return	the self-assessment tax return is issued annually to certain taxpayers – it is divided into a common section, plus supplementary pages that relate to the taxpayer's circumstances
exempt income	income that is not chargeable to income tax and should therefore not be shown on the tax return or in the tax computation

Student Activities

NOTE: an asterisk (*) after the activity number means that the solution to the question is given at the back of this book.

Note: in these Student Activities the words 'year end' are abbreviated to 'y/e' and dates are quoted in the format '30/9/06'.

1.1* The following are statements made by a trainee in the tax department:

(a) One of the reasons that income is divided into categories is so that the correct rules can be applied to each type of income. TRUE

(b) When examining the tax rules for 2007/08, the only law that is relevant is the Finance Act 2007. NO

(c) Every individual will receive a tax return each year that they must complete. NO

(d) All income must be declared on the tax return and used in the income tax computation. NO

(e) Taxable income is the name given to total income (apart from exempt income) after basic personal allowances have been subtracted. TRUE

(f) An individual with only general taxable income of £1,500 in 2007/08 would pay income tax of £150. TRUE   1500 × 10% = 150

(g) It is the job of a tax practitioner to ensure that his client pays the least amount of tax. This may involve bending the rules, or omitting certain items from a tax computation. NO

(h) Most self-employed people pay tax under PAYE and so don't have to worry about completing tax returns. NO

Required

Select those statements that are true.

1.2* Mary has the following income:

Salary of £1,000 per month from her employment throughout 2007 and 2008, plus bonuses paid as follows:

£300 paid in May 2007 re y/e 31/12/06 ✓

£500 paid in May 2008 re y/e 31/12/07 ✗

Mary had £1,289 deducted under PAYE during 2007/08. ✓

Part time self-employed business – profits as follows:

y/e 30/9/07 £2,800 ✓

y/e 30/9/08 £2,750 ✗

She also rents out a property that she owns. She received £4,500 in rent for the period 6/4/07 – 5/4/08 after deducting allowable costs.

Required:

Using an Income Tax Computation for 2007/08, calculate Mary's total income tax liability, and how much of it has not been paid.

1.3* The following is a list of the sources of Sue's income for the tax year.

(a) Dividends from shares in UK companies

(b) Income from employment as a Sales Manager

(c) Interest from a TESSA

(d) Interest from a bank deposit account

(e) Winnings from a bet on the Grand National

(f) Rent received from a property let to students

Required

For each income source either state which category it should be included under, or state that it is exempt from income tax.

1.4* John has the following income:

- Wages from employment £660 per month.

- Rental income from a house left to him by his Grandmother, due on the last day of each month. The £250 per month for the months of April 2007 - February 2008 were paid on time. The £250 for March 2008 was paid on 30/4/08 along with the April rent.

- There were no allowable expenses to be deducted from this rental income.

- Interest Earned on ISA with B&B Building Society, £230.

John paid £325 during 2007/08 under PAYE.

Required:

Using an Income Tax Computation for the tax year, calculate John's total income tax liability, and how much of it has not been paid.

1.5*   Megan has the following income:

Salary of £1,800 per month from her employment throughout 2007 and 2008, plus bonuses paid as follows:

£800 paid in September 2007 re y/e 31/3/07

£500 paid in September 2008 re y/e 31/3/08

Megan had £3,511 deducted under PAYE during 2007/08.

Income from writing articles for technical magazines, categorised as trading income, as follows:

year ended 31/12/07   £4,700

year ended 31/12/08   £6,350

Required:

Using an Income Tax Computation for the tax year, calculate Megan's total income tax liability, and how much of it has not been paid.

2 Income from property

In this chapter we examine:

* how we tax property income
* expenditure that is allowable
* expenditure that is not allowable
* calculating the profit or loss for property income
* dealing with property losses
* completing the tax return supplementary pages for property income
* keeping records

PERFORMANCE CRITERIA COVERED

unit 19: PREPARING PERSONAL TAXATION COMPUTATIONS

element 19.2 calculate property and investment income

B   prepare schedules of property income and determine profits or losses

D   apply deductions and reliefs and claim loss set-offs

E   record relevant details of property and investment income accurately and legibly in the tax return

F   make computations and submissions in accordance with current tax law and take account of current Inland Revenue practice

H   give timely and constructive advice to clients on the recording of information relevant to tax returns

HOW PROPERTY INCOME IS TAXED

what does Property Income cover?

Property income can include:

- income from renting out land
- income from renting out unfurnished property
- income from renting out furnished property

The term 'property' is used to mean buildings, either residential (flats, houses, etc) or commercial (offices etc). Running a hotel or guest house would not fall under this category, but would instead be considered a trade.

Furnished holiday letting income is also taxed as property income, although it is treated in many respects like trading income. The general rules that we will study in this chapter apply to holiday lettings as well as other property rentals.

You are most likely to be asked to calculate the amount assessable relating to one or more properties that are rented out by a client. The client is usually the owner of the properties, but it would be possible for him to have rented them from another landlord.

accruals basis of calculation

You may remember from the last chapter that a 'basis of assessment' sets out the way that income is calculated and linked to tax years. The basis of assessment for property income is **profits** from land and property **for the tax year**, calculated on an **accruals** basis.

This means the income should therefore relate to the tax year in which it will be assessed. For example, for the tax year 2007/08 this would be the period 6/4/07 to 5/4/08.

You need to be clear about the distinction between:

- the accruals basis that we must use here. (This is the same basis that applies to profit and loss accounts under normal financial accounting rules), and
- the receipts (or cash) basis that does not apply to this category, but applies (for example) to salaries and wages

Because property income is calculated on an accruals basis, the assessable rental income is that which **relates to the tax year**. So, for example, (assuming an ongoing tenancy):

- If a tenant had paid more than one year's worth of rent during the tax year, only the amount that related to the tax year would be assessable in the tax year.

- If a tenant had fallen behind with his rental payments, the amount that related to the tax year would still be assessable in that year, even though it hadn't all been received. This is provided the tenant was able to pay it eventually.

One issue to be careful about is where an unpaid amount of rent is considered 'irrecoverable'. In these circumstances the irrecoverable amount can be deducted from the rental income. This is exactly the same logic that occurs in financial accounting, when 'bad debts' are written off.

Case Study

MINNIE STREET: ASSESSABLE RENT

Minnie Street rents out two unfurnished properties to tenants. Each has a monthly rental of £500, payable in advance on the 6th day of each month.

From January 2007 onwards, the following rents were paid:

The tenant of property one paid the rent on time every month during 2007. On 6th January 2008 he paid six months rent in advance since he was going on a long holiday.

The tenant of property two also paid the rent on time every month during 2007. During 2008 he failed to pay any rent. He left the property on 5th March, without leaving a forwarding address or paying the rent that he owed. Minnie has been unable to locate him since then. Property two was re-let to another tenant in May 2008.

required

Calculate the assessable amount under property income for Minnie Street for the tax year 2007/08.

solution

The assessable amount for **property one** is 12 x £500 = £6,000. The extra rent paid in advance by the tenant that relates to the period after 6/4/2008 will be assessable in the following tax year.

The assessable amount for **property two** is calculated as:

Relating to the period of occupation		
6/4/2007 – 5/3/2008	11 x £500	= £5,500
Less irrecoverable amounts (relating to		
rent due in January and February but not paid)	2 x £500	= £1,000
		£4,500

Since property two is not rented out in the period 6/3/2008 to 5/4/2008 there is no assessable amount for this month.

The total amount assessable as property income for Minnie Street for 2007/08 is therefore £6,000 + £4,500 = £10,500.

EXPENDITURE THAT IS ALLOWABLE

'Allowable' expenditure is expenditure that can be deducted from the rental income to arrive at the assessable property income.

Note that some expenditure that is quite proper from an accounting point of view may not be 'allowable' for taxation purposes. This does not mean that the accounts produced are necessarily wrong, but we will need to make adjustments before they are suitable for our tax work.

The general rule for expenditure to be allowable in a property income calculation is that it must be:

- revenue rather than capital in nature, and
- 'wholly and exclusively' for the purpose of lettings

Allowable expenditure may include:

- business rates, water rates and council tax – this would apply where the landlord has paid these items, effectively on behalf of the tenant – the rent would have been set at such a level to allow for the fact that the landlord was paying this cost
- rent paid to a 'superior' landlord – this would apply only if the property did not belong to the client, but was rented from someone else, the situation would therefore be one of 'subletting'
- interest paid on a loan or mortgage to buy the property – this applies where the client is the owner; where payments are made to the lender that include both interest and repayment of the amount borrowed, only the interest part is allowable
- insurance and management expenses
- costs of advertising for tenants
- ongoing repairs, maintenance and redecoration costs (but not those of a *capital* nature – see next page)
- irrecoverable rent (as discussed above)
- wear and tear allowance, if the property is rented out on a furnished basis (see next page)

Expenditure that satisfies the above rules and is incurred before the premises are rented out or in periods in between rental periods ('void' periods) is also generally allowable.

wear and tear allowance

For furnished lettings only, **wear and tear allowance** is a reflection of the costs involved in providing and maintaining suitable furniture and other items in the property.

Wear and tear allowance is calculated as:

10% of the assessable rent (after deducting only rates (general and water) and council tax (where applicable) from the rent)

Wear and tear allowance is a broad measure that is easy to calculate and simply provides some recognition that costs are incurred in the provision of furniture. The logic for deducting rates or council tax before applying the 10% in the calculation is that the rent would have been artificially increased to cover them in the first place, since they are normally the tenant's responsibility. It would therefore be unfair to allow more wear and tear allowance just because the landlord was effectively collecting and paying out these amounts.

Note that the calculation does not take account of how much the landlord spends on furniture, nor how he depreciates it in his accounts.

EXPENDITURE THAT IS NOT ALLOWABLE

Since only revenue expenditure is allowable, it follows that any capital expenditure will not be allowable. Non-allowable capital expenditure includes the following:

- The **cost of the property itself** together with any furniture etc. Also considered as capital will be the costs connected with the purchase, including the legal and professional fees incurred in buying the property.
- The **cost of improvements**. This will apply when expenditure is incurred in upgrading or extending the property. For example, replacing single glazing with double-glazing is an improvement, as is the installation of central heating where none existed previously. Note that normal ongoing repairs and maintenance when the property is simply brought back to its previous condition are allowable.
- The **cost of renovations** carried out before a property is rented out for the first time. One argument for viewing this expenditure as capital is that the need for the renovations will have been reflected in the lower purchase price of the property.

Other costs that are not allowable include the following:

- depreciation of any kind relating to capital expenditure
- expenditure not connected with the business of lettings (for example, expenditure on a private part of the property)

CALCULATING THE PROFIT OR LOSS UNDER PROPERTY INCOME

To arrive at the profit or loss under property income we need to:

- determine the assessable rents receivable, and
- deduct any allowable expenditure

The calculation of the profit or loss is known as a **property income computation**.

dealing with a single property

We will now present a Case Study involving a single property to show how this calculation can be carried out. We will use the information regarding allowable expenditure to help us (see pages 2.3 and 2.4).

Case Study

UNA LODGE:
CALCULATING ASSESSABLE PROPERTY INCOME

Una Lodge rents out one furnished property. The following is a statement compiled from her accounting records relating to the period 6/4/2007 – 5/4/2008.

	£	£
Rental Income Receivable		12,000
less expenditure:		
Council Tax	800	
Water Rates	400	
Irrecoverable Rent	600	
Insurance	300	
Installing Central Heating	2,000	
Depreciation of Furniture	900	
Managing Agent's Charges	600	
		5,600
Profit		6,400

required

Calculate the assessable property income for Una Lodge.

solution

We can re-draft the profit statement, incorporating only allowable expenditure and deductions as follows:

Property Income Computation

	£	£
Rental Income		12,000
less allowable expenditure:		
Council Tax	800	
Water Rates	400	
Irrecoverable Rent	600	
Insurance	300	
Managing Agent's Charges	600	
Wear & Tear Allowance	1,080	
		3,780
Assessable		8,220

Notes

- The installation of central heating is capital expenditure, and therefore not allowable for tax purposes.
- Depreciation is never allowable.
- The wear and tear allowance is calculated as

  10% x (£12,000 - £800 council tax - £400 water rates) = £1,080.

an alternative approach to calculation

Assuming we are given a statement in the form of a profit and loss account, an alternative approach is to start with the profit figure, and adjust it by

- **adding** any non-allowable expenditure items that were originally deducted, and
- **deducting** allowable items that were not originally deducted

This approach would save having to draft a whole new statement. However it is not recommended if you need to go on to complete the rental section of a tax return, since the full analysis needs to be shown on that document.

If you refer to the 'Una Lodge' Case Study, this calculation method would provide the same assessable amount, as follows:

Property Income Computation

	£
Profit per original statement	6,400
Add non-allowable expenditure deducted in statement:	
Installing Central Heating	2,000
Depreciation of Furniture	900
Deduct wear & tear allowance (as calculated above)	(1,080)
Assessable	8,220

Here, non-allowable items are added to the original profit to cancel them out, and items like the wear and tear allowance are then deducted.

Either approach is acceptable, but you need to be clear about which you are using so that you don't confuse the two methods.

several properties

When there is more than one property, the best approach is to draw up a statement with one column for each property. The addition of a total column provides a means of double-checking your arithmetic, and sets out the figures needed for the tax return. Each property can then be dealt with in turn, and the overall result incorporated into one property income assessment figure. If one property then incurs a loss after adjustment for tax purposes, it should be offset against the assessable profits from the other properties. Using a columnar format like this enables the net result to be calculated quite easily, as in the Case Study which follows.

In the next section (page 2.9) we will go on to see how to deal with a situation where the net effect of all the properties is a loss.

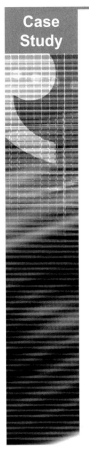

Case Study

ANDY LORD:
PROFITS FROM SEVERAL PROPERTIES

Andy Lord rents out three properties in High Street. Property number 1 is unfurnished, while properties 2 and 3 are furnished.

Andy has provided the following statement of income and expenditure on the properties for the period 6/4/2007 – 5/4/2008.

	Property 1 £	Property 1 £	Property 2 £	Property 2 £	Property 3 £	Property 3 £
Rental Income		5,000		6,000		4,300
Less expenses:						
Council Tax	500		450		400	
Loan Interest	3,600		2,000		-	
Rent Payable	-		-		2,500	
Property Insurance	200		200		200	
Bad Debt	600		-		-	
Roof Repairs	700		300		-	
Other Repairs	2,900		450		200	
Professional Fees for Debt Recovery	150		-		-	
Depreciation	500		500		500	
		9,150		3,900		3,800
Profit / (Loss)		(4,150)		2,100		500

You have also determined the following facts:

- The loan interest relates to mortgages obtained to purchase properties number one and two.
- The rent payable relates to property number three that is not owned by Andy Lord.
- The bad debt and the professional fees for attempted debt recovery relate to a problem with a tenant for property number one who left whilst owing rent. He cannot be traced.
- 'Roof Repairs' relates to the cost of repairing damage that occurred during a storm. This amount was not covered by the insurance policy.
- 'Other Repairs' includes £2,900 paid to install double-glazing in property number one to replace the single glazed windows.

required

Calculate the amount of assessable property income.

solution

	Property 1 £	Property 2 £	Property 3 £	Total £
Rental Income	5,000	6,000	4,300	15,300
Less allowable expenses:				
Council Tax	500	450	400	1,350
Loan Interest	3,600	2,000	-	5,600
Rent Payable	-	-	2,500	2,500
Property Insurance	200	200	200	600
Bad Debt	600		-	600
Roof Repairs	700	300	-	1,000
Other Repairs	-	450	200	650
Professional Fees for Debt Recovery	150	-	-	150
Wear & Tear Allowance	-	555	390	945
Assessable amount	(750)	2,045	610	1,905

Notes

- The bad debt for property No. 1 is considered as irrecoverable rent and is therefore allowable.
- The professional fees for attempting to recover the debt are wholly and exclusively for the rental business and therefore allowable.
- The roof repairs are allowable as revenue expenditure.

- The 'other repairs' are allowable, with the exception of the installation of double-glazing that is considered an improvement and therefore capital in nature.
- Depreciation is not allowable.
- The wear and tear allowance is calculated as 10% of the rent less council tax. There is no wear and tear allowance for property No.1, since it is let unfurnished.
- The loss for property No. 1 is offset against the profits on the other properties to give a 'property income' figure of £1,905.

DEALING WITH PROPERTY LOSSES

In the last section we saw how a loss when renting one property is offset against profits for other properties in the same tax year.

However, if *either*

- there are no other properties with profits in that tax year, *or*
- the net result from all the properties is a loss

then the following occurs:

- the property income assessment for the tax year is nil, and
- the loss must be carried forward until there is sufficient future property income to offset it.

The property loss can only be set against future property income. If there are insufficient property income profits in the tax year that follows the loss, then the balance of the loss is carried forward again until it can be relieved.

The following Case Study demonstrates how this works.

Case Study

IVOR COST:
DEALING WITH LOSSES

Ivor Cost rents out several properties. After amalgamating the rents from all his properties, and deducting all allowable expenses he has arrived at the following figures:

Tax Year	Profit / (Loss)
	£
2006/07	(5,500)
2007/08	3,800
2008/09	6,400

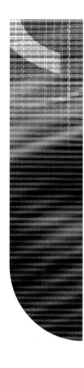

required

Calculate the assessable property income for each of the three tax years referred to.

solution

Tax Year	Working	Property Income Assessment
2006/07	loss of £5,500 carried forward to next year	Nil
2007/08	£3,800 of loss used against profit of £3,800. Balance of loss carried forward	Nil
2008/09	Profit £6,400 less balance of loss £1,700	£4,700

COMPLETING THE RELEVANT PARTS OF THE TAX RETURN

In the first chapter we saw that a tax return consists of a main section that is common to all taxpayers, plus 'supplementary pages' that relate to specific situations. Details of property income or losses are entered on the 'Land and Property' supplementary pages that we will look at now.

There are only two Land and Property pages. We will ignore the topics covered on the first page, and just look at how to complete page L2, headed 'Other property income'. This page of the return could form the basis of an examination task. **You should be careful in an examination if you are presented with both pages to only complete page L2** (unless you are dealing with holiday lets – which is unlikely). The 2006/07 tax year version is shown on the next page.

The page broadly follows the format of a property income computation, with sections for:

- income,
- expenses, and
- tax adjustments

These will enable us to arrive at an adjusted profit or loss.

There is then a short section where losses carried forward can be noted.

Other property income (not including dividends from a UK Real Estate Investment Trust - go to box 13.1 - 13.3 on page 5 of the Tax Return)

■ *Income*

- Furnished holiday lettings profits   copy from box 5.14 | 5.19 £

- Rents and other income from land and property | 5.20 £   Tax taken off | 5.21 £

- Chargeable premiums | 5.22 £

- Reverse premiums | 5.22A £   boxes 5.19 + 5.20 + 5.22 + 5.22A | 5.23 £

■ *Expenses* (do not include figures you have already put in boxes 5.2 to 5.7 on Page L1)

- Rent, rates, insurance, ground rents etc. | 5.24 £

- Repairs, maintenance and renewals | 5.25 £

- Finance charges, including interest | 5.26 £

- Legal and professional costs | 5.27 £

- Costs of services provided, including wages | 5.28 £

- Other expenses | 5.29 £   total of boxes 5.24 to 5.29 | 5.30 £

Net profit (put figures in brackets if a loss)   box 5.23 minus box 5.30 | 5.31 £

■ *Tax adjustments*

- Private use | 5.32 £

- Balancing charges - including those arising under Business Premises Renovation Allowance which should also be included in box 23.8 | 5.33 £   box 5.32 + box 5.33 | 5.34 £

- Rent a Room exempt amount | 5.35 £

- Capital allowances - including those arising under Business Premises Renovation Allowance which should also be included in box 23.7 | 5.36 £

- Tick box 5.36A if box 5.36 includes a claim for 100% capital allowances for flats over shops | 5.36A

- Tick box 5.36B if box 5.36 includes enhanced capital allowances for designated environmentally beneficial plant and machinery | 5.36B

- Landlord's Energy Saving Allowance | 5.36C £

- 10% wear and tear | 5.37 £

- Furnished holiday lettings losses   copy from box 5.18 | 5.38 £   total of boxes 5.35 to 5.38 | 5.39 £

Adjusted profit (if a loss, enter '0' in box 5.40 and put the loss in box 5.41)   boxes 5.31 + 5.34 minus box 5.39 | 5.40 £

Adjusted loss (if you have entered '0' in box 5.40)   boxes 5.31 + 5.34 minus box 5.39 | 5.41 £

- Loss brought forward from previous year | 5.42 £

Profit for the year   box 5.40 minus box 5.42 | 5.43 £

■ *Losses etc.*

- Loss offset against total income - read the note on page LN8 | 5.44 £

- Loss to carry forward to following year | 5.45 £

- Tick box 5.46 if these Pages include details of property let jointly | 5.46

- Tick box 5.47 if all property income ceased in the year to 5 April 2007 and you do not expect to receive such income again, in the year to 5 April 2008 | 5.47

Now fill in any other supplementary Pages that apply to you.
Otherwise, go back to page 2 of your Tax Return and finish filling it in.   © Crown Copyright

Since the tax form is designed to deal with more complicated situations than we need to study, you will find that we will not need some of the boxes. It is quite acceptable to leave boxes blank that do not apply.

Each box on the form is numbered for reference, and the notes that follow should help you understand how the form works.

Further guidance is available from the 'Notes on Land and Property' document (SA105) that can be found on the HM Revenue & Customs website (www.hmrc.gov.uk), but note that such documents cannot be used in an examination.

Income Section

Here you will only need to complete box 5.20 with the rent receivable, and repeat the figure in box 5.23.

Expenses Section

You should analyse the expenses (excluding any wear and tear allowance) into boxes 5.24 to 5.29. Make sure that the figures reconcile with your workings, and put the total of these figures in box 5.30. Deduct box 5.30 from box 5.23, and put the net figure into box 5.31 (as instructed on the form).

Tax Adjustments

The only box that you will need in this section is box 5.37 for the wear and tear allowance figure. The figure is repeated in box 5.39, and deducted from box 5.31 to provide the adjusted profit (box 5.40) or loss (box 5.41).

Any loss brought forward is entered into box 5.42 and the resulting property income profit is entered in box 5.43. If there is a loss to be carried forward this is shown in box 5.45 (and then box 5.43 must be nil).

Once you have finished filling in this page

- make sure that the figures agree with your earlier workings, and that the arithmetic is accurate

- make sure that you have completed all the 'sub total' and 'total' boxes that are required; these are 5.23, 5.30, 5.31, 5.39, 5.40 (or 5.41) and 5.43

- if you have been asked to complete page 2 from the main return, you should now tick the box there to indicate that you have completed these supplementary pages

We will now see how a completed page looks by using the data from the earlier Case Study 'Andy Lord'.

Case Study

ANDY LORD:
COMPLETING THE RELEVANT TAX RETURN PAGES

Andy Lord rents out three properties in High Street. Two of the properties are furnished. The following is a computation of his property income (using the total column taken from the solution to the Case Study on page 2.8).

	£	£
Rental Income		15,300
less allowable expenses:		
Council Tax	1,350	
Loan Interest	5,600	
Rent Payable	2,500	
Property Insurance	600	
Bad Debt	600	
Roof Repairs	1,000	
Other Repairs	650	
Professional Fees for Debt Recovery	150	
Wear & Tear Allowance	945	
		13,395
Assessable amount		1,905

required
Complete page L2 of the tax return for Andy Lord.

solution
The completed document is reproduced on the next page. The following workings explain how each figure reconciles with the property income computation.

Box No.	Workings and Comments
5.20	Rental Income (before any deductions) £15,300.
5.23	Figure repeated from box 5.20.
5.24	Council Tax £1,350 + Rent Payment £2,500 + Property Insurance £600 = £4,450.
5.25	Roof Repairs £1,000 + Other Repairs £650 = £1,650.
5.26	Loan Interest £5,600.
5.27	Professional Fees for Debt Recovery £150.
5.29	Bad Debt £600.
5.30	Total of boxes 5.24 to 5.29 = £12,450.
5.31	Box 5.23 £15,300 minus box 5.30 £12,450 = £2,850.
5.37	Wear & Tear Allowance £945.
5.39	Figure repeated from box 5.37.

5.40   Box 5.31 £2,850 minus box 5.39 £945 = £1,905. This agrees with the assessable amount from the computation.

5.43   Figure repeated from box 5.40, since there are no losses brought forward in this case.

Other property income (not including dividends from a UK Real Estate Investment Trust - go to box 13.1 - 13.3 on page 5 of the Tax Return)

Income

		copy from box 5.14		Tax taken off	
Furnished holiday lettings profits	5.19	£			
Rents and other income from land and property	5.20	£ 15,300	5.21	£	
Chargeable premiums	5.22	£			
Reverse premiums	5.22A	£		boxes 5.19 + 5.20 + 5.22 + 5.22A 5.23	£ 15,300

Expenses (do not include figures you have already put in boxes 5.2 to 5.7 on Page L1)

Rent, rates, insurance, ground rents etc.	5.24	£ 4,450			
Repairs, maintenance and renewals	5.25	£ 1,650			
Finance charges, including interest	5.26	£ 5,600			
Legal and professional costs	5.27	£ 150			
Costs of services provided, including wages	5.28	£			
Other expenses	5.29	£ 600		total of boxes 5.24 to 5.29 5.30	£ 12,450

Net profit (put figures in brackets if a loss)   box 5.23 m minus box 5.30 **5.31** £ 2,850

Tax adjustments

Private use	5.32	£			
Balancing charges - including those arising under Business Premises Renovation Allowance which should also be included in box 23.8	5.33	£		box 5.32 + box 5.33 5.34	£
Rent a Room exempt amount	5.35	£			
Capital allowances - including those arising under Business Premises Renovation Allowance which should also be included in box 23.7	5.36	£			
Tick box 5.36A if box 5.36 includes a claim for 100% capital allowances for flats over shops	5.36A				
Tick box 5.36B if box 5.36 includes enhanced capital allowances for designated environmentally beneficial plant and machinery	5.36B				
Landlord's Energy Saving Allowance	5.36C	£			
10% wear and tear	5.37	£ 945			
Furnished holiday lettings losses	copy from box 5.18 5.38	£		total of boxes 5.35 to 5.38 5.39	£ 945

Adjusted profit (if a loss, enter '0' in box 5.40 and put the loss in box 5.41)   boxes 5.31 + 5.34 m minus box 5.39 **5.40** £ 1,905

Adjusted loss (if you have entered '0' in box 5.40)   boxes 5.31 + 5.34 minus box 5.39 **5.41** £

Loss brought forward from previous year   **5.42** £

Profit for the year   box 5.40 minus box 5.42 **5.43** £ 1,905

Losses etc.

Loss offset against total income - read the note on page LN8	5.44	£
Loss to carry forward to following year	5.45	£

KEEPING RECORDS

Records for property income must normally be kept for five years after the online tax return is due to be submitted. For the tax year 2007/08 the return is due on 31 January 2009, and so the records must be kept until 31 January 2014. Note that this is longer than non-business records need to be kept for tax purposes (one year after the final online tax return submission date).

The records should be able to substantiate the entries on the tax return, and would therefore typically include:

- accounting records including cash books and bank statements
- rental agreements and other records of tenancies
- invoices or receipts for expenses paid
- working papers for computations
- copies of tax returns

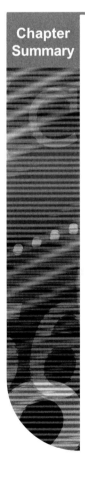

Chapter Summary

- Income from renting land and property is assessed under 'property income'. The basis of assessment for this is the income relating to the tax year, less allowable expenses, calculated on an accruals basis. The calculation of the assessable amount is known as a property income computation.

- Allowable expenses are those wholly and exclusively for the business of lettings. Irrecoverable rent is an allowable expense, as is a 'wear and tear allowance' for property that is let furnished.

- Expenditure that is not allowable includes capital expenditure and any form of depreciation.

- Where more than one property is let, the results are combined and any individual losses netted off against other properties with profits. Where the overall result is a loss, this is carried forward against future property income profits.

- There are supplementary pages in the tax return that relate to land and property. These must be completed accurately and agree with the computation. The relevant records must be retained for five years after the submission date for the online tax return.

Key Terms		
	Property Income	the term used to categorise income from land and property (typically rental income)
	Accruals Basis	this is where normal accountancy rules are followed, so that income and expenditure is matched to the period of time that it relates to; property income must be calculated by using the accruals basis, matching the profits to the tax year
	Allowable Expenditure	expenditure that may be deducted from income in the calculation of profits or losses for tax purposes
	Wear and Tear Allowance	an allowable deduction from income when property is rented on a furnished basis. It is calculated as 10% of the rent received after deducting council tax and rate

Student Activities

NOTE: an asterisk (*) after the activity number means that the solution to the question is given at the back of this book.

2.1* Julie rented out her unfurnished property from 6/7/2007, and received £5,000 for 12 month's rent in advance on that day. She also set up a direct debit payment of £25 per month for property insurance. In December 2007 she spent £200 for repairs following a burst pipe.

Calculate the assessable property income for 2007/08.

2.2* Dave bought an unfurnished office on 6/11/2007, and immediately let it to a tenant for £400 per month, payable monthly. Dave paid £2,000 legal fees to acquire the office, and paid monthly mortgage interest relating to the office of £150. He also paid £30 per month property insurance.

Dave used the services of an agent to collect the rent and liaise with the tenant. The agent charged £1,200 per year for this service.

Calculate the assessable property income for 2007/08.

2.3* Anna Partement rents out one furnished property. The following is a statement compiled from her accounting records relating to the tax year:

	£	£
Rental Income Receivable		10,000
less expenditure:		
Council Tax	700	
Water Rates	300	
Insurance	400	
Cost of New Carpets	2,500	
Depreciation of Furniture	800	
Managing Agent's Charges	1,000	
		5,700
Profit		4,300

Required

Calculate the property income for Anna for the tax year.

2.4 Sonny Hill rents out three country cottages. All properties are furnished.

He has provided the following statement of income and expenditure on the properties for the tax year:

	Property 1		Property 2		Property 3	
	£	£	£	£	£	£
Rental Income		8,000		6,000		5,500
Less expenses:						
Council Tax	800		650		400	
Loan Interest	3,600		2,000		4,000	
Property Insurance	400		300		250	
Redecoration	-		600		-	
Repainting Windows	500		450		500	
Other Repairs	2,900		400		200	
Accountancy Fees	150		150		150	
Depreciation	500		500		500	
		8,850		5,050		6,000
Profit / (Loss)		(850)		950		(500)

You have also determined the following facts:

- The loan interest relates to mortgages obtained to purchase the properties.

- 'Other Repairs' includes £2,600 paid to install central heating in property number one where none had previously existed.

- Sonny Hill has an unrelieved property income loss of £1,000 brought forward from the previous tax year.

Required:

1 Calculate the property income for the tax year.

2 Complete the blank supplementary page from the tax return (see opposite page).

2.5 Maisey Nett rents out one furnished property. The following is a statement compiled from her accounting records relating to the tax year.

	£	£
Rental Income Receivable		11,500
less expenditure:		
Accountancy Fees	400	
Council Tax	650	
Water Rates	350	
Insurance	300	
Cost of New Furniture	2,000	
Mortgage Interest	2,300	
Managing Agent's Charges	1,000	
		7,000
Profit		4,500

Maisey also had gross income of £31,500 in the tax year from her job as a legal executive. She paid £5,513 income tax under PAYE.

Required

1 Calculate the property income for Maisey.

2 Calculate Maisey's total income tax liability for the tax year, and the part of that amount that she has yet to pay.

Other property income *(not including dividends from a UK Real Estate Investment Trust - go to box 13.1 - 13.3 on page 5 of the Tax Return)*

■ *Income*

copy from box 5.14

● Furnished holiday lettings profits — 5.19 £

● Rents and other income from land and property — 5.20 £   Tax taken off 5.21 £

● Chargeable premiums — 5.22 £

● Reverse premiums — 5.22A £   boxes 5.19 + 5.20 + 5.22 + 5.22A 5.23 £

■ *Expenses* (do not include figures you have already put in boxes 5.2 to 5.7 on Page L1)

● Rent, rates, insurance, ground rents etc. — 5.24 £

● Repairs, maintenance and renewals — 5.25 £

● Finance charges, including interest — 5.26 £

● Legal and professional costs — 5.27 £

● Costs of services provided, including wages — 5.28 £

● Other expenses — 5.29 £   total of boxes 5.24 to 5.29 5.30 £

Net profit (put figures in brackets if a loss)   box 5.23 minus box 5.30 5.31 £

■ *Tax adjustments*

● Private use — 5.32 £

● Balancing charges - including those arising under Business Premises Renovation Allowance which should also be included in box 23.8 — 5.33 £   box 5.32 + box 5.33 5.34 £

● Rent a Room exempt amount — 5.35 £

● Capital allowances - including those arising under Business Premises Renovation Allowance which should also be included in box 23.7 — 5.36 £

● Tick box 5.36A if box 5.36 includes a claim for 100% capital allowances for flats over shops — 5.36A

● Tick box 5.36B if box 5.36 includes enhanced capital allowances for designated environmentally beneficial plant and machinery — 5.36B

● Landlord's Energy Saving Allowance — 5.36C £

● 10% wear and tear — 5.37 £

copy from box 5.18

● Furnished holiday lettings losses — 5.38 £   total of boxes 5.35 to 5.38 5.39 £

Adjusted profit (if a loss, enter '0' in box 5.40 and put the loss in box 5.41)   boxes 5.31 + 5.34 minus box 5.39 5.40 £

Adjusted loss (if you have entered '0' in box 5.40)   boxes 5.31 + 5.34 minus box 5.39 5.41 £

● Loss brought forward from previous year — 5.42 £

Profit for the year   box 5.40 minus box 5.42 5.43 £

■ *Losses etc.*

● Loss offset against total income - read the note on page LN8 — 5.44 £

● Loss to carry forward to following year — 5.45 £

● Tick box 5.46 if these Pages include details of property let jointly — 5.46

● Tick box 5.47 if all property income ceased in the year to 5 April 2007 and you do not expect to receive such income again, in the year to 5 April 2008 — 5.47

Now fill in any other supplementary Pages that apply to you. Otherwise, go back to page 2 of your Tax Return and finish filling it in.

3 Income from savings and investments

this chapter covers . . .

In this chapter we examine:

- the basis of assessment for savings and dividend income
- income received gross and net
- tax bands and rates for savings and dividend income
- tax free investment income
- completing the UK savings and investments page of the tax return
- keeping records

PERFORMANCE CRITERIA COVERED

unit 19: PREPARING PERSONAL TAXATION COMPUTATIONS

element 19.2 calculate property and investment income

A   prepare schedules of dividends and interest received on shares and securities

C   prepare schedules of investment income from other sources

E   record relevant details of property and investment income accurately and legibly in the tax return

F   make computations and submissions in accordance with current tax law and take account of current Inland Revenue practice

H   give timely and constructive advice to clients on the recording of information relevant to tax returns

THE BASIS OF ASSESSMENT FOR SAVINGS AND INVESTMENT INCOME

In this chapter we will examine savings and investment income and see how it is taxed. There are two types of savings and investment income. They are:

- interest received from various sources
- dividends from shares held in limited companies

Examples from which interest is received are:

- bank and building society deposit or savings accounts
- National Savings & Investments accounts
- government securities ('Gilts')
- loans to local authorities
- loans to limited companies (Debentures)

Examples of companies from which dividends are received are:

- PLC's such as 'British Airways plc'
- private limited companies such as 'Osborne Books Ltd'

The basis of assessment for both interest and UK dividends is the gross equivalent of the amount *received in the tax year*. Notice that this receipts basis applies to most types of income, but is different from property income which is calculated on an accruals basis. The period that the interest is based on is therefore irrelevant. Amounts received include money credited to an individual's bank or building society accounts during the tax year. There are no allowable expenses that can be deducted in the calculation of savings and investment income.

TAX DEDUCTED AT SOURCE

Most (but not all) of the savings and investment income that we will come across is received after some tax has effectively been deducted from the amount that will count as income. This works as follows:

- interest is often received after 20% of the gross amount has been deducted
- interest from some sources can be received as a gross amount without any deduction
- dividends will always be received after a notional 10% 'tax credit' has been effectively deducted

Note that both percentages relate to the 'gross' amounts, and are not percentages of the amounts that are actually received. We will see in the next section how these percentages link into the tax rates that apply to these forms of income.

Tax deducted from interest received and tax credits on dividends have the same general effect – they are both treated as part of the individual's tax liability **that has already been paid**. In this way it is similar to tax deducted under PAYE. The main difference between tax credits and other tax deducted is that tax credits are not repayable if it turns out that the individual has paid too much income tax.

Apart from tax-free income, (which we will examine later in this chapter) it is always the gross amount that is assessable for tax purposes. This is irrespective of whether the investment income is received 'net' or 'gross'. The gross figure is therefore the amount included in the individual's income tax computation.

You will be expected to know the main sources of savings and investment income, and how to calculate the assessable amounts and any tax deduction or tax credits that apply. These details are outlined in the following table.

Type of Savings and Investment Income	Received	Tax Deduction
Interest from:		
National Savings & Investments (NS&I)Accounts	Gross	None
Government Securities ('Gilts')	Gross	None
Bank & Building Society Accounts	Net	20%
Limited Company Loans	Net	20%
Local Authority Loans	Net	20%
Dividends from UK Company Shares	Net	10%

calculating the gross and tax amounts

We may be provided, on a tax voucher, for example, with a full analysis of the gross amount, the deduction and the net figure received.

For example, interest received of

Net Amount Received	£640.00	
Tax Deducted	£160.00	(20% of £800.00)
Gross Amount	£800.00	

or dividends received of:

Amount Received	£720.00	
Tax Credit	£80.00	(10% of £800.00)
Dividend + Tax Credit	£800.00	

Notice that the percentage deductions (20% for the interest and 10% for the dividends) both relate to the 'gross' figures. Many references do not use the term 'gross' in relation to dividends – the preferred expression is 'dividend plus tax credit', as we will see later when completing the tax return.

If we are only presented with the figures for the amounts received then (unless the income is received gross) we will need to calculate the tax deducted and gross amounts, as in the examples just given. This calculation is carried out as follows:

For **interest** that is received net, 20/80 of the net amount must be added for the tax deducted.

For **dividends**, 10/90 of the amount received must be added for the tax credit.

Alternatively, the assessable figure can be calculated by multiplying net interest by 100/80 and dividends by 100/90.

This diagram illustrates these principles:

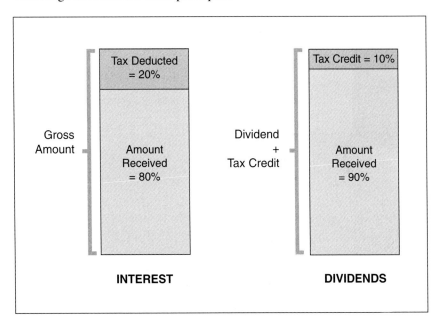

Using the interest example given above, the tax deducted could be calculated as 20/80 x £640.00 = £160.00. Added to the net amount of £640.00 this gives the gross figure of £800.00.

Similarly, the tax credit on the dividend can be worked out as £720.00 x 10/90 = £80.00.

We will now use a Case Study to see how the principles studied so far in this chapter can be applied in practice.

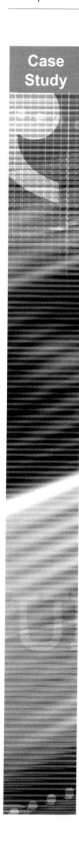

Case Study

ANNE INVESTOR:
CALCULATING SAVINGS AND DIVIDEND INCOME

Anne has provided you with the following details of the amounts that she has received during 2007 and part of 2008 from her various investments.

Date Received	Details	Amount Rec'd
		£
31/3/2007	Callifax Bank Deposit Account Interest	120.00
31/5/2007	Dividend from Gloxxo plc	1,800.00
30/6/2007	Newtown Building Society A/C Interest	1,200.00
31/8/2007	Dividend from CIC plc	6,750.00
30/9/2007	Interest from CIC plc Debenture	5,000.00
31/12/2007	National Savings & Investments (NS&I) - Investment A/C Interest	800.00
31/1/2008	Bank of Cambria Deposit A/C Interest	6,500.00
31/3/2008	Callifax Bank Deposit Account Interest	300.00
31/5/2008	Dividend from Gloxxo plc	1,600.00

required

Produce schedules of the amounts of savings and dividend income assessable in 2007/08, and the amounts of tax deducted at source and tax credits.

solution

1 The first step is to make sure that we only include amounts received between 6/4/2007 and 5/4/2008 in our calculation for 2007/08. This means that we can ignore the first Callifax interest of £120, and the last Gloxxo plc dividend of £1,600.

2 The second step is to categorise the receipts into savings and dividend income, and to produce schedules showing the amounts received, the tax deducted or tax credit, and the assessable amounts. This format will be useful if we have to complete a tax return. We must be careful to check the source of each savings income to determine whether it will have been received net or gross. In this Case Study the only amount received gross is the National Savings & Investments account interest.

This provides us with the following analysis.

SAVINGS INCOME

Date	Details	Amount Received	Tax Deducted	Assessable Amount
		£	£	£
30/6/07	Newtown BS	1,200.00	300.00	1,500.00
30/9/07	CIC Debenture	5,000.00	1,250.00	6,250.00
31/12/07	NS&I Inv A/C	800.00	-	800.00
31/1/08	Bank of Cambria	6,500.00	1,625.00	8,125.00
31/3/08	Callifax Bank	300.00	75.00	375.00
Total		13,800.00	3,250.00	17,050.00

DIVIDEND INCOME

Date	Details	Amount Received	Tax Credit	Assessable Amount
		£	£	£
31/5/07	Gloxxo plc	1,800.00	200.00	2,000.00
31/8/07	CIC plc	6,750.00	750.00	7,500.00
Total		8,550.00	950.00	9,500.00

Remember that the assessable amounts would be included in Anne's tax computation for 2007/08, and the tax deducted and tax credits would be treated as payments of tax already made.

TAX BANDS AND RATES FOR SAVINGS AND DIVIDEND INCOME

You may well have wondered why the tax amounts in the last section were based on 20% or 10% when general income tax rates are 10%, 22% and 40%. The reason is that these general income tax rates do not apply to savings or dividend income. Instead savings income and dividend income each have their own tax rates that apply in the various tax bands.

Income from savings and dividends are the only exceptions to the general income tax rates that we saw in Chapter 1. We therefore have a total of three categories of income that have different tax rates:

- general income
- savings income, and
- dividend income

General income is any income except that from savings or dividends.

The following chart shows the tax bands and rates for these three types of income, and is based on the tax year 2007/08.

Tax bands and tax rates, 2007/08			
Higher Rate	40%	40%	32.5%
£34,600			
Basic Rate	22%	20%	10%
£2,230			
Starting Rate	10%	10%	10%
£0			
	General Income	**Savings Income**	**Dividend Income**

using the rates and bands

It is vital when working out an individual's tax that the taxable income is analysed into these three categories, and a specific order is followed when working up through the tax bands. This order is:

- general income
- savings income
- dividend income

Dividend income is considered the 'top slice' of an individual's taxable income, with savings income the next slice down.

Suppose someone has taxable income (after deducting the personal allowance) as follows for the tax year 2007/08:

- general income   £15,000
- savings income   £12,000
- dividend income   £10,000

The bands would be worked through starting with the general income amounts and rates, then moving up through the savings income rates, and finally using the dividend income rates.

The band levels apply to the whole income, so each time we move into the next type of income we use the cumulative effect of the income to determine the rate. In our example, this would work as follows:

General Income	£2,230 x 10%	= £223.00
	£12,770 x 22% (the rest of the £15,000)	= £2,809.40
Savings Income	£12,000 x 20% (all at the basic rate)	= £2,400.00
Dividend Income	£7,600 x 10% (up to £34,600 cumulative)	= £760.00
	£2,400 x 32.5% (the rest of the dividends)	= £780.00
Total tax liability		£6,972.40

The diagram below (which is not to scale) illustrates how the system works, using the figures shown above. Notice how the bar representing each type of income starts at the level that the previous one ended. This is the key to understanding the system.

The personal allowance is deducted from the general income when analysing the taxable income. If there is insufficient general income to do this then the savings income is used, and so on.

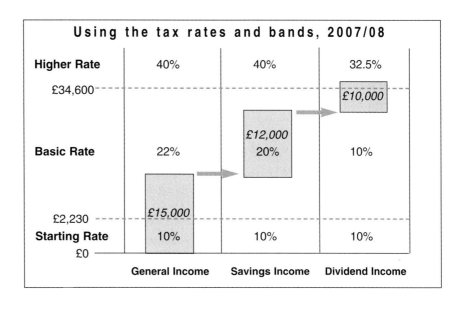

To summarise:

- always work up the bands, following the order:
  - general income
  - savings income
  - dividend income
- always use the cumulative taxable income totals to determine the bands

We can now build on the last Case Study to look at a more comprehensive income tax computation.

ANNE INVESTOR:
INCOME TAX COMPUTATION

Anne Investor has investment income for 2007/08 (see page 3.4) that has been summarised as follows:

Savings Income

	Amount Received £	Tax Deducted £	Assessable Amount £
Total	13,800.00	3,250.00	17,050.00

Dividend Income

	Amount Received £	Tax Credit £	Assessable Amount £
Total	8,550.00	950.00	9,500.00

Anne also has gross income from employment for 2007/08 of £15,000, from which £1,883.00 was deducted under PAYE.
She is entitled to the normal personal allowance of £5,225.

required
Using an income tax computation, calculate the income tax liability for 2007/08, and the amount of tax that Anne has not yet paid.

solution

Income Tax Computation 2007/08

	Income	Tax already paid
	£	£
Employment Income	15,000	1,883
Savings income (as above)	17,050	3,250
Dividend income (as above)	9,500	950
Total Income	41,550	6,083
Less Personal Allowance	5,225	
Taxable Income	36,325	

Analysis of Taxable Income:

General Income	(£15,000 - £5,225)	£9,775
Savings Income		£17,050
Dividend Income		£9,500
		£36,325

Income Tax Calculation:

General Income:

		£	£
£2,230 x 10%		223.00	
£7,545 x 22%	(the rest of £9,775)	1,659.90	
£9,775			1,882.90

Savings Income:

£17,050 x 20%	(all in the basic rate band)	3,410.00	
			3,410.00

Dividend Income:

£7,775 x 10%	(£34,600 − (£9,775 + £17,050))	777.50	
£1,725 x 32.5%	(the rest of £9,500)	560.62	
£9,500			1,338.12
	Income Tax Liability		6,631.02
	Less Paid		6,083.00
	Income Tax to Pay		548.02

ASSESSMENT SUMMARY

As you can see, the income tax computation in the Case Study is more complicated than the calculations that we saw in the earlier chapters. The way the tax is calculated for each category of income by working up through the bands is illustrated in the chart shown below. Make sure that you can follow the logic, since it is very important for your success in this unit that you can carry out computations like this accurately.

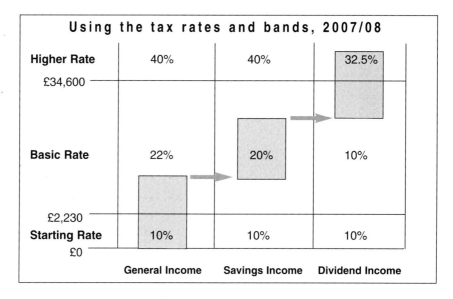

Using the tax rates and bands, 2007/08			
Higher Rate	40%	40%	32.5%
£34,600			
Basic Rate	22%	20%	10%
£2,230			
Starting Rate	10%	10%	10%
£0			
	General Income	**Savings Income**	**Dividend Income**

TAX-FREE INVESTMENT INCOME

Some specific types of investment income are exempt from income tax. You may recall that this was referred to in Chapter 1. The implications of having tax-free investment income are that:

- the tax-free income is not included in the income tax computation, and
- the tax-free income is not recorded on the tax return

In an examination you may be asked to comment on specific types of tax-free income. Alternatively you may be given a situation where an individual's income includes some from tax-free sources. You would then need to identify that income and exclude it from your income tax computation.

The following list covers the main sources of tax-free investment income. Some are investments managed by National Savings & Investments on behalf of the Government, while ISAs and PEPs are managed by commercial organisations in accordance with government rules.

- increases in value of National Savings Certificates
- Premium Bond prizes
- income from Individual Savings Accounts (ISAs)
- income from Personal Equity Plans (PEPs)

Note that the interest from the National Savings and Investments 'Easy Access Savings Account' that has replaced the Ordinary Account is all taxable, with no exempt portion. Like other National Savings and Investments Accounts, the interest is paid gross.

ISAs were introduced in 1999, and were designed to replace the previous tax-free investment vehicles of PEPs. However existing PEPs will maintain their tax-free status.

An investment of up to £7,000 can be made into an ISA in a tax year. This is divided into cash, life insurance and stocks and shares. The maximum that can be invested in the cash component (eg designated bank or building society accounts) is currently £3,000 in a tax year.

Where shares are owned through a PEP or an ISA, any income from dividends is free of income tax, and you should therefore ignore it in any tax computation.

COMPLETING THE RELEVANT TAX RETURN PAGE

Income from UK investments (savings and dividends) is recorded on page 3 of the common part of the tax return. The page starts with the question 'Did you receive any income from UK savings and investments?' If there is any of this income, the 'yes' box is ticked and the page needs to be completed.

Most of the page is made up of lines consisting of three boxes. These represent 'net', tax deducted and 'gross' amounts. This means that if your workings are laid out as shown earlier in this chapter, the form should be easy to complete.

Where figures include pence, throughout the tax return, income should be *rounded down* to the £. This applies to the 'gross' and 'net' amounts that are required on page 3. Tax deducted and tax credits should be *rounded up* to the next £. This may mean that the figures don't quite cross-cast. Where such rounding is necessary, it is carried out after any totalling necessary to calculate the figures for each box.

INCOME *for the year ended 5 April 2007*

Q10 Did you receive any income from UK savings and investments?   YES ☐

If yes , tick this box and then fill in boxes 10.1 to 10.26 as appropriate. Include only your share of any joint savings and investments. If not applicable, go to Question 11.

■ *Interest and alternative finance receipts*

● Interest and alternative finance receipts from UK banks or building societies including UK Internet accounts.
   If you have more than one bank or building society account enter totals in the boxes.

- enter any bank or building society interest and alternative finance receipts that have not had tax taken off . (Interest and alternative finance receipts are usually taxed before you receive them so make sure you should be filling in box 10.1, rather than boxes 10.2 to 10.4.) Enter other types of interest and alternative finance receipts in boxes 10.5 to 10.14, as appropriate.

Taxable amount
10.1 £

- enter details of taxed bank or building society interest and taxed alternative finance receipts. The Working Sheet on page 11 of your Tax Return Guide will help you fill in boxes 10.2 to 10.4.

	Amount after tax taken off	Tax taken off	Gross amount before tax
	10.2 £	**10.3** £	**10.4** £

● Interest distributions from UK authorised unit trusts and open-ended investment companies (dividend distributions go below)

	Amount after tax taken off	Tax taken off	Gross amount before tax
	10.5 £	**10.6** £	**10.7** £

● National Savings & Investments (other than First Option Bonds and Fixed Rate Savings Bonds and the first £70 of interest from an Ordinary Account)

Taxable amount
10.8 £

● National Savings & Investments First Option Bonds and Fixed Rate Savings Bonds

	Amount after tax taken off	Tax taken off	Gross amount before tax
	10.9 £	**10.10** £	**10.11** £

● Other income from UK savings and investments (except dividends)

	Amount after tax taken off	Tax taken off	Gross amount before tax
	10.12 £	**10.13** £	**10.14** £

■ *Dividends*

● Dividends and other qualifying distributions from UK companies (enter distributions from the tax exempt profits of a Real Estate Investment Trust at Q13)

	Dividend/distribution	Tax credit	Dividend/distribution plus credit
	10.15 £	**10.16** £	**10.17** £

● Dividend distributions from UK authorised unit trusts and open-ended investment companies

	Dividend/distribution	Tax credit	Dividend/distribution plus credit
	10.18 £	**10.19** £	**10.20** £

● Stock dividends from UK companies

	Dividend	Notional tax	Dividend plus notional tax
	10.21 £	**10.22** £	**10.23** £

● Non-qualifying distributions and loans written off

	Distribution/loan	Notional tax	Taxable amount
	10.24 £	**10.25** £	**10.26** £

© Crown Copyright

Page 3 of the form is reproduced on the previous page. The boxes that we are most likely to use are:

- box numbers 10.2, 10.3, and 10.4 for bank and building society interest.
- box number 10.8 for National Savings & Investments account interest.
- box numbers 10.12, 10.13, and 10.14 for interest from government securities ('gilts') and loans to local government or companies.
- box numbers 10.15, 10.16, and 10.17 for dividend income.

We will now use the data from the Case Study to demonstrate how the page is completed.

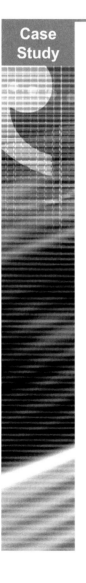

Case Study

ANNE INVESTOR:
COMPLETING THE TAX RETURN

The 2007/08 investment income for Anne Investor (see page 3.5) has been analysed as follows:

SAVINGS INCOME

Date	Details	Amount Received	Tax Deducted	Assessable Amount
		£	£	£
30/6/07	Newtown BS	1,200.00	300.00	1,500.00
30/9/07	CIC Debenture	5,000.00	1,250.00	6,250.00
31/12/07	NS&I Inv A/C	800.00	-	800.00
31/1/08	Bank of Cambria	6,500.00	1,625.00	8,125.00
31/3/08	Callifax Bank	300.00	75.00	375.00
Total		13,800.00	3,250.00	17,050.00

DIVIDEND INCOME

Date	Details	Amount Received	Tax Credit	Assessable Amount
		£	£	£
31/5/07	Gloxxo plc	1,800.00	200.00	2,000.00
31/8/07	CIC plc	6,750.00	750.00	7,500.00
Total		8,550.00	950.00	9,500.00

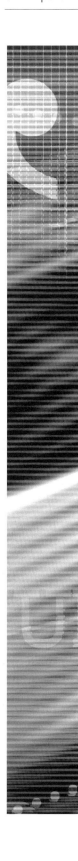

required

Complete page 3 of the 2007/08 tax return, using the above information.

solution

The income needs to be analysed further, in line with the requirements of the form.

Boxes 10.2 – 10.4

Date	Details	Amount Received	Tax Deducted	Assessable Amount
		£	£	£
30/6/07	Newtown BS	1,200.00	300.00	1,500.00
31/1/08	Bank of Cambria	6,500.00	1,625.00	8,125.00
31/3/08	Callifax Bank	300.00	75.00	375.00
		8,000	2,000	10,000

Box 10.8

31/12/07	NS&I Inv A/C	£800

Boxes 10.12 – 10.14

Date	Details	Amount Received	Tax Deducted	Assessable Amount
		£	£	£
30/9/07	CIC Debenture	5,000	1,250	6,250

Boxes 10.15 – 10.17

Date	Details	Amount Received	Tax Credit	Assessable Amount
		£	£	£
31/5/07	Gloxxo plc	1,800.00	200.00	2,000.00
31/8/07	CIC plc	6,750.00	750.00	7,500.00
Total		8,550	950	9,500

Always check to make sure that the total of the boxes running down the right hand side of the tax return page equals the total assessable amount of savings and dividend income. In this case they both amount to £26,550.

The completed page is shown opposite.

Q10 Did you receive any income from UK savings and investments?   YES ✔   If yes , tick this box and then fill in boxes 10.1 to 10.26 as appropriate. Include only your share of any joint savings and investments. If not applicable, go to Question 11.

- ### *Interest and alternative finance receipts*

- Interest and alternative finance receipts from UK banks or building societies including UK Internet accounts.
  If you have more than one bank or building society account enter totals in the boxes.

  - enter any bank or building society interest and alternative finance receipts that have not had tax taken off . (Interest and alternative finance receipts are usually taxed before you receive them so make sure you should be filling in box 10.1, rather than boxes 10.2 to 10.4.) Enter other types of interest and alternative finance receipts in boxes 10.5 to 10.14, as appropriate.

    Taxable amount
    10.1 £

  - enter details of taxed bank or building society interest and taxed alternative finance receipts. The Working Sheet on page 11 of your Tax Return Guide will help you fill in boxes 10.2 to 10.4.

	Amount after tax taken off	Tax taken off	Gross amount before tax
	10.2 £ 8,000	**10.3** £ 2,000	**10.4** £ 10,000

- Interest distributions from UK authorised unit trusts and open-ended investment companies (dividend distributions go below)

	Amount after tax taken off	Tax taken off	Gross amount before tax
	10.5 £	**10.6** £	**10.7** £

- National Savings & Investments (other than First Option Bonds and Fixed Rate Savings Bonds and the first £70 of interest from an Ordinary Account)

    Taxable amount
    10.8 £ 800

- National Savings & Investments First Option Bonds and Fixed Rate Savings Bonds

	Amount after tax taken off	Tax taken off	Gross amount before tax
	10.9 £	**10.10** £	**10.11** £

- Other income from UK savings and investments (except dividends)

	Amount after tax taken off	Tax taken off	Gross amount before tax
	10.12 £ 5,000	**10.13** £ 1,250	**10.14** £ 6,250

- ### *Dividends*

- Dividends and other qualifying distributions from UK companies (enter distributions from the tax exempt profits of a Real Estate Investment Trust at Q13)

	Dividend/distribution	Tax credit	Dividend/distribution plus credit
	10.15 £ 8,550	**10.16** £ 950	**10.17** £ 9,500

- Dividend distributions from UK authorised unit trusts and open-ended investment companies

	Dividend/distribution	Tax credit	Dividend/distribution plus credit
	10.18 £	**10.19** £	**10.20** £

- Stock dividends from UK companies

	Dividend	Notional tax	Dividend plus notional tax
	10.21 £	**10.22** £	**10.23** £

- Non-qualifying distributions and loans written off

	Distribution/loan	Notional tax	Taxable amount
	10.24 £	**10.25** £	**10.26** £

KEEPING RECORDS

Records of savings and dividend income need to be kept approximately 22 months after the end of the tax year to which they relate. This means that 2007/08 records need to be retained until 31/01/10 – one year after the final submission date for the online tax return.

Typical records that should be retained include:

- interest statements or tax deduction certificates
- dividend vouchers
- account details
- working papers for investment income
- copies of tax returns

The first two items on this list would normally be provided automatically by the organisation making the payments.

Chapter Summary

- Interest and dividends are categorised as 'Savings and Investment Income'. The basis of assessment is the gross equivalent of the amounts received in the tax year. Most interest is received net of a 20% income tax deduction, although interest from some sources is received gross. Dividends are always received after a notional 10% tax credit has been deducted from the assessable amount.

- Savings income and dividend income are both taxed at different rates from general income, although they share the same tax bands. The rates for savings income are 10%, 20% and 40%, while the rates for dividend income are 10%, 10% and 32.5%. Dividend income is considered the top slice of an individual's income, with savings income forming the next slice. This means that great care must be taken when calculating an individual's tax liability if income of these types is included.

- The details of savings and dividend income are recorded on page 3 of the common part of an individual's tax return. The documentation to substantiate the income must be retained for one year after the final submission date for the online tax return.

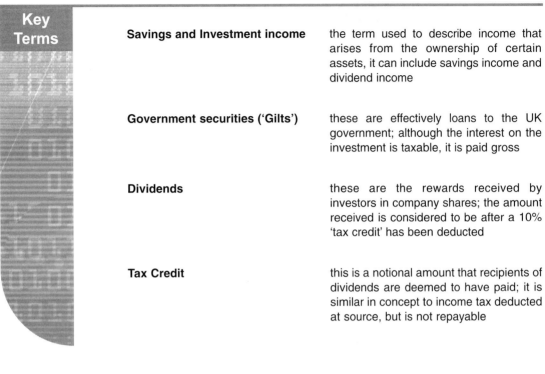

Key Terms		
Savings and Investment income	the term used to describe income that arises from the ownership of certain assets, it can include savings income and dividend income
Government securities ('Gilts')	these are effectively loans to the UK government; although the interest on the investment is taxable, it is paid gross
Dividends	these are the rewards received by investors in company shares; the amount received is considered to be after a 10% 'tax credit' has been deducted
Tax Credit	this is a notional amount that recipients of dividends are deemed to have paid; it is similar in concept to income tax deducted at source, but is not repayable

Student Activities

NOTE: an asterisk (*) after the activity number means that the solution to the question is given at the back of this book.

3.1* Anna Mount received the following amounts from her investments during 2007/08:

Date Received	Details	Amount Received
30/6/07	Nat East Bank Interest	£1,600
30/9/07	Osborne plc Dividends	£2,700
31/12/07	National Savings & Investments (NS&I):	
	Easy Access Savings Account Interest	£30
31/12/07	National Savings & Investments:	
	Investment Account Interest	£300

Required

Calculate the assessable amounts of savings and dividend income for 2007/08, and the associated amounts of tax deducted at source and tax credits.

3.2* Max Growth has provided you with the following details of the amounts that he has received during 2007/08 from his various investments.

Date Received	Details	Amount Rec'd
		£
31/5/2007	Dividend from PCR plc	1,440.00
30/6/2007	Oldport Building Society A/C Interest	1,680.00
30/9/2007	Interest from PCR plc Debenture	2,000.00
31/12/2007	National Savings & Investments Investment A/C Interest	100.00
31/1/2008	Exchequer Stock (Gilt) Interest	6,500.00
31/3/2008	Premium Bond Prize	5,000.00

Required

(a) Produce schedules of the amounts of savings and dividend income assessable in 2007/08, and the amounts of tax deducted at source and tax credits.

(b) Enter the necessary data onto page 3 of Max's income tax return for 2007/08 (see next page)

3.3* Sophie had the following income in 2007/08:

Income from Employment (gross amount)	£28,500
Building Society Interest (net amount received)	£1,200
Dividends from UK Companies (amount received)	£3,600
Property Income (agreed assessable amount)	£1,900

Sophie had income tax deducted under PAYE of £4,853. She is entitled to the normal personal allowance of £5,225.

Prepare Sophie's Income Tax Computation for the tax year, including calculations of her total income tax liability, and the part of this amount that has yet to be paid.

3.4 Brian had the following income in 2007/08:

Salary of £1800 per month (gross) from his employment.	
Dividends from UK companies (amount received)	£2,700
Interest on National Savings & Investments Accounts (amounts received):	
Easy Access Savings Account	£65
Investment Account	£300
Bank Deposit Account Interest (amount received)	£1,600

Brian had £3,335 deducted during 2007/08 under PAYE. He is entitled to a personal allowance of £5,225.

Prepare Brian's Income Tax Computation for the tax year, including calculations of his total income tax liability, and the part of this amount that has yet to be paid.

Q10 Did you receive any income from UK savings and investments?   YES

If yes , tick this box and then fill in boxes 10.1 to 10.26 as appropriate. Include only your share of any joint savings and investments. If not applicable, go to Question 11.

■ *Interest and alternative finance receipts*

● Interest and alternative finance receipts from UK banks or building societies including UK Internet accounts.
If you have more than one bank obuilding society account entetotals in the boxes.

- enter any bank or building society interest and alternative finance receipts that have not had tax taken off . (Interest and alternative finance receipts are usually taxed before you receive them so make sure you should be filling in box 10.1, rather than boxes 10.2 to 10.4.) Enter other types of interest and alternative finance receipts in boxes 10.5 to 10.14, as appropriate.

Taxable amount
10.1 £

- enter details of taxed bank or building society interest and taxed alternative finance receipts. The Working Sheet on page 11 of your Tax Return Guide will help you fill in boxes 10.2 to 10.4.

	Amount after tax taken off	Tax taken off	Gross amount before tax
	10.2 £	**10.3** £	**10.4** £

● Interest distributions from UK authorised unit trusts and open-ended investment companies (dividend distributions go below)

	Amount after tax taken off	Tax taken off	Gross amount before tax
	10.5 £	**10.6** £	**10.7** £

● National Savings & Investments (other than First Option Bonds and Fixed Rate Savings Bonds and the first £70 of interest from an Ordinary Account)

Taxable amount
10.8 £

● National Savings & Investments First Option Bonds and Fixed Rate Savings Bonds

	Amount after tax taken off	Tax taken off	Gross amount before tax
	10.9 £	**10.10** £	**10.11** £

● Other income from UK savings and investments (except dividends)

	Amount after tax taken off	Tax taken off	Gross amount before tax
	10.12 £	**10.13** £	**10.14** £

■ *Dividends*

● Dividends and other qualifying distributions from UK companies (enter distributions from the tax exempt profits of a Real Estate Investment Trust at Q13)

	Dividend/distribution	Tax credit	Dividend/distribution plus credit
	10.15 £	**10.16** £	**10.17** £

● Dividend distributions from UK authorised unit trusts and open-ended investment companies

	Dividend/distribution	Tax credit	Dividend/distribution plus credit
	10.18 £	**10.19** £	**10.20** £

● Stock dividends from UK companies

	Dividend	Notional tax	Dividend plus notional tax
	10.21 £	**10.22** £	**10.23** £

● Non-qualifying distributions and loans written off

	Distribution/loan	Notional tax	Taxable amount
	10.24 £	**10.25** £	**10.26** £

3.5   Major Player had employment income of £23,000 (gross) in 2007/08, on which he paid £3,643 under PAYE. He has provided you with the following details of the amounts that he has received from his investments. He is entitled to a personal allowance of £5,225.

Date Received	Details	Amount Rec'd
		£
31/3/2007	Osborne Bank Deposit Account Interest	190.00
31/5/2007	Dividend from Growth plc	3,600.00
30/6/2007	3.5% War Loan Interest ('Gilt')	1,500.00
30/9/2007	Interest from Nationside cash ISA	300.00
31/12/2007	National Savings & Investments –	
	Investment A/C Interest	500.00
31/1/2008	Bank of Northumberland Deposit A/C Interest	9,500.00
31/3/2008	Osborne Bank Deposit Account Interest	600.00
30/6/2008	Dividend from Growth plc	1,600.00

Required

(a)   Produce schedules of the amounts of savings and dividend income assessable in the tax year, and the amounts of tax deducted at source and tax credits.

(b)   Prepare an Income Tax Computation for the tax year, including calculations of his total income tax liability, and the part of this amount that has yet to be paid.

(c)   Complete page 3 of Major Player's tax return for the tax year (see next page).

| Q10 | Did you receive any income from UK savings and investments? | YES | If yes , tick this box and then fill in boxes 10.1 to 10.26 as appropriate. Include only your share of any joint savings and investments. If not applicable, go to Question 11. |

■ *Interest and alternative finance receipts*

● Interest and alternative finance receipts from UK banks or building societies including UK Internet accounts.
If you have more than one bank or building society account enter totals in the boxes.

- enter any bank or building society interest and alternative finance receipts that have not had tax taken off . (Interest and alternative finance receipts are usually taxed before you receive them so make sure you should be filling in box 10.1, rather than boxes 10.2 to 10.4.) Enter other types of interest and alternative finance receipts in boxes 10.5 to 10.14, as appropriate.

Taxable amount
10.1 £

- enter details of taxed bank or building society interest and taxed alternative finance receipts. The Working Sheet on page 11 of your Tax Return Guide will help you fill in boxes 10.2 to 10.4.

Amount after tax taken off	Tax taken off	Gross amount before tax
10.2 £	10.3 £	10.4 £

● Interest distributions from UK authorised unit trusts and open-ended investment companies (dividend distributions go below)

Amount after tax taken off	Tax taken off	Gross amount before tax
10.5 £	10.6 £	10.7 £

● National Savings & Investments (other than First Option Bonds and Fixed Rate Savings Bonds and the first £70 of interest from an Ordinary Account)

Taxable amount
10.8 £

● National Savings & Investments First Option Bonds and Fixed Rate Savings Bonds

Amount after tax taken off	Tax taken off	Gross amount before tax
10.9 £	10.10 £	10.11 £

● Other income from UK savings and investments (except dividends)

Amount after tax taken off	Tax taken off	Gross amount before tax
10.12 £	10.13 £	10.14 £

■ *Dividends*

● Dividends and other qualifying distributions from UK companies (enter distributions from the tax exempt profits of a Real Estate Investment Trust at Q13)

Dividend/distribution	Tax credit	Dividend/distribution plus credit
10.15 £	10.16 £	10.17 £

● Dividend distributions from UK authorised unit trusts and open-ended investment companies

Dividend/distribution	Tax credit	Dividend/distribution plus credit
10.18 £	10.19 £	10.20 £

● Stock dividends from UK companies

Dividend	Notional tax	Dividend plus notional tax
10.21 £	10.22 £	10.23 £

● Non-qualifying distributions and loans written off

Distribution/loan	Notional tax	Taxable amount
10.24 £	10.25 £	10.26 £

4 Income from employment

In this chapter we examine:

*   the basis of assessment for employment income
*   benefits in kind
*   allowable expenses and deductions
*   completing the employment section of the tax return
*   the keeping of records

PERFORMANCE CRITERIA COVERED

unit 19: PREPARING PERSONAL TAXATION COMPUTATIONS

element 19.1 calculate income from employment

A   prepare accurate computations of emoluments, including benefits in kind

B   list allowable expenses and deductions

C   record relevant details of income from employment accurately and legibly in the tax return

D   make computations and submissions in accordance with current tax law and take account of current Inland Revenue practice

F   give timely and constructive advice to clients on the recording of information relevant to tax returns

THE BASIS OF ASSESSMENT FOR EMPLOYMENT INCOME

Income from employment is assessed under 'Employment, Pensions and Social Security Income', and the income tax is normally collected through Pay-As-You-Earn (PAYE). We will generally include this in the income tax computation simply as 'employment income'. The basis of assessment is:

	gross income **received** in the tax year
plus	the assessable value of any benefits in kind,
less	any allowable deductions
equals	assessable income from employment

You will notice that (like savings and investment income) we are using a **cash basis** to determine which tax year any receipts are linked to, not an accruals basis. The period in which the income was earned may therefore not always be the one in which it is assessed; this could apply for example to commissions or bonuses that are earned in one period, but paid to the employee in a later one. You should therefore disregard any reference to the period in which employment income was earned, and concentrate just on when it was received. As well as income from current employment, this category of income also includes pensions received and certain social security benefits.

employment and self-employment

The income from employment includes salaries, wages, bonuses, commissions, fees and gratuities (tips) where they relate to a job or office. It is important to distinguish between the concept of being employed (and having employment income) and being self-employed, the income from which is assessed as 'trading income'. Employment income results from an employment contract (even an implied one) where the employer exerts control over the employee. A self-employed person or contractor has much more control over the way he or she operates.

pay as you earn

PAYE (Pay-As-You-Earn) is the system that HM Revenue & Customs uses to deduct tax at source from payments from employers to employees. It works by allocating a code number – a **tax code** – to every employee. This code is based on personal allowances and possibly other adjustments. For example, someone with just the normal personal allowance of £5,225 would have a code including the number 522. The number ensures the employer deducts income tax by using a proportion of the available tax allowances every time the employee is paid.

The tax code can be adjusted to take account of benefits in kind or allowable deductions, and therefore should ensure that an appropriate amount of tax is deducted. In this chapter we will provide information about tax deducted under PAYE, and use it in our computations (as we have already) to calculate any final balance of tax to be paid or repaid.

PAYE uses certain documents that you need to be aware of, and may need to extract information from. The forms that we will describe briefly now are the P45, the P60 and the P11D.

The **P45** form is used when an employee leaves a job. It records the pay and tax to date for the current tax year, and also the employee's tax code. A copy of the form is sent to HM Revenue & Customs when the employee leaves, and the remaining parts of the form are given to the employee to pass on to his new employer. In this way the new employer should have all the relevant information to deduct an appropriate amount of tax from the first payment to the new employee. A P45 is shown on the next page.

The **P60** is a summary of pay, income tax and national insurance for the tax year. All employees must be provided with a P60 shortly after the end of the tax year. A P60 is shown on page 4.4.

The **P11D** (see pages 4.14 - 4.15 for the 2006/07 version) is a summary of benefits in kind that must be issued by employers to all relevant employees who earn over £8,500 pa (including the value of their benefits). You will not be expected to complete a P11D in your examination. We will see how this form works later in this chapter.

We will now examine benefits in kind.

BENEFITS IN KIND

You will have noticed that employment income includes the assessable value of '**benefits in kind**'. This is the term used to describe any reward that an employee receives because of his employment that is not paid in money. It can therefore apply to a range of 'non-cash' items ranging from use of a company car to holidays paid for by the employer.

There are some situations where a payment on behalf of an employee may count as a benefit in kind, but the expense incurred would also be considered an **allowable deduction**, thereby cancelling out the effect of any tax charge. We will examine these situations in the 'allowable deductions' section later in this chapter.

Inland Revenue

Details of employee leaving work
Copy for Inland Revenue office
P45
Part 1

1 PAYE Reference

Office number   Reference number

2 Employee's National Insurance number

(Mr Mrs Miss Ms Other)

3 Surname
(in CAPITALS)

First name(s)
(in CAPITALS)

4 Leaving date
(in figures)

Day   Month   Year

5 Continue Student
Loan Deductions(Y)

6 Tax Code at leaving date. *If Week 1 or Month 1 basis applies, write 'X' in the box marked* Week 1 or Month 1.

Code   Week 1 or Month 1

7 Last entries on *Deductions Working Sheet* (P11). **Complete only if Tax Code is cumulative.** *Make no entry here if Week 1 or Month 1 basis applies. Go to item 8.*

Week or month number

Week   Month

Total pay to date £   p

Total tax to date £   p

8 This employment pay and tax. ■ *No entry is needed if Tax Code is cumulative and amounts are the same as item 7 entry.*

Total pay in this employment £   p

Total tax in this employment £   p

9 Works number/
Payroll number

10 Department or
branch, if any

11 Employee's private address and Postcode

FOR INFORMATION ONLY

12 I certify that the details entered above in items 1 to 10 are correct.

Employer's name, address and Postcode

Date

To the employer   **Please complete with care ★**   For IR office use

- Complete this form following the 'What to do when an employee leaves' instructions in the Employer's Help Book, *'Day-to-day payroll, E13'*.
  ★ Make sure the details are clear on all four parts of this form. Make sure your name and address is shown on Parts 1 and 1A.

- Detach Part 1 and send it to your

Inland Revenue office immediately.

- Hand Parts 1A, 2 and 3 (unseparated) to your employee when he or she leaves.

- If the employee has died, write 'D' in this box and send all four parts of this form (unseparated) to your Inland Revenue office immediately.

P45   BS12/01

P60 End of Year Certificate

Tax year to 5 April | **2007**

To the employee:

Please keep this certificate in a safe place as **you will need it if you have to fill in a Tax Return or make a claim for Tax Credits.**

It also helps you check that your employer is using the correct National Insurance number and deducting the right rate of National Insurance contributions.

By law you are required to tell HM Revenue & Customs about any income that is not fully taxed, even if you are not sent a Tax Return.

HM REVENUE & CUSTOMS

The figures marked ★ should be used for your Tax Return, if you get one

Employee's details

Surname

Forenames or initials

National Insurance number

Works/payroll number

Pay and Income Tax details

	Pay		Tax deducted	
	£	p	£	p
In previous employment(s)				
			if refund mark 'R'	
★ In this employment		—		
Total for year				

Employee's Widows & Orphans/Life Assurance contributions in this employment ★

Final tax code

National Insurance contributions in this employment

NIC table letter	Earnings up to and including the Earnings Threshold (where earnings are equal to or exceed the Lower Earnings Limit)		Earnings above the Earnings Threshold, up to and including the Upper Earnings Limit	Employee's contributions	
	£		£	£	p

Statutory payments
included in the pay 'In this employment' figure above

	£	p		£	p		£	p
Statutory Maternity Pay			Statutory Paternity Pay			Statutory Adoption Pay		

Other details

Student Loan Deductions in this employment *(whole £s only)*

£

To employee

Your employer's full name and address (including postcode)

Employer PAYE reference

Certificate by Employer/Paying Office:

This form shows your total pay for Income Tax purposes in this employment for the year.
Any overtime, bonus, commission etc, Statutory Sick Pay, Statutory Maternity Pay, Statutory Paternity Pay or Statutory Adoption Pay is included.

Originally, benefits were assessed based on the cash cost to the employer of providing the employee with the benefit. While this rule is still used in some situations, there are now many types of benefit where specific rules are used to calculate the assessable amounts. Through this section we will now look at the more important benefits and how they are assessed. Although this is a complicated area you must learn how to deal with all these examples, as they are popular examination topics.

company cars

A car owned (or leased) by the employer, but available for both business and private use by an employee is an assessable benefit. Most company cars have at least some private use, since the journey to and from work is considered private rather than business mileage. The way that the benefit is calculated is very specific, and is divided into two separate types of benefit:

- **A scale charge for having private use of the car** – the assessable amount is a percentage of the car's list price, and is deemed to include all the costs of the car, except fuel. It therefore includes road tax, insurance, repairs and servicing etc, and none of these costs are assessable separately.

- **A scale charge for using fuel for private motoring** if this is paid for by the employer.

We will describe the two benefits in turn.

scale charges for private use of cars

The scale charge for having use of the car depends on:

- the list price of the car when new, and

- the car's carbon dioxide emissions, measured in grams per kilometre (g/km), and

- whether the car is petrol or diesel.

The system works by using percentages linked to emission levels. The appropriate percentage (between 15% and 35%) is then applied to the list price of the car when new, and the result forms the assessable amount of the benefit. The percentages are different for each tax year, since it is expected that typical emission levels will generally fall as new models are introduced.

For **2007/08** the 15% charge for petrol cars relates to emissions of up to 140 g/km, and increase by 1% for every 5 g/km over 140 g/km up to a maximum level of 35%. Before calculating the percentage, the car's emission level is rounded down to a multiple of 5 (eg 199 would be rounded down to 195).

---

example

If an employee is provided with a petrol engine car with a list price of £20,000, and an emission level of 203 g/km throughout 2007/08, then the assessable benefit would be calculated as:

Percentage: 15% + (1% x (200 – 140) / 5)

                    = 15% + 12%   = 27%.

The 27% is then multiplied by the list price of the car:

Benefit: £20,000 x 27% = £5,400.

The percentages that apply to diesel cars are 3% more than those for petrol powered cars. This is because diesel cars naturally have slightly lower emission levels than similar petrol models.

Both petrol and diesel cars are subject to a maximum percentage of 35%.

---

example

If an employee is provided with a diesel engine car with a list price of £15,000, and an emission level of 177 grams per kilometre throughout 2007/08, then the assessable benefit would be:

£15,000 x (15% + 7% + 3% = 25%) = £3,750.

You will need to remember how to carry out the calculations for petrol and diesel cars. In an examination you are likely to be given the base figure of 140g/km.

The figure calculated is adjusted in the following circumstances:

- where the car is not available to the employee for the whole tax year, the assessable amount is time-apportioned
- where the employee makes a *revenue* contribution to the employer for the use of the car, this is deducted from the assessable amount that would otherwise apply
- where the employee makes a *capital* contribution towards the cost of the car, this is deducted from the list price before the appropriate percentage is applied
- where the list price of the car is over £80,000, then £80,000 is used instead of the actual price in the calculation

fuel benefit for private use of company cars

When an employee is provided with a company car, the employer may agree to pay for the fuel that the employee uses for private mileage as well as for business use. If this happens, a further assessable benefit arises, calculated as follows:

In **2007/08** the same percentage as is applied to the car (based on its emissions), is multiplied by a fixed amount of £14,400.

---

example

If an employee is provided with a petrol engine car with a list price of £20,000, and an emission level of 203 g/km throughout 2007/08, then the assessable **fuel benefit** would be:

- £14,400 x 27% = £3,888 (by applying the emission percentage to the fixed amount of £14,400).

The fuel charge is time-apportioned if the car, for which private fuel is provided, is not available for the whole tax year. Note however that the same fuel charge applies if the employee has **any** fuel provided for private mileage, no matter how little or how much. Unlike the car benefit itself, making a contribution to the employer will have no effect on the assessable benefit for fuel. The only way for an employee to avoid the charge is to pay privately (or reimburse the employer) for **all** private fuel that has been used.

pool cars

Pool cars are cars whose use is shared amongst employees for business purposes. There is no assessable benefit for employees who use pool cars, but the definition of a pool car is strict. To qualify as a non-assessable pool car it must:

- be primarily used for business purposes and any private use must be incidental
- be used by several employees, and
- not normally be kept at an employee's home

vans

Where an employer provides a small van that can be used privately there is a scale charge. The assessable benefit for 2007/08 is £3,000 (previously it was either £500 or £350). This amount includes any private fuel, and so is probably less than the benefit assessed on a car. Where the employee uses the van between home and work but no other private use, this will not be classed as a benefit.

cheap (or 'beneficial') loans

Where a loan is granted to an employee and charged at less than the HM Revenue & Customs official interest rate, there may be an assessable benefit. This official rate is currently 5%.

The benefit is calculated as the difference between the interest charge that would be generated by using the official rate, and the actual interest charged. However, there is no assessable benefit if the loan (or total loans) outstanding is £5,000 or less throughout the tax year.

If a loan is written-off by the employer then the whole amount is assessable.

---

example

An employer provides his employee with a £10,000 loan at an interest rate of 2% per year. The actual interest charge would be £200 per year, assuming no capital repayments. The assessable benefit would therefore be (£10,000 x 5%) minus £200 = £300.

---

living accommodation

Where the employer provides free accommodation for an employee, this can result in an assessable benefit. Unless an exemption applies (as we will see later in this section), the assessable benefit works as follows:

- The assessable amount for the accommodation itself is normally the amount of the 'annual value' (based on the rateable value).

- Where the accommodation was purchased by the employer, and cost more than £75,000 then an additional assessment is applied. This is based on the excess of the purchase price over £75,000 multiplied by the HM Revenue & Customs official interest rate. This is the same rate (currently 5%) that is used to calculate the benefit of cheap loans as described above.

- The cost of any other living expenses paid by the employer would be added to the assessment (for example electricity costs). Furniture and other assets provided by the employer will also result in an assessable benefit as we will see in the next section.

- If an employee does not have use of the accommodation for the whole tax year, then any assessable benefit (as described above) would be time-apportioned.

---

example

An employee is allowed to live in a company flat free of charge throughout the tax year. The annual value of the flat is £1,500, and the employer also pays the heating costs of the flat which amount to £600 per year.

The flat cost the employer £100,000 when it was originally purchased.

Assuming that the employee could not claim any exemption from the flat being assessable, the amount would be calculated as follows:

Annual value	£1,500
Additional charge (£100,000 - £75,000) x 5%	£1,250
Other expenses paid by employer	£600
Total assessable benefit	£3,350

If the accommodation was only available to the employee for 6 months of the tax year the benefit would be £3,350 x 6/12 = £1,675.

For the accommodation itself to result in no assessable benefit one of the following situations must apply:

- the employee is a representative occupier (for example a caretaker)
- it is customary to provide the employee with accommodation in that particular job (for example a vicar)
- the accommodation is provided for security reasons

Note that in these situations the annual value and additional charge for properties over £75,000 is not applied. However any running expenses of the accommodation that are paid for by the employer will still result in an assessable benefit. In these circumstances the benefit of such costs will be restricted to a maximum of 10% of the employee's earnings from the job.

provision of other assets

Where an asset is given to an employee then the assessable benefit is the market value of the asset at that time. Apart from vehicles, if an asset is provided for an employee's private use (but remains belonging to the employer) then there is an assessable benefit of 20% of the market value of the asset when first provided. This benefit would apply to each tax year that it was used by the employee.

If an asset that was provided in this way is subsequently given to the employee (or he/she buys it from the employer) then a further benefit may arise based on the higher of:

- market value at the date of the transfer, and
- market value when first provided, less assessments already applied

From the higher of these figures is deducted any amount paid by the employee.

---

example

An employee is provided with the use of a home entertainment system, when its market value was £1,000. Two years later he buys it from the employer, paying £100, when its market value was £300.

The assessment for each year that it was owned by the employer and the employee used it would be £1,000 x 20% = £200.

The assessment upon purchase would be the higher of:

- market value at the date of the transfer, (£300), and
- market value when first provided, less assessments already applied (£1,000 - £200 - £200 = £600)

ie £600, minus amount paid by the employee of £100 = £500.

These calculations would also apply to furniture owned by the employer in accommodation used by an employee.

In the case of a computer provided to an employee until 2005/06, there was no assessable benefit when the computer has a value of £2,500 or less. For 2006/07 and later years that exemption has been withdrawn, and all computers provided to employees for private use are assessable.

vouchers, credit cards, and other benefits paid by the employer

Where an employee is provided with a voucher that can be spent in a specified way, the benefit is the cost to the employer of providing the voucher. This may be less than the face value of the voucher.

For example, suppose an employer gave his employee a £500 voucher at Christmas to spend in a particular store. If the voucher cost the employer £470 then this amount would be the assessable benefit.

If an employee has use of a company credit card then any expenditure will be assessable, except:

- business expenditure that qualifies as an allowable deduction (see next section), and
- expenditure on benefits that are assessed separately (for example in connection with a company car or its fuel)

Where an employer provides an employee with goods or services for private use, the cost to the employer is the assessable amount. This could arise if an employer paid for a holiday for an employee, or paid their train fare from home to work.

tax-free benefits

The following is a summary of the main benefits that do not give rise to any assessment. They are tax-free.

- childcare provided by the employer (eg a workplace creche) – this exemption does not apply to cash or payment of employees' childcare expenditure
- workplace parking
- staff canteen (provided it is available to all staff)
- in-house sports facilities
- counselling services
- employers' contributions to pension schemes
- mobile telephones (limited to one per employee)
- reimbursement of expenses that are an allowable deduction (see next section)

Case Study

BENNY FITT: EMPLOYMENT INCOME INCLUDING BENEFITS IN KIND

Benny Fitt works as a Sales Manager for ESP Limited. He was employed throughout 2007/08 at a basic salary of £25,000 per year, plus a six-monthly bonus dependent on his performance. He received the following bonus payments:

Period related to bonus	Amount	Date Received
July – Dec 2006	£2,000	28/2/07
Jan – June 2007	£2,400	31/8/07
July – Dec 2007	£2,700	28/2/08
Jan – June 2008	£3,000	31/8/08

He was provided with a Hexus Demon company car and free private fuel throughout the tax year. The car had a petrol engine with an emission rating of 210 g/km, and a list price of £18,500.

He was granted an interest-free loan of £12,000 by ESP Limited on 6/4/07. He had not made any repayments by 5/4/08.

Benny was also provided with a home cinema system on 6/4/06 with a value of £800 at that time. On 6/4/07 he bought the system from the company for £250, when its second-hand value was £400.

required

Calculate the assessable amount of employment income for Benny for the tax year 2007/08. Assume that the HM Revenue & Customs official interest rate is 5% throughout the year.

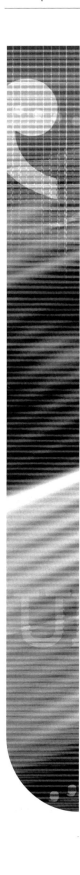

solution

salary and bonuses:

The date that the money was received determines which tax year it is assessed in. This gives the following figures for 2007/08:

		£
Basic Salary		25,000
Bonuses –	rec'd 31 August 07	2,400
	rec'd 28 Feb 08	2,700
		30,100

The other bonuses are assessed before or after the year that we are concerned with.

company car

Here we use the emission level calculation to determine the percentages to apply to the list price of £18,500, as follows.

% (based on 210 g/km) (15% + 14%)	29%
Assessable benefit of car	£5,365

car fuel

benefit based on 29% x fixed amount of £14,400	£4,176

interest-free loan

Since the full amount is outstanding throughout the year, and no interest is charged, the benefit is based on the amount lent multiplied by the official rate.

£12,000 x 5%	£600

home cinema

In the first year (2006/07) 20% of the value is charged (£160). In the second year (2007/08) the charge is based on the original value less previous benefit, since this is greater than the second-hand value.

(£800 – £160) minus £250 paid by Benny	£390

Employment Income Summary

	£
Salary & Bonuses	30,100
Company Car	5,365
Car Fuel	4,176
Loan	600
Home Cinema	390
Employment income assessable amount	40,631

form P11D

Form P11D is an HM Revenue & Customs form which summarises an employee's benefits in kind. Please now look at the next two pages. Using the data from the Case Study, this P11D form shows how Benny's employer lists his benefits in kind. Note that the 2006/07 tax form is used here because the 2007/08 form was not available when this book went to press.

ALLOWABLE DEDUCTIONS

We will now examine the amounts that can be deducted from the income and benefits received in respect of employment, and therefore reduce the employment income assessment. These are specific amounts that the employee has paid out in connection with the employment.

The general rule is that to be allowable against employment income, expenditure must be incurred **wholly, exclusively and necessarily** in the performance of the duties of the employment. You may recognise part of this phrase from our studies of property income; but here the word 'necessarily' is added. This means that strictly speaking allowable expenditure must be for something that the employment duties could not be carried out without – not just that the job is carried out more easily or efficiently because of the expenditure. For example, personal clothing is not an allowable deduction, even if it was bought especially for work and only worn to work. There are specific instances where expenditure is allowable outside this stringent test, but you should use this basic rule when you come across expenditure that you are unsure how to treat.

expenditure reimbursed by the employer

When an employee's expenditure is reimbursed (usually through an 'expenses' claim) the following tax implications are possible:

- Where there is a **'dispensation'** in force from HM Revenue & Customs, it means that it is agreed in advance that expenses will only be paid for allowable expenditure. This means that the reimbursement automatically cancels out the original expenditure and there is no effect on tax and no need to enter the details on a tax return.

- If there isn't a dispensation in force, the reimbursement may still be for expenditure that is allowable. This means that the amount received from the employer is treated as a benefit, but the expenditure by the employee is an allowable deduction. If these amounts are identical they will cancel each other out, but they still need to be shown separately on the tax return, as we will see later. *continued on page 4.16. . .*

HM Revenue & Customs

P11D EXPENSES AND BENEFITS 2006–07

Please ensure your entries are clear on both sides of the form.

Employer details

Employer name

| ESP LIMITED |

Employer PAYE reference

Note to employer
Complete this return for a director, or an employee who earned at a rate of £8,500 a year or more during the year to 5 April 2007.

Note to employee
Your employer has filled in this form, keep it in a safe place. You will need it to complete your 2006–07 Tax Return if you get one.

Employee details

Employee name

| BENNY FITT | If a director tick here ▶

Works number/department   National Insurance number

Date of birth *in figures (if known)*

| D | D | M | M | Y | Y | Y | Y |

Sex **M** – Male **F** – Female

Employers pay Class 1A National Insurance contributions on most benefits. These are shown in boxes which are brown and have a **1A** indicator

A Assets transferred (cars, property, goods or other assets)

		Cost/Market value	Amount made good or from which tax deducted		Cash equivalent	
Description of asset	HOME CINEMA	£ 640	– £ 250	= **1.12**	£ 390	**1A**

B Payments made on behalf of employee

Description of payment		**1.12** £	—
Tax on notional payments not borne by employee within 90 days of receipt of each notional payment		**1.12** £	—

C Vouchers or credit cards

	Gross amount	Amount made good or from which tax deducted	Cash equivalent
Value of vouchers and payments made using credit cards or tokens (for qualifying childcare vouchers the excess over £55 a week)	£	– £	= **1.13** £ —

D Living accommodation

	Cash equivalent	
Cash equivalent of accommodation provided for employee, or his/her family or household	**1.14** £ —	**1A**

E Mileage allowance and passenger payments

	Taxable amount
Amount of car and mileage allowances paid to employee for business travel in employee's own vehicle, and passenger payments, in excess of maximum exempt amounts (See P11D Guide for 2006–07 exempt rates)	**1.15** £ —

F Cars and car fuel *If more than two cars were made available, either at the same time or in succession, please give details on a separate sheet*

	Car 1	Car 2
Make and Model	HEXUS DEMON	—
Date first registered	1/1/04	/ /
Approved CO$_2$ emissions figure for cars registered on or after 1 January 1998 *Tick box if the car does not have an approved CO$_2$ figure*	210 g/km	*See P11D Guide for details of cars that have no approved CO$_2$ figure*
		g/km *See P11D Guide for details of cars that have no approved CO$_2$ figure*
Engine size	1950 cc	cc
Type of fuel or power used *Please use the key letter shown in the P11D Guide*	P	
Dates car was available *Only enter a 'from' or 'to' date if the car was first made available and/or ceased to be available in 2006–07*	From 6/4/07 to 5/4/08	From / / to / /
List price of car *Including car and standard accessories only: if there is no list price, or if it is a classic car, employers see booklet 480*	£ 18,500	£
Accessories *All non-standard accessories, see P11D Guide*	£ —	£
Capital contributions (maximum £5,000) the employee made towards the cost of car or accessories	£ —	£
Amount paid by employee for private use of the car	£ —	£
Date free fuel was withdrawn *Tick if reinstated in year (see P11D Guide)*	/ /	/ /
Cash equivalent of each car	£ 5,365	£ —
Total cash equivalent of all cars available in 2006–07		**1.16** £ 5,365 **1A**
Cash equivalent of fuel for each car	£ 4,176	£ —
Total cash equivalent of fuel for all cars available in 2006–07		**1.17** £ 4,176 **1A**

P11D(2007) DRAFT HMRC 11/06

© Crown Copyright

G Vans

Cash equivalent of all vans made available for private use   **1.18** £ ⬚ 1A

H Interest-free and low interest loans
If the total amount outstanding on all loans does not exceed £5,000 at any time in the year, there is no need to complete this section.

	Loan 1	Loan 2
Number of joint borrowers *(if applicable)*	⬚	⬚
Amount outstanding at 5 April 2006 or at date loan was made if later	£ 12,000	£
Amount outstanding at 5 April 2007 or at date loan was discharged if earlier	£ 12,000	£
Maximum amount outstanding at any time in the year	£ 12,000	£
Total amount of interest paid by the borrower in 2006–07 – *enter "NIL" if none was paid*	£ NIL	£
Date loan was made in 2006–07 if applicable	6/4/07	/ /
Date loan was discharged in 2006–07 if applicable	/ /	/ /
Cash equivalent of loans after deducting any interest paid by the borrower	**1.19** £ 600 1A	**1.19** £ —— 1A

I Private medical treatment or insurance

	Cost to you	Amount made good or from which tax deducted	Cash equivalent
Private medical treatment or insurance	£	– £	= **1.21** £ —— 1A

J Qualifying relocation expenses payments and benefits
Non-qualifying benefits and expenses go in sections M and N below

Excess over £8,000 of all qualifying relocation expenses payments and benefits for each move   **1.22** £ —— 1A

K Services supplied

	Cost to you	Amount made good or from which tax deducted	Cash equivalent
Services supplied to the employee	£	– £	= **1.22** £ —— 1A

L Assets placed at the employee's disposal

	Annual value plus expenses incurred	Amount made good or from which tax deducted	Cash equivalent
Description of asset ⬚	£	– £	= **1.22** £ —— 1A

M Other items (including subscriptions and professional fees)

	Cost to you	Amount made good or from which tax deducted	Cash equivalent
Description of other items ⬚	£	– £	= **1.22** £ —— 1A
Description of other items ⬚	£	– £	= **1.22** £ ——

			Tax paid
Income tax paid but not deducted from director's remuneration			**1.22** £ ——

N Expenses payments made to, or on behalf of, the employee

	Cost to you	Amount made good or from which tax deducted	Taxable payment
Travelling and subsistence payments *(except mileage allowance payments for employee's own car - see section E)*	£	– £	= **1.23** £ ——
Entertainment *(trading organisations read P11D Guide and then enter a tick or a cross as appropriate here)* ⬚	£	– £	= **1.23** £
General expenses allowance for business travel	£	– £	= **1.23** £ ——
Payments for use of home telephone	£	– £	= **1.23** £
Non-qualifying relocation expenses *(those not shown in sections J or M)*	£	– £	= **1.23** £
Description of other expenses ⬚	£	– £	= **1.23** £ ——

We will now look at how to deal with some specific types of expenditure. These items may or may not be reimbursed by an employer.

using your own transport for business

This relates to travelling within the job, (eg journeys from one site to another) not for travelling from home to the normal workplace (which counts as private motoring). HM Revenue & Customs has published mileage rates that constitute allowable expenditure as follows.

Cars and vans:	First 10,000 miles in tax year	40p per mile
	Additional mileage	25p per mile
Motor cycles:		24p per mile
Bicycles:		20p per mile

Note that this does not apply to company cars – only for use of the employees' own transport. It may well be that the employer reimburses a mileage allowance. Where this is exactly in line with these figures the benefit received cancels out the allowable expenditure, but if it is at a higher rate the excess is a net taxable benefit. If the rates paid by the employer are lower (or expenses are not reimbursed at all) then the shortfall is a net allowable deduction. This system is known as 'Approved Mileage Allowance Payments' (AMAP).

entertaining and subsistence

Where an employee incurs expenditure on the costs of spending time away from his/her normal place of work, these costs are normally allowable. Entertaining of the employer's clients is only allowable if the employer has reimbursed the employee, and then the benefit will not be chargeable.

professional fees & subscriptions

Where an employee pays a professional fee or subscription to an organisation that is relevant to his or her employment the cost is an allowable expense. HM Revenue & Customs has a list of approved bodies (available on its website), and the AAT is amongst the accountancy bodies on the list. Where the employer pays the subscription for the employee the benefit received is cancelled out by the allowable deduction.

pension contributions

Contributions that an employee makes to an approved pension scheme are allowable deductions within employment income. If the contributions are made to a scheme run by the employer, then the deduction will often be made automatically before PAYE is operated on the balance of income. If this is the situation, then amounts shown on an employee's P45 and P60 will represent income after the employee's pension contribution has been deducted. You may recall that the employer's contribution to an approved pension scheme is not taxable as a part of an employee's income, so the employee gains two advantages if both he/she and his/her employer contribute to such a scheme.

payroll giving scheme

Where an arrangement has been made between an employer and an approved charity agency, employees can authorise deductions (without limit) through the payroll of donations to charities. This is allowed as a deduction from earnings, and the employer is able to operate PAYE on the income after the donation has been deducted – just like employees' pension contributions. The employee therefore gets tax relief on his/her donations, and the employer passes the gross amount of the donations onto the charity agency, and this organisation distributes the amounts to the named charities.

Case Study

AL LOWE:
BENEFITS AND ALLOWABLE DEDUCTIONS

Al is employed as an administrator by Spencer & Company, and is paid a gross salary of £22,000 per year. He makes a contribution of 5% of his salary to the company pension scheme, (a scheme that is approved by HM Revenue & Customs). Spencer & Company also pays a contribution into the pension fund of 8% of Al's salary.

As a bonus, he was given vouchers to spend on a holiday with a particular travel agent. The retail value of the vouchers was £1500, and these cost Spencer & Company £1350.

Al is required to undertake business journeys in his own car, for which the company agreed to reimburse him at a rate of 50p per mile. Al used his car for 7,500 business miles during the tax year, and the company paid him the agreed amounts. He also claimed £300 for subsistence allowances while away on company business, and this was also paid to him. Spencer & Company has a dispensation in force with HM Revenue & Customs regarding payments for subsistence.

Al pays an annual subscription to the Association of Administrative Managers (a professional body, approved by HM Revenue & Customs). This amounted to £140. Spencer & Company did not reimburse him for this.

Al also pays £30 per month to Oxfam under the 'payroll giving scheme' organised by Spencer & Company. This amount is deducted each month from his salary.

required

Calculate the assessable amount of employment income for Al for the tax year.

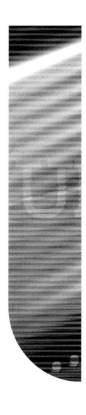

solution

	£
Gross Salary	22,000
less	
5% pension contribution	(1,100)
payroll giving scheme	(360)
Amount used for PAYE purposes	20,540
add benefits:	
Mileage paid in excess of IR approved rate	
7,500 x (50p – 40p)	750
Cost of holiday vouchers	1,350
less allowable deduction:	
Professional fee paid	(140)
Assessable amount	22,500

Note that

- the employer's contribution to the pension scheme is not included as a benefit.

- the subsistence allowance is covered by a dispensation, and so does not need to be considered further.

COMPLETING THE EMPLOYMENT PAGES OF THE TAX RETURN

The tax return supplementary pages relating to employment consist of two pages (E1 and E2), as illustrated on the next two pages. One pair of pages needs to be completed for each separate employment carried out during the tax year. There are four parts to these pages that we need to know about:

- The '**details of employer**' section is at the top of page E1. Boxes 1.1 to 1.5 require the reference number and name and address of the employer, together with start and finish dates if the employment did not continue throughout the tax year. Box 1.6 relates to directors, and box 1.7 can be ignored.

- The remainder of the form requires details of **assessable income**, and commences with boxes 1.8 to 1.11, which relate to income in the form of money. Note that box 1.8 is for the gross pay, although it will be the figure after most company pension contributions and any payroll giving donations have been deducted. The tax deducted under PAYE is inserted in box 1.11. This is the only box in the income section that will not form part of the employment income figure.

Please note that the 2006/07 tax form is used here because the 2007/08 form was not available when this book went to press.

continued on page 4.21 . . .

Income for the year ended 5 April 2007

HM Revenue & Customs

EMPLOYMENT

Name

Tax reference

Fill in these boxes first

If you want help, look up the box numbers in the Notes.

Details of employer

Employer's PAYE reference - the 'HM Revenue & Customs office number and reference' on your P60 or 'PAYE reference' on your P45

1.1

Employer's name

1.2

Date employment started
(only if between 6 April 2006 and 5 April 2007)

1.3 / /

Date employment finished
(only if between 6 April 2006 and 5 April 2007)

1.4 / /

Employer's address

1.5

Postcode

Tick box 1.6 if you were a director of the company

1.6

and, if so, tick box 1.7 if it was a close company

1.7

Income from employment

■ **Money** - see Notes, page EN3.

Before tax

● Payments from P60 (or P45)   1.8 £

● Payments not on P60, etc.   - tips   1.9 £

                                 - other payments (excluding expenses entered below and lump sums and compensation payments or benefits entered overleaf)   1.10 £

Tax taken off

● UK tax taken off payments in boxes 1.8 to 1.10   1.11 £

■ **Benefits and expenses** - see Notes, pages EN3 to EN6. If any benefits connected with termination of employment were received, or enjoyed, after that termination and were from a   former employer you need Help Sheet IR204, available from   the Orderline. Do not enter such benefits here.

	Amount			Amount
● Assets transferred/ payments made for you	1.12 £		● Vans	1.18 £
● Vouchers, credit cards and tokens	1.13 £		● Interest-free and low-interest loans see Notes, page EN5.	1.19 £
● Living accommodation	1.14 £		box 1.20 is not used.	
● Excess mileage allowance and passenger payments	1.15 £		● Private medical or dental insurance	1.21 £
● Company cars	1.16 £		● Other benefits	1.22 £
● Fuel for company cars	1.17 £		● Expenses payments received and balancing charges	1.23 £

© Crown Copyright

Income from employment continued

■ *Lump sums and compensation payments or benefits including such payments and benefits from a former employer*

You must read pages EN6 and EN7 of the Notes before filling in boxes 1.24 to 1.30.

Reliefs

- £30,000 exception — **1.24** £
- Foreign service and disability — **1.25** £
- Retirement and death lump sums — **1.26** £
- Exempt employer's contributions to an overseas pension scheme — **1.26A** £

Taxable lump sums

- From box B of Help Sheet IR204 — **1.27** £
- From box K of Help Sheet IR204 — **1.28** £
- From box L of Help Sheet IR204 — **1.29** £

- Tax taken off payments in boxes 1.27 to 1.29 - leave blank if this tax is included in the box 1.11 figure but tick box 1.30A. — Tax taken off **1.30** £

- Tick this box if you have left box 1.30 blank because the tax is included in the box 1.11 figure — **1.30A**

■ *Foreign earnings not taxable in the UK in the year ended 5 April 2007* - see Notes, page EN7. — **1.31** £

■ *Expenses you incurred in doing your job* - see Notes, pages EN7 and EN8.

- Travel and subsistence costs — **1.32** £
- Fixed deductions for expenses — **1.33** £
- Professional fees and subscriptions — **1.34** £
- Other expenses and capital allowances — **1.35** £
- Tick box 1.36 if the figure in box 1.32 includes travel between your home and a permanent workplace — **1.36**

■ *Seafarers' Earnings Deduction*
   - enter the amount of the earnings that attract the deduction, not the tax
   - enter ship names in box 1.40 (see Notes, page EN8 and Help Sheet IR205) — **1.37** £

■ *Foreign tax for which tax credit relief not claimed* — **1.38** £

Student Loans

■ *Student Loans repaid by deduction by employer* - see Notes, page EN8. — **1.39** £

- Tick box 1.39A if your income is under Repayment of Teachers' Loans Scheme — **1.39A**

1.40 *Additional information*

Now fill in any other supplementar y Pages that apply to you.
Otherwise, go back to page 2 in your Tax Return and finish filling it in.

- **Benefits and expenses** received are entered into boxes 1.12 to 1.23. It is important that the correct box is used for each category, and that the figures used are the assessable amounts. Note that in box 1.15 only the excess of mileage allowances over the approved level are entered. For other situations (except where there is a dispensation) when an employer pays an amount to an employee that is also an allowable deduction, it should be entered both in this section, and on page E2 as a deduction.

- **Allowable expenses and deductions** are entered on page E2 into boxes 1.32 to 1.36 (towards the bottom of the page). These figures are all items that reduce the employment income assessment. If they have been reimbursed they will have already appeared in earlier boxes as well, but if the employee has borne the cost they will just appear here.

You will not need to use boxes 1.24 to 1.31 or 1.37 onwards, since these are outside your area of study.

It is vital that the data entered on the employment pages reconciles with the employment income computation that will have been completed. With the exception of the tax paid amount in box 1.11, you should check that the total amounts entered in the boxes on page E1, minus the entries under 'expenses' on page E2 equal the assessable amount.

We will now demonstrate how to complete the employment pages by using the data from the two Case Studies that were used earlier in this chapter.

Case Study

BENNY FITT:
COMPLETING THE TAX RETURN EMPLOYMENT PAGES

Benny Fitt works as a Sales Manager for ESP Limited. His assessable amount of employment income for 2007/08 has already been calculated (see pages 4.11 - 4.12), and is summarised as follows.

Employment Income Summary

	£
Salary & Bonuses	30,100
Company Car	5,365
Car Fuel	4,176
Loan	600
Home Cinema	390
Assessable amount	40,631

required

Complete the relevant employment pages for Benny for 2007/08. (Please note that the 2006/07 tax form is used here because the 2007/08 form was not available when this book went to press.)

Income for the year ended 5 April 2007

HM Revenue & Customs

EMPLOYMENT

Fill in these boxes first

Name

BENNY FITT

Tax reference

If you want help, look up the box numbers in the Notes.

Details of employer

Employer's PAYE reference - the 'HM Revenue & Customs office number and reference' on your P60 or 'PAYE reference' on your P45

1.1

Employer's name

1.2 ESP LIMITED

Date employment started
(only if between 6 April 2006 and 5 April 2007)

1.3   /   /

Employer's address

1.5

Date employment finished
(only if between 6 April 2006 and 5 April 2007)

1.4   /   /

Tick box 1.6 if you were a director of the company

1.6

and, if so, tick box 1.7 if it was a close company

1.7

Postcode

Income from employment

■ *Money* - see Notes, page EN3.

		Before tax
• Payments from P60 (or P45)	1.8	£ 30,100
• Payments not on P60, etc. - tips	1.9	£
- other payments (excluding expenses entered below and lump sums and compensation payments or benefits entered overleaf)	1.10	£

Tax taken off

• UK tax taken off payments in boxes 1.8 to 1.10   1.11 £

■ *Benefits and expenses* - see Notes, pages EN3 to EN6. If any benefits connected with termination of employment were received, or enjoyed, after that termination and were from a former employer you need Help Sheet IR204, available from the Orderline. Do not enter such benefits here.

	Amount		Amount
• Assets transferred/ payments made for you	1.12 £ 390	• Vans	1.18 £
• Vouchers, credit cards and tokens	1.13 £	• Interest-free and low-interest loans see Notes, page EN5.	1.19 £ 600
• Living accommodation	1.14 £	box 1.20 is not used.	
• Excess mileage allowance and passenger payments	1.15 £	• Private medical or dental insurance	1.21 £
• Company cars	1.16 £ 5,365	• Other benefits	1.22 £
• Fuel for company cars	1.17 £ 4,176	• Expenses payments received and balancing charges	1.23 £

solution

The completed form is shown on the opposite page. In this case study only page E1 needs completing, since Benny does not have any allowable deductions. We have not been given full employment details or a figure for income tax deducted in this case, so boxes 1.1, 1.5, and 1.11 have been left blank.

Most of the entries are self-explanatory, but note that the transfer of the home cinema is shown in box 1.12 If the form related to the previous year, when Benny just had use of the home cinema then the benefit would be shown in box 1.22.

Check to make sure that you can follow how the form has been completed, so that you could complete a similar exercise if required.

Case Study

AL LOWE:
COMPLETING THE TAX RETURN EMPLOYMENT PAGES

Al Lowe is an administrator, employed by Spencer & Company. His employment income computation for 2007/08 has already been produced from information provided and is summarised below:

Gross Salary	22,000
less	
5% pension contribution	(1,100)
payroll giving scheme	(360)
Amount used for PAYE purposes	20,540
add benefits:	
Mileage paid in excess of	
IR approved rate	
7,500 x (50p – 40p)	750
Cost of holiday vouchers	1,350
less allowable deduction:	
Professional fee paid	(140)
Assessable amount	22,500

The completed form is shown on the next page. You should note the following:

- the amount shown in box 1.8 is after deducting pension contributions and donations under the 'payroll giving scheme'
- the excess only of the mileage payments is shown in box 1.15. If he had not been reimbursed the allowed amount, any shortfall could be claimed in box 1.32
- the professional fees paid are claimed in box 1.34. If his employer had paid these for him they would also need to be entered in box 1.23
- the subsistence payments have not been entered on the form, as there is a dispensation in force. If this were not the case they would normally be shown in both boxes 1.23 and 1.32 to cancel out their effect

Income for the year ended 5 April 2007

HM Revenue & Customs

EMPLOYMENT

Fill in these boxes first

Name

AL LOWE

Tax reference

If you want help, look up the box numbers in the Notes.

Details of employer

Employer's PAYE reference - the 'HM Revenue & Customs office number and reference' on your P60 or 'PAYE reference' on your P45

1.1

Employer's name

1.2 SPENCER & COMPANY

Date employment started
(only if between 6 April 2006 and 5 April 2007)

1.3 / /

Employer's address

1.5

Date employment finished
(only if between 6 April 2006 and 5 April 2007)

1.4 / /

Tick box 1.6 if you were a director of the company

1.6

and, if so, tick box 1.7 if it was a close company

1.7

Postcode

Income from employment

■ **Money** - see Notes, page EN3.

Before tax

● Payments from P60 (or P45)

1.8 £ 20,540

● Payments not on P60, etc. - tips

1.9 £

- other payments (excluding expenses entered below and lump sums and compensation payments or benefits entered overleaf)

1.10 £

Tax taken off

● UK tax taken off payments in boxes 1.8 to 1.10

1.11 £

■ **Benefits and expenses** - see Notes, pages EN3 to EN6. If any benefits connected with termination of employment were received, or enjoyed, after that termination and were from a former employer you need Help Sheet IR204, available from the Orderline. Do not enter such benefits here.

	Amount			Amount
● Assets transferred/ payments made for you	1.12 £		● Vans	1.18 £
● Vouchers, credit cards and tokens	1.13 £ 1,350		● Interest-free and low-interest loans see Notes, page EN5.	1.19 £
● Living accommodation	1.14 £		box 1.20 is not used.	
● Excess mileage allowance and passenger payments	1.15 £ 750		● Private medical or dental insurance	1.21 £
● Company cars	1.16 £		● Other benefits	1.22 £
● Fuel for company cars	1.17 £		● Expenses payments received and balancing charges	1.23 £

Income from employment   continued

■ *Lump sums and compensation payments or benefits including such payments and benefits from a former employer*

You must read pages EN6 and EN7 of the Notes before filling in boxes 1.24 to 1.30.
Reliefs

- £30,000 exception — **1.24** £
- Foreign service and disability — **1.25** £
- Retirement and death lump sums — **1.26** £
- Exempt employer's contributions to an overseas pension scheme — **1.26A** £

Taxable lump sums

- From box B of Help Sheet IR204 — **1.27** £
- From box K of Help Sheet IR204 — **1.28** £
- From box L of Help Sheet IR204 — **1.29** £

- Tax taken off payments in boxes 1.27 to 1.29 - leave blank
  if this tax is included in the box 1.11 figure but tick box 1.30A. — Tax taken off **1.30** £

- Tick this box if you have left box 1.30 blank because the tax is
  included in the box 1.11 figure — **1.30A**

■ *Foreign earnings not taxable in the UK in the year ended 5 April 2007*
  - see Notes, page EN7. — **1.31** £

■ *Expenses you incurred in doing your job* - see Notes, pages EN7 and EN8.

- Travel and subsistence costs — **1.32** £
- Fixed deductions for expenses — **1.33** £
- Professional fees and subscriptions — **1.34** £   140
- Other expenses and capital allowances — **1.35** £
- Tick box 1.36 if the figure in box 1.32 includes travel between your home and a permanent workplace — **1.36**

■ *Seafarers' Earnings Deduction*
  - enter the amount of the earnings that attract the deduction, not the tax
  - enter ship names in box 1.40 (see Notes, page EN8 and Help Sheet IR205) — **1.37** £

■ *Foreign tax for which tax credit relief not claimed* — **1.38** £

Student Loans

■ Student Loans repaid by deduction by employer - see Notes, page EN8. — **1.39** £

- Tick box 1.39A if your income is under Repayment of Teachers' Loans Scheme — **1.39A**

1.40   *Additional information*

Now fill in any other supplementar y Pages that apply to you.
Otherwise, go back to page 2 in your Tax Return and finish filling it in.

KEEPING RECORDS

Employment income records, like those for savings and dividend income, need to be kept for at least a year after the online tax return must be submitted. For example, the employment income records for the tax year 2007/08 would need to be kept by the employee until at least 31/1/10.

Typical records that an employee should keep to substantiate his or her tax position include:

- P60 form(s) that summarise income and tax from the employment(s)
- P11D form(s) that give details of benefits and expenses of the employment(s) (where applicable)
- receipts or invoices to substantiate payments made that count as allowable deductions
- a copy of the employment pages of the tax return

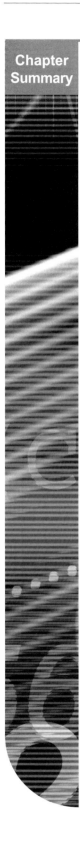

Chapter Summary

- Income from employment is categorised as 'Income from Employment, Pensions and Social Security'. The basis of assessment is the gross income received in the tax year, plus the assessable value of any benefits in kind, less any allowable deductions. Employers are required to operate the PAYE system whereby tax is deducted from payments made to employees throughout the tax year.

- Benefits in kind are generally assessed on the cost to the employer of providing the benefit. However many more specific rules have been developed to calculate the assessable amount of certain benefits.

- Company cars that are available for an employee's private use have an assessable amount based on a percentage of the list price of the car. The percentage will depend on the carbon dioxide emission rating of the car, and whether it has a petrol or diesel engine. Fuel for private motoring is assessed using the same percentage that applies to the car, but multiplied by a fixed amount. Pool cars are not assessable, but the conditions to qualify are stringent.

- Cheap or interest free loans of over £5,000 are assessable on the difference between the 'official' interest rate and the interest charged. Living accommodation may be non-assessable, but otherwise is based on the annual value of the property, plus a supplementary charge for 'expensive' properties owned by the employer. Other assets provided for employees' private use are generally charged at 20% of their value. There are also some specific tax-free benefits.

- Allowable deductions are generally expenditure that is incurred wholly, exclusively and necessarily in the performance of the duties of the employment. There are also examples of certain expenditure that is allowable, including mileage payments at specified rates, professional fees and subscriptions, and pension contributions. Employees can also make tax-free donations to charities via a 'payroll giving scheme' operated by their employer.

- Employees who need to complete a tax return must fill in the supplementary pages E1 and E2. Records must be kept for one year after the latest date for filing the online return.

Pay As You Earn (PAYE)

the system that employers must operate whereby income tax is deducted at source from payments made to employees

benefits in kind

any reward from employment that an employee receives that is not in the form of money

company car

a car owned (or leased) by the employer that is normally available for both business and private use by an employee

pool car

a non-assessable car that is available for primarily business use by a range of employees, and is not kept at any employee's home

beneficial loan

a loan that is at a low interest rate, or is interest free, granted to an employee by an employer

allowable deductions

expenditure that the employee has incurred that can be deducted in the calculation of the employment income assessable amount

dispensation

an agreement between HM Revenue & Customs and an employer that certain expenses payments will only be made if they are for costs that form allowable deductions; where a dispensation is in force, the expenditure covered does not need to be entered on an employee's tax return

payroll giving scheme

a scheme whereby employees can make tax-free donations to charity through their employer's payroll system

Student Activities

NOTE: an asterisk (*) after the activity number means that the solution to the question is given at the back of this book.

4.1* James is employed as a salesman. He receives a basic salary of £18,000 per year, plus commission that is paid on a quarterly basis in arrears.

During the period 1/1/2007 to 30/6/2008 he earned the following commissions, and received the amounts on the dates shown.

Period Commission Earned	Amount	Date Received
Jan – March 2007	£1,200	30/4/07
April – June 2007	£1,450	31/7/07
July – Sept 2007	£1,080	31/10/07
Oct – Dec 2007	£1,250	31/1/08
Jan – March 2008	£1,390	30/4/08
April – June 2008	£1,710	31/7/08

Required:

Calculate the assessable amount of employment income for 2007/08.

4.2* Analyse the following list of benefits in kind into those that are assessable, and those that are tax-free.

(a) Free meals in a staff canteen available to all staff

(b) Use of a company car (including private use)

(c) Free use of a company flat by the company accountant

(d) A £6,000 loan provided by the employer at 6% p.a. interest

(e) Free health insurance

(f) A £2,000 computer available to take home and use privately

(g) Mileage payments at a rate of 40p per mile for using own car to drive to and from permanent workplace

4.3* Julie Payd works as an Accounting Technician for IOU Limited. She was employed throughout the year at a basic salary of £20,000 per year, plus various benefits as follows:

She was provided with a company car and free private fuel throughout the tax year. The car had a 1,350cc petrol engine with an emission rating of 174 grams per km, and a list price of £11,500.

She had use of a company credit card to pay for fuel for the car. The amounts charged to the card for fuel amounted to £1,100 during the year. At Christmas she also spent £100 on private goods through the credit card with her employer's agreement.

She had her private healthcare insurance premium of £730 paid by IOU Ltd.

Required

Calculate the assessable amount of employment income for Julie for the tax year.

4.4 Sue Mee is employed as a solicitor by Contrax & Company, and is paid a gross salary of £28,000 per year. She makes a contribution of 6% of her salary to an approved company pension scheme. Contrax & Company also pays a contribution into the pension fund of 7% of Sue's salary.

As a bonus, she was given vouchers to spend in a particular department store. The retail value of the vouchers was £1,000, and these cost Contrax & Company £850.

Sue is required to undertake business journeys in her own car, for which the company agreed to reimburse her at a rate of 60p per mile. She used her car for 11,500 business miles, and the company paid her the agreed amounts.

Sue pays an annual subscription to the Association of Executive Solicitors (a professional body, approved by HM Revenue & Customs). This amounted to £170. Contrax & Company did not reimburse her for this.

Sue was reimbursed £250 for hotel accommodation that she had paid for while on business trips. This was agreed as necessary business expenditure.

Required

1   Calculate the employment income for Sue for the tax year.

2   Complete pages E1 and E2 of Sue's tax return (shown on the next two pages).

Please note that the 2006/07 tax form is used here because the 2007/08 form was not available when this book went to press.

Income for the year ended 5 April 2007

HM Revenue & Customs

EMPLOYMENT

Fill in these boxes first

Name

Tax reference

If you want help, look up the box numbers in the Notes.

Details of employer

Employer's PAYE reference - the 'HM Revenue & Customs office number and reference' on your P60 or 'PAYE reference' on your P45

1.1

Employer's name

1.2

Date employment started
(only if between 6 April 2006 and 5 April 2007)

1.3 / /

Date employment finished
(only if between 6 April 2006 and 5 April 2007)

1.4 / /

Employer's address

1.5

Postcode

Tick box 1.6 if you were a director of the company

1.6

and, if so, tick box 1.7 if it was a close company

1.7

Income from employment

■ *Money* - see Notes, page EN3.

Before tax

- Payments from P60 (or P45) **1.8** £

- Payments not on P60, etc. - tips **1.9** £

  - other payments (excluding expenses entered below and lump sums and compensation payments or benefits entered overleaf) **1.10** £

Tax taken off

- UK tax taken off payments in boxes 1.8 to 1.10 **1.11** £

■ *Benefits and expenses* - see Notes, pages EN3 to EN6. If any benefits connected with termination of employment were received, or enjoyed, after that termination and were from a former employer you need Help Sheet IR204, available from the Orderline. Do not enter such benefits here.

- Assets transferred/ payments made for you

  Amount **1.12** £

- Vouchers, credit cards and tokens

  Amount **1.13** £

- Living accommodation

  Amount **1.14** £

- Excess mileage allowance and passenger payments

  Amount **1.15** £

- Company cars

  Amount **1.16** £

- Fuel for company cars

  Amount **1.17** £

- Vans

  Amount **1.18** £

- Interest-free and low-interest loans see Notes, page EN5.

  Amount **1.19** £

  box 1.20 is not used.

- Private medical or dental insurance

  Amount **1.21** £

- Other benefits

  Amount **1.22** £

- Expenses payments received and balancing charges

  Amount **1.23** £

SA101

HMRC 12/06 net

TAX RETURN ■ EMPLOYMENT: PAGE E1

Please turn over

© Crown Copyright

Income from employment continued

■ *Lump sums and compensation payments or benefits including such payments and benefits from a former employer*

You must read pages EN6 and EN7 of the Notes before filling in boxes 1.24 to 1.30.

Reliefs

- £30,000 exception — 1.24 £
- Foreign service and disability — 1.25 £
- Retirement and death lump sums — 1.26 £
- Exempt employer's contributions to an overseas pension scheme — 1.26A £

Taxable lump sums

- From box B of Help Sheet IR204 — 1.27 £
- From box K of Help Sheet IR204 — 1.28 £
- From box L of Help Sheet IR204 — 1.29 £

- Tax taken off payments in boxes 1.27 to 1.29 - leave blank if this tax is included in the box 1.11 figure but tick box 1.30A.
  Tax taken off — 1.30 £

- Tick this box if you have left box 1.30 blank because the tax is included in the box 1.11 figure — 1.30A

■ *Foreign earnings not taxable in the UK in the year ended 5 April 2007*
- see Notes, page EN7. — 1.31 £

■ *Expenses you incurred in doing your job* - see Notes, pages EN7 and EN8.

- Travel and subsistence costs — 1.32 £
- Fixed deductions for expenses — 1.33 £
- Professional fees and subscriptions — 1.34 £
- Other expenses and capital allowances — 1.35 £
- Tick box 1.36 if the figure in box 1.32 includes travel between your home and a permanent workplace — 1.36

■ *Seafarers' Earnings Deduction*
- enter the amount of the earnings that attract the deduction, not the tax
- enter ship names in box 1.40 (see Notes, page EN8 and Help Sheet IR205) — 1.37 £

■ *Foreign tax for which tax credit relief not claimed* — 1.38 £

Student Loans

■ *Student Loans repaid by deduction by employer* - see Notes, page EN8. — 1.39 £

- Tick box 1.39A if your income is under Repayment of Teachers' Loans Scheme — 1.39A

1.40 *Additional information*

Now fill in any other supplementar y Pages that apply to you.
Otherwise, go back to page 2 in your Tax Return and finish filling it in.

4.5   Lettie Housego was employed by Fease & Company as an estate agent throughout 2007/08. She was paid a salary of £20,000 p.a., and contributed 5% of this to the approved company pension scheme. She paid tax through PAYE of £3,350 during 2007/08, although she suspects that the tax code used was incorrect.

Lettie was provided with an 1800cc company car throughout the year. The car had a diesel engine with an emission rating of 224 grams per kilometre, and a list price of £17,000. She paid Fease & Company £50 per month as a contribution for use of the car. She was also entitled to free fuel (including for private mileage).

The company pays for private dental treatment for Lettie. This cost £500.

Lettie had bought her own house through a mortgage arranged by Fease & Company. The £60,000 mortgage is on an interest only basis at a rate of 5.5% p.a.

Lettie also had dividend income of £1,800 (the amount received), and net interest of £1,200 from a savings account with NatEast Bank.

Required

1   Calculate the assessable amount of employment income for Lettie for the tax year.

2   Calculate the assessable amounts of savings and dividend income for the tax year, and the amount of tax that has effectively been paid on this income.

3   Using an income tax computation for the tax year, calculate the amount of income tax for the year that is still owed by Lettie, or due to her.

Preparing income tax computations

this chapter covers . . .

In this chapter we cover the following areas:

- a review of assessable income

- expenditure that reduces total income tax

- comprehensive income tax computations

- a review of payment dates

- interest and penalties

PERFORMANCE CRITERIA COVERED

unit 19: PREPARING PERSONAL TAXATION COMPUTATIONS

element 19.3 prepare income tax computations

A   list general income, savings income and dividend income and check for completeness

B   calculate and deduct charges and personal allowances

C   calculate Income Tax payable

D   record income and payments legibly and accurately in the tax return

E   make computations and submissions in accordance with current tax law and take account of current Inland Revenue practice

A REVIEW OF ASSESSABLE INCOME

what we have covered so far

In **Chapter 1** we took an overview of assessable income, and looked in outline at how the income tax computation works. We saw that assessable income is divided into categories so that distinct rules can be applied to each source of income.

The analysis of income that we need to be familiar with is repeated here:

'Property Income'	Rental income from land and property.
'Trading Income'	Profits from trades and professions (the self-employed and those in partnership).
'Savings and Investment Income'	UK Interest and UK Dividends.
'Employment, Pensions and Social Security Income'	Income from employment. Income tax is deducted from employment income under the system known as Pay As You Earn (PAYE).

In **Chapter 2** we looked at income from land and property, and how it is assessed. We also saw how the assessable amount is calculated.

In **Chapter 3** we examined 'savings and investment income' in the form of savings income and dividend income. Again we saw how the basis of assessment is applied, and also learned that savings income and dividend income use different tax rates to other (general) income. These different rates, and the order in which income must be treated in the computation are vital if tax is to be calculated accurately.

In **Chapter 4** we explained income from employment. This is a complex area, and we saw how benefits in kind are assessed, and what allowable deductions can be made from employment income.

The only category of income from the above list that we have not looked at in detail is 'profits from trades and professions' that is assessed as 'trading income'. We do not need to look in any detail at this type of income in this unit, since instead it forms a major part of Unit 18, covered by Osborne Books' 'Business Taxation' text. We just need to include the assessable amount in an income tax computation where appropriate (see Chapter 1, pages 1.11 - 1.12).

summary of tax rates for different sources of income

Set out below is a summary of what we have covered so far and a reminder of the type of income to decide the tax rate used for each source of income.

Assessable Income	Coverage in this book	Type of Income
Property Income Rental income (less allowable expenses), for the tax year, calculated on an accruals basis.	Chapter 2	general
Trading Income Profits (after deducting allowable expenses) for the accounting year that ends in the tax year.	outline only	general
Savings and Investment Income: • Gross interest received in the tax year. • Dividends received in the tax year, plus the related tax credits.	Chapter 3	savings dividend
Employment Income Amounts received in the tax year from employment, plus the assessable value of any benefits, less any allowable deductions.	Chapter 4	general

At this stage it is worth reminding ourselves of the different tax rates for general, savings, and dividend income. These rates all use common bands, but we must work up through the bands starting with general income, followed by savings income, and then dividend income.

	General Income	Savings Income	Dividend Income
Higher Rate	40%	40%	32.5%
Basic Rate	22%	20%	10%
Starting Rate	10%	10%	10%

If you feel unsure about how the system works, now would be a good point to look again at Chapter 3, where it is explained in detail.

We will shortly be using the mechanism described there to carry out some comprehensive tax computations. Before we do that there are a couple of further topics regarding tax computations that we must be able to deal with.

EXPENDITURE THAT REDUCES TOTAL INCOME TAX

When we described property income and employment income we saw that some allowable expenditure can be deducted from the income within the category to arrive at the assessable amount. We are now going to look at two specific types of expenditure that reduce the total amount of income tax. They both use the same mechanism for obtaining the tax saving.

The system used is similar but *opposite to* the way that building society interest is received. You will remember that bank and building society interest (being taxable) is received *after* tax has been taken off. The specific payments that we are now going to look at (being tax allowable) are similarly paid after tax has been taken off. This effectively reduces the cost to the individual making the payment.

gift aid payments

Gift aid is a government scheme that allows taxpayers to donate any amount to a charity and obtain tax relief at the highest rate that they pay.

The system operates by allowing the payer to deduct tax at 22% from the amount of the gift. The charity then claims the tax amount from HM Revenue & Customs.

Suppose, for example, a taxpayer makes a donation of £78 to a charity. The effect is to treat the payment as a gift of £100 and the charity will be able to reclaim the £22 from HM Revenue & Customs. Such donations can be for any amount, and can be either a one-off gift or a regular payment. The taxpayer simply has to make a declaration to the charity that the donation(s) are to be considered as falling under the gift aid rules, and provide their name and address.

The tax treatment of gift aid payments in the individual's tax computation is as follows:

- Unless the taxpayer pays tax at the higher rate, nothing needs to be done. The payer obtains tax relief by the deduction from the payment.
- Where the taxpayer does pay tax at higher rate, then in addition to the 22% tax relief obtained when making the payment, the basic rate band is increased by the *gross* amount of the gift. This gives further tax saving by moving income from the higher rate into the basic rate.

So, for our example of a payment of £78 to a charity (gross equivalent of £100) the taxpayer's basic rate band would be increased in 2007/08 from £34,600 to £34,700. This will result in extra income being taxed at 22%, not 40%. The adjustment of the band enables the taxpayer to save a further (40% − 22% = 18%) tax. In this example the extra tax saving is £18. This makes the effective cost of the donation only £60 (ie the total tax saving will be £22 + £18).

Note that gift aid is a separate scheme from payroll giving that we looked at in Chapter 4, although an individual can make donations through both schemes if desired.

personal pension plan payments

All pension schemes work in the same general way from a tax point of view. Contributions to the schemes are allowed tax relief, but when the pension is drawn, the regular proceeds are treated as taxable.

We saw in Chapter 4 that payments to approved **occupational pension schemes** (organised by the employer) are usually given tax relief by deducting an employee's contributions in the calculation of their assessable employment income.

Personal pension plans (PPPs) may be set up by individuals who are employees or self-employed. The term also includes **stakeholder pensions** that were introduced as a government initiative, and are not dependent on the contributor being an employee or self-employed.

The mechanism for obtaining tax relief for PPPs is different from that used for an occupational pension scheme. Instead it is dealt with in the same way as donations under the gift aid scheme.

Contributions are made as net amounts − after 22% tax relief has been deducted from the gross amount payable. As with gift aid donations, the gross amount can be calculated by multiplying the net amount by 100/78. The basic rate tax band is increased by the gross amount of the taxpayer's contribution, and this enables higher rate taxpayers to obtain further relief. There is no other action to be taken in the tax computation.

Suppose a taxpayer, Tom, wanted to make gross contributions to a personal pension plan of £2,500 per year. He would make payments of £2,500 x 78% = £1,950 to his pension provider, who would reclaim the tax of £550, and invest £2,500 in the pension fund.

If he is a basic rate taxpayer, then that is the end of the matter – he has obtained the right amount of tax relief through making payments net. If he is a higher rate taxpayer then a further tax saving will arise through moving £2,500 of his income into the basic rate band from the higher rate band. This extra saving would amount to £2,500 x (40% - 22%) = £450.

gift aid and pension payments on the tax return

Both gift aid payments and personal pension scheme contributions are entered on the main (common) part of the tax return. The questions relating to these payments occur separately on the form, several questions after the section on savings and dividend income.

On the return Q14 (on page 5) asks 'Do you want to claim relief for your pension contributions?'. Having ticked the 'yes' box, you would then proceed to box 14.1 where the gross amount of the PPP is entered.

Please note that the 2006/07 tax form is used here because the 2007/08 form was not available when this book went to press.

Q14 Do you want to claim relief for your pension contributions? YES

If yes , tick this box and then fill in boxes 14.1 to 14.4 as appropriate.
If not applicable, go to Question 15.

If your pension contributions are taken off your pay before it is taxed, no more tax relief is due – leave Question 14 blank. If you make any other type of pension contribution read page 21 of the Tax Return Guide and then complete Question 14.

■ *Contributions you paid with basic rate tax deducted (called relief at source)* – contributions paid to a personal pension or stakeholder pension scheme, or group personal pension; contributions paid to a Free-standing AVC Scheme; contributions paid to other pension schemes after deducting basic rate tax.

• Enter the full amount of the contribution and add back the basic rate tax deducted. Read the notes on page 21 of your Tax Return Guide.   **14.1** £

■ *Contributions you paid in full* – Enter the amount of contributions you paid. Read the notes on page 21 of the Tax Return Guide

• Contributions under a retirement annuity contract paid in full without deducting basic rate tax   **14.2** £

• Contributions paid to your employer's occupational pension scheme which were not deducted from your pay before tax   **14.3** £

• Contributions paid to a non-UK registered overseas pension scheme which are eligible for tax relief, and were not deducted from your pay before tax   **14.4** £

© Crown Copyright

Question 15A on the following page asks 'Have you made any gifts to charity?'. Box 15A.1 is then used for the total actually paid (the 'net' amount) to charity during the year. If this includes any one-off amounts, the total for these is also stated in box 15A.2.

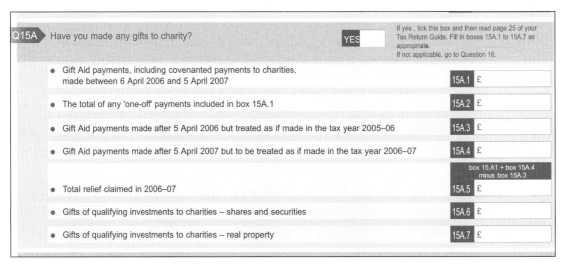

We will now use a Case Study to demonstrate how this mechanism works for these two types of payment – pension contributions and gift aid – and show how the relevant parts of the tax return are completed.

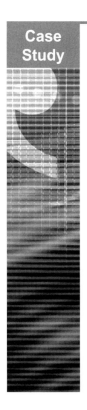

Case Study

DEE D'UCT:
EXPENDITURE THAT SAVES TAX

Dee is self-employed, with assessable profits for 2007/08 of £28,000. She also has rental income, with an agreed property income of £15,000 for 2007/08.

Dee has various investments, and these provided the following amounts in 2007/08:

	Amount Received	Tax Paid / Credit	Assessable Amount
Interest	£ 8,000	£2,000	£10,000
Dividends	£ 5,400	£600	£6,000

required

1   Using an income tax computation, calculate the total tax liability for 2007/08, and the part of this amount that Dee has yet to pay.

Assume that Dee has made no gift aid or personal pension payments.

2   Now assume that in 2007/08 Dee made the following payments:

  • regular gift aid payments totalling £780 net (gross equivalent £1,000)

  • personal pension plan payments of £1,248 net (equivalent to £1,600 gross)

  You are to recalculate Dee's income tax computation to take account of these two payments, and explain how the tax relief has been obtained.

3   Show the relevant extracts from Dee's tax return relating to the pension payments and the gift aid.

solution

Task 1   **Income Tax Computation 2007/08**

	£	£
		Tax Paid
Property Income	15,000	-
Trading Income	28,000	-
Interest rec'd (as above)	10,000	2,000
Dividend income (as above)	6,000	600
Total Income	59,000	2,600
less Personal Allowance	5,225	
Taxable Income	53,775	

Analysis of Taxable Income:

	£
General Income (£15,000 + £28,000 - £5,225)	37,775
Savings Income	10,000
Dividend Income	6,000
	53,775

Income Tax Calculation:

General Income:

	£	£
£2,230 x 10%	223.00	
£32,370 x 22% (to £34,600 cumulative)	7,121.40	
£3,175 x 40% (the rest of the £37,775)	1,270.00	
£37,775		8,614.40

Savings Income:

	£	£
£10,000 x 40% (all in this top band)	4,000.00	
		4,000.00

continued...

Dividend Income:

	£6,000 x 32.5% (all in this top band)	1,950.00
		1,950.00
	Income Tax Liability	14,564.40
	less Paid	2,600.00
	Income Tax to Pay	11,964.40

The way the tax is calculated for each category of income by working up through the bands is illustrated by the following chart (a format already seen in Chapter 3):

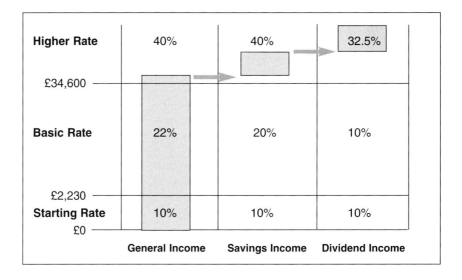

Task 2

Note firstly that the amounts payable as gift aid (£1,000) and pension plan contributions (£1,600) have only cost Dee £780 + £1,248 = £2,028.

The difference of £2,600 − £2,028 = £572 is the tax relief (22% of £2,600) that she obtained when making the payments.

The income tax computation in this case follows the same principles as it did in Task 1:

Analysis of Taxable Income (as previously):	£
General Income (£15,000 + £28,000 − £5,225)	37,775
Savings Income	10,000
Dividend Income	6,000
	53,775

Because of the payments under gift aid and to the personal pension plan, the basic rate band is now extended by (£1,000 + £1,600) from £34,600 to £37,200 cumulative. This is used as follows:

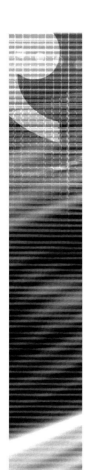

Income Tax Calculation:

General Income:	£	£
£2,230 x 10%	223.00	
£34,970 x 22% (to £37,200 cumulative)	7,693.40	
£575 x 40%	230.00	
£37,775		8,146.40
Savings Income:		
£10,000 x 40% (all in this top band)	4,000.00	
		4,000.00
Dividend Income:		
£6,000 x 32.5% (all in this top band)	1,950.00	
		1,950.00
Income Tax Liability		14,096.40
Less Paid		2,600.00
Income Tax to Pay		11,496.40

In this situation Dee now has to pay £11,496.40.

This compares with a payment of £11,964.40 in Task 1, a tax saving of £468 (18% of £2,600), which when added to the £572 tax relief given on the payments (see above) gives a total tax saving of £1,040 (£2,600 x 40%).

Task 3

The tax return extracts are as shown below. Please note that the 2006/07 tax form is used here because the 2007/08 form was not available when this book went to press.

Q14 Do you want to claim relief for your pension contributions?   YES ✓
If your pension contributions are taken off your pay before it is taxed, no more tax relief is due – leave Question 14 blank. If you make any other type of pension contribution read page 21 of the Tax Return Guide and then complete Question 14.

If yes , tick this box and then fill in boxes 14.1 to 14.4 as appropriate.
If not applicable, go to Question 15.

- *Contributions you paid with basic rate tax deducted (called relief at source)* – contributions paid to a personal pension or stakeholder pension scheme, or group personal pension; contributions paid to a Free-standing AVC Scheme; contributions paid to other pension schemes after deducting basic rate tax.

- Enter the full amount of the contribution and add back the basic rate tax deducted. Read the notes on page 21 of your Tax Return Guide.   **14.1** £ 1,600

- *Contributions you paid in full* – Enter the amount of contributions you paid. Read the notes on page 21 of the Tax Return Guide

- Contributions under a retirement annuity contract paid in full without deducting basic rate tax   **14.2** £

- Contributions paid to your employer's occupational pension scheme which were not deducted from your pay before tax   **14.3** £

- Contributions paid to a non-UK registered overseas pension scheme which are eligible for tax relief, and were not deducted from your pay before tax   **14.4** £

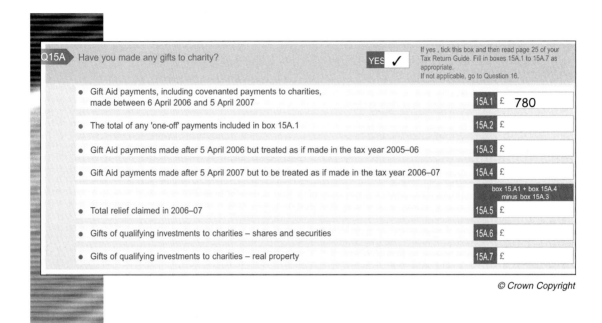

COMPREHENSIVE TAX COMPUTATIONS

We have now examined all the issues that we need to understand to produce comprehensive income tax computations. Although in an examination you may be asked to work out assessable income for various categories and then combine the information in a tax computation, the problem will be broken down into separate manageable tasks.

We will now take this approach with the following Case Study. All the topics covered here have been looked at already in this book, and it should therefore provide a good way of starting revision.

Case Study

MAX CASE:
COMPREHENSIVE TAX COMPUTATION

Max received rent from furnished property in the tax year of £10,800. He paid out allowable expenses of £500 in relation to the property, and also intends to claim wear and tear allowance. He has £750 of losses from property income carried forward from the previous tax year.

Max is employed as an administrator, at a basic gross salary of £25,500 per year. Out of this his employer deducts £100 per month contribution to an approved pension scheme. Max paid £5,880 under PAYE.

He is also provided with a 1500cc petrol engine company car. It had a list price of £15,600 when new, and has an emission rating of 215 grams of carbon dioxide per kilometre. Max is entitled to fuel for the car paid for by his employer for business and private motoring. Max pays an annual subscription of £130 to the Association of Company Administrators (an approved professional body).

Max has various investments, and during the tax year he received £1,080 dividends from UK companies, plus £1,120 interest (after deduction of tax) from his bank accounts. He also received £100 interest from his National Savings and Investment, Investment Account.

Max made a £390 donation to charity under the gift aid scheme during the tax year. Max uses paper-based tax returns.

required

1   Calculate the assessable property income.

2   Calculate the assessable employment income.

3   Calculate the assessable savings and dividend income and the tax that has effectively been paid on this.

4   Using an income tax computation, calculate the total tax liability for the tax year, and the amount that has yet to be paid.

5   State the date by which the final tax payment must be made, and the final date for submitting Max's 2007/08 tax return.

solution

We will deal with each task in turn, selecting the appropriate data. In this Case Study the information is provided in the same order as the tasks to make the process clearer.

Task 1

Property Income	£
Rental received	10,800
less	
allowable expenditure	500
wear & tear allowance (£10,800 x 10%)	1,080
	9,220
less loss brought forward	750
Assessable amount	8,470

Task 2

Employment Income	
Basic salary	25,500
less pension contribution	1,200
Salary per P60	24,300
add benefits:	
Company car (£15,600 x 30%)	4,680
Company car fuel (£14,400 x 30%)	4,320
	33,300
less allowable expenses (professional fees)	130
Assessable amount	33,170

Task 3

Savings and Dividend Income

	Amount Rec'd £	Tax £	Assessable £
Bank Interest	1,120	280	1,400
NSI Investment A/c interest	100	nil	100
			1,500
Dividends	1,080	120	1,200

Task 4   **Income Tax Computation 2007/08**

	£	£ Tax Paid
Property Income	8,470	-
Employment Income	33,170	5,880
Savings and Investment Income:		
(interest rec'd)	1,500	280
(dividend income)	1,200	120
Total Income	44,340	6,280
Less Personal Allowance	5,225	
Taxable Income	39,115	

Analysis of Taxable Income:

General Income (£8,470 + £33,170 - £5,225)	36,415
Savings Income	1,500
Dividend Income	1,200
	£39,115

The basic rate band will be increased by the gross equivalent of the gift aid payment (£390 x 100/78 = £500).

This makes the new top of the band £34,600 + £500 = £35,100.

Income Tax Calculation:

General Income:	£	£
£2,230 x 10%	223.00	
£32,870 x 22% (to £35,100 cumulative)	7,231.40	
£1,315 x 40% (the rest of the £36,415)	526.00	
		7,980.40
Savings Income (£1,500 x 40%)		600.00
Dividend Income (£1,200 x 32.5%)		390.00
Income tax liability		8,970.40
less paid		6,280.00
Balance to pay		2,690.40

Task 5

Final payment must be made by 31/1/09, and the paper-based tax return must be filed by 31/10/08.

entering the tax due on the tax return

Once a full computation has been finalised, and all the assessable figures and claims entered on the tax return, there is one final section of the return to complete. This is where the final tax to be paid is entered.

On the tax return Q18 asks 'Do you want to calculate your tax.....?' After answering 'yes', box 18.3 can be completed with the final figure from the tax computation.

The extract shown below illustrates how the last Case Study figure would be entered. Note that the amount is rounded down to the £ below. Please note again that the 2006/07 tax form is used here because the 2007/08 form was not available when this book went to press.

Q18	Do you want to calculate your tax and, if appropriate, Class 4 National Insurance contributions and Student Loan Repayment?	YES ✔	Use your Tax Calculation Guide then fill in boxes 18.1 to 18.8 as appropriate.

- Underpaid tax for earlier years included in your tax code for 2006-07 — **18.1** £
- Underpaid tax for 2006–07 included in your tax code for 2007–08 — **18.2** £
- Student Loan Repayment due — **18.2A** £
- Class 4 NICs due — **18.2B** £
- Pension charges due- enter the amount from box 32 of the Pensions supplementary Page — **18.2C** £
- Total tax, Class 4 NICs and Student Loan Repayment due for 2006–07before you made any payments on account (put the amount in brackets if an overpayment.) — **18.3** £ 2,690
- Tax due calculated by reference to earlier years- see the notes on page 10 of your Tax Calculation Guide (SA151W). — **18.4** £
- Reduction in tax due calculated by reference to earlier years- see the notes on page 10 of your Tax Calculation Guide (SA151W). — **18.5** £
- Tick box 18.6 if you are claiming to reduce your 2007–08 payments on account. Make sure you enter the reduced amount of your first payment in box 18.7. Then, in the 'Additional information' box, box 23.9 on page 10, say why you are making a claim — **18.6**
- Your first payment on account for 2007–08 (please include the pence.) — **18.7** £
- Any 2007–08 tax you are reclaiming now — **18.8** £

HMRC 12/06 net   TAX RETURN: PAGE 7   Please turn over

A REVIEW OF PAYMENT DATES

In Chapter 1 we saw that the final date for payment of income tax is 31 January following the end of the tax year (eg 31/1/09 for 2007/08). We also discussed briefly the timing of payments on account that are sometimes due. We will now look a little more closely at these interim payments.

payments on account

The two payments on account are calculated as follows:

Each payment on account is based on half the income tax amount due for the previous year, (after deducting tax paid under PAYE and other income tax deducted at source).

Suppose, for example, the total income tax for 2006/07 was £7,000, of which £4,000 had been paid via PAYE. Each of the two payments on account for 2007/08 would be:

$$\frac{£7,000 - £4000}{2} \; = \; \frac{£3,000}{2} \; = \; £1,500$$

As with all income tax payments amounts on account are rounded down to the nearest £ if required.

These payments on account for 2007/08 would be made on

*   31 January 2008
*   31 July 2008

If the amount of income tax paid each year is quite similar, there would not be much left to pay (or have refunded) on the final date of 31 January 2009.

Payments on account are not always required. They do not have to be made if, for example, the taxpayer makes a claim that his tax will be less than the previous year and therefore a payment on account is not needed.

INTEREST AND PENALTIES

interest payable

Interest is payable on late payment of tax, and also on any underpayment of the amount due on account. The rates are different to those used for assessing beneficial loans, and are usually a little higher. The rate is 7.5% at the time of going to press.

penalties

Penalties are payable for:

Late submission of the tax return:

- an automatic penalty of £100 for missing the 31 January online deadline (taxpayers missing the paper-based deadline of 31 October can simply submit online in the next 3 months)
- possibly £60 per day (if the tax owed is believed to be substantial)
- a further £100 if the tax return is still outstanding on 31 July
- up to 100% of the unpaid tax if the return is still outstanding 12 months after it should have been submitted

Late payment of the balancing payment by more than 28 days:

- 5% of the tax due, plus
- a further 5% of the tax due if the balancing payment is still unpaid by 31 July

Note that the penalties are in addition to the interest charges.

The fixed penalties for late submission of the tax return cannot, however, exceed the tax unpaid on the date that the return is due. If no tax is due there cannot therefore be a penalty.

incorrect returns

If, after submitting a tax return, the taxpayer discovers that he/she has made an error or omission, he/she should notify HM Revenue & Customs as soon as possible. If the alteration results in less tax being payable than was originally thought, the taxpayer will receive a refund. Where additional tax is due this will of course need to be paid, plus interest that will run from the normal payment date.

If the notification takes place more than one year after the normal 31st January return date, a penalty of up to 100% of this tax can also be imposed.

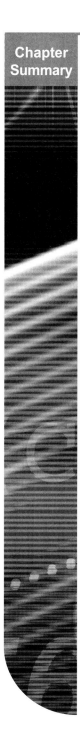

Chapter Summary

- The income tax computation is used to bring together income from various sources and calculate the tax. We have studied in some detail income from property, income from savings and investments, together with income from employment. We only need to have an outline understanding of profits from self-employment or partnership (trading income).

- Income tax is calculated by working up through the bands, looking at general income, followed by savings income, and finally dividend income. Each of these classifications of income use their own tax rates, but share the same bands.

- Payments to charities under the gift aid scheme, and to pension providers for personal pension plan contributions are made net, which provides tax relief at basic rate. Further tax relief is provided for higher rate taxpayers by increasing the basic rate tax band by the gross amounts of these types of payment.

- Final payment of tax is due by 31st January following the end of the tax year. Some taxpayers are also required to make estimated payments on account based on the previous year's tax amount. Payments on account are due on the 31st January in the tax year, plus the 31st July following the tax year.

- Penalties are payable for late submission of returns, and interest and penalties are payable for late payments.

Key Terms	Gift Aid	a scheme whereby individuals can make payment(s) to charities as net amounts, and the charity can claim the income tax back; higher rate taxpayers get further relief through their tax computations
	Personal pension plan	a type of pension plan (including a stakeholder pension) arranged for an individual – basic rate tax relief is provided by making payments net of 22% income tax while higher rate taxpayers get further relief through their tax computations

Student Activities

NOTE: an asterisk (*) after the activity number means that the solution to the question is given at the back of this book.

5.1* Jo paid £1,950 (net) under the gift aid scheme and £2,964 (net) to her pension provider as personal pension plan contributions. Her total taxable pay is £50,000 (all general income).

Calculate:

(a) the gross equivalent of each payment

(b) the effective cost to her of each payment, after taking into account higher rate tax relief

5.2* Matt has the following assessable income for the tax year:

Rental Income	£8,400
Employment Income	£16,500 (tax paid under PAYE £2,213)
Gross Interest Received	£5,000 (tax deducted £1,000)
Dividends + Tax Credits	£12,000

He paid £2,340 (net) to a personal pension plan during the tax year.

Required:

(a) Using an income tax computation, calculate the income tax liability and the amount of tax that is outstanding.

(b) Calculate whether any payments on account are required for the next tax year, and if so how much would need to be paid, and when.

5.3 John had a balance of income tax to pay for 2007/08 of £400. However he did not send in his online tax return or pay this amount until 31/3/09.

Assume that the HM Revenue & Customs interest rate is 7.5%, and that they will not impose the £60 per day additional penalty. Interest calculations can be made on a monthly basis.

Calculate (in £) the total interest and penalties due.

5.4 Mike received rent from furnished property in 2007/08 of £6,300. He paid out insurance of £350 in relation to the property, and also intends to claim wear and tear allowance. He has £250 of losses against property income carried forward from the previous year.

Mike is employed as an accounting technician, at a basic gross salary of £18,500 per year. He paid £2,653 under PAYE in 2007/08.

Mike uses his own car for occasional company business trips. During 2007/08 he travelled 2,000 business miles, and was reimbursed by his employer at 80p per mile. Mike paid his membership fees of £104 to the Association of Accounting Technicians in 2007/08.

Mike has various investments, and during 2007/08 he received £1,260 in dividends from UK companies, plus £800 interest (after deduction of tax) from his bank accounts. He also received £300 interest from his National Savings & Investments investment account.

Mike paid a total of £1,872 (net) to his pension provider as contributions to his personal pension plan during 2007/08.

Required:

(a) Calculate the assessable property income.

(b) Calculate the assessable employment income.

(c) Calculate the assessable savings and dividend income, and the tax that has effectively been paid on this.

(d) Using an income tax computation, calculate the total tax liability for 2007/08, and the amount that has yet to be paid.

(e) State the date by which the final tax payment must be made, and the final date for submitting his 2007/08 paper-based tax return.

6 Capital gains tax – the main principles

this chapter covers . . .

In this chapter we provide an introduction to capital gains tax and examine:

- chargeable and exempt assets

- capital gains tax calculations

- the computation of each gain

- the way in which gains and losses are brought together

PERFORMANCE CRITERIA COVERED

unit 19: PREPARING PERSONAL TAXATION COMPUTATIONS

element 19.4 prepare capital gains tax computations

A   identify and value disposed of personal assets

C   calculate chargeable gains and allowable losses

D   apply reliefs and exemptions correctly

E   calculate Capital Gains Tax payable

G   make computations and submissions in accordance with current tax law and take account of current Inland Revenue practice

AN INTRODUCTION TO CAPITAL GAINS TAX

Capital Gains Tax (CGT) applies in certain circumstances to individuals who dispose of capital assets that they have previously acquired. It often applies to the sale or gift of an asset that may have been owned for quite some time. This can result in what is called a 'chargeable gain'. Note that CGT does not apply to trading assets, where items are regularly bought and sold to make a profit, as these are not classed as capital assets.

Although capital gains tax applies to both personal assets and business assets, we are only going to examine how it applies to personal assets in this book. Gains on the disposal of business assets are dealt with in Unit 18 'Preparing Business Taxation Computations' (see Osborne Books' *Business Taxation*).

basis of assessment

Capital gains tax is applied to individuals by using the same tax years as those used for income tax. The basis of assessment for capital gains tax is the **chargeable gains less capital losses** arising from disposals that occur during the tax year.

We will look at how losses are dealt with later in this chapter. The main issues to understand at this point are that the tax is based on the total (or aggregate) of gains that have occurred, and that a gain can only arise when a **disposal** has taken place.

disposals

A disposal arises when an asset is

- sold (or part of it is sold), or
- given away, or
- lost, or
- destroyed

Most of the situations that we will come across will be based on the sale or gift of an asset. You should remember, however, that a disposal can also result from loss or destruction of an asset. In the case of loss and destruction, the value of the asset is most likely to be assessed as zero.

Two special situations where disposals do not give rise to capital gains tax are:

- disposals arising because the owner has died, and
- any disposal between spouses (husband and wife)

CHARGEABLE AND EXEMPT ASSETS

For capital gains tax to arise, the asset that has been disposed of must be a 'chargeable' asset. Exempt assets are entirely outside the CGT system. Instead of there being a long list of the assets that are chargeable, there is a fairly short list of assets that are exempt.

The simple rule is that if an asset is not exempt, then it must be chargeable!

A list of the main exempt assets is set out below:

exempt assets

- principal private residence (we will look at the rules for this later)
- cars
- wasting chattels (chattels are tangible, movable items; wasting means they have an estimated life of less than 50 years)
- chattels bought and sold for £6,000 or less (there are also some special rules for those sold for more than £6,000 that we will look at later)
- Government Securities (Gilts)

chargeable assets

Some typical personal assets that are chargeable and regularly feature in examination tasks include:

- antique furniture and paintings (since they have already lasted over 50 years)
- holiday homes
- land (eg a field not part of a main residence)
- shares

You must remember that these are only examples – all assets are chargeable unless they are exempt.

CALCULATION OF CAPITAL GAINS TAX

All individuals are entitled to an annual exempt amount – an **annual exemption** – for each tax year. This works in a similar way to a personal allowance under income tax. The exempt amount is deducted from the total net gains that have been calculated on the individual assets that have been disposed of during the year. Capital gains tax is then worked out on the balance.

The exempt amount is £9,200 in 2007/08. The exempt amount can only be used against capital gains (not set against income), and cannot be carried back or forward and used in another tax year.

Once the exempt amount has been deducted, the balance of the gains is subject to capital gains tax. Although this is a separate tax from income tax it shares the same tax bands. Gains are treated as if they were added on top of taxable income, and the rates of 10%, 20%, and 40% are applied through the bands. You will recognise these rates as being the same as those that apply to savings income.

Because almost every individual that is liable to CGT also has some income in the same tax year, the rate of 10% is rarely used for capital gains tax. If the individual is already a higher rate taxpayer under income tax, he/she will automatically pay 40% capital gains tax, and this is quite often the case.

example

Rashid has total income in 2007/08 of £35,225, made up of £15,225 general income, £12,000 savings income and £8,000 dividend income. In the same year he sells a single chargeable asset that generates a gain of £29,200.

After deducting the personal allowance from the income, and the exempt amount from the gain, the amounts subject to tax would be as follows:

	£
Total Income	35,225
less personal allowance	5,225
Taxable income	30,000
Gain	29,200
less exempt amount	9,200
Amount subject to CGT	20,000

The amounts of the two taxes payable would be calculated as follows:

Income Tax	£	£
On General Income of £10,000		
(ie £15,225 - £5,225)		
£2,230 x 10%	223.00	
£7,770 x 22%	1,709.40	
		1,932.40

b/f	1,932.40
On Savings Income of £12,000 (£12,000 x 20%)	2,400.00
On Dividend Income of £8,000 (£8,000 x 10%)	800.00
Total Income Tax	5,132.40
Capital Gains Tax	
On amount of £20,000	
£4,600 x 20% (to £34,600 cumulative) 920.00	
£15,400 x 40% 6,160.00	
Total Capital Gains Tax	7,080.00

We can use the type of diagram (not to scale) that we used earlier to demonstrate the computation process, but now we add an extra column for the gains:

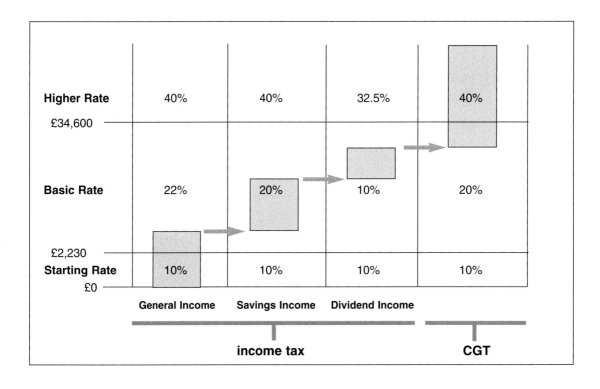

We must now turn our attention to how to calculate the chargeable gain or loss on each separate disposal.

THE COMPUTATION OF EACH GAIN

Each disposal of a chargeable asset requires a calculation to determine the amount of any gain or loss. This computation follows a standard format that is in effect a mini profit & loss account for the item disposed of. There are some minor variations to this format in particular circumstances, as we will see later.

The basic format is as follows:

	£
Proceeds on disposal	X
less	
Incidental costs of disposal	(x)
Net proceeds	X
less	
Original cost	(x)
Incidental costs of acquisition	(x)
Unindexed gain	X
less	
Indexation allowance	(x)
Gain before taper relief	X

We will explain how to work out indexation and taper relief later in this chapter.

The procedure following a number of these computations would be to group the results together and apply taper relief as necessary, before deducting the annual exempt amount and then calculating the tax.

We will now look at the components of the individual gain computation in more detail.

proceeds on disposal

This normally refers to the amount that the asset realised when it was disposed of – ie the selling price. However there are some special situations where the figure used is different:

- if the asset was given away, or sold to a 'connected' person at less than the market value, the **market value** is used in the computation instead of the actual amount received

- if the asset has been lost or destroyed then the asset will have been disposed of for zero proceeds, and zero will be used in the computation – the exception to this would be if an insurance claim has been made, in which case the amount of the claim proceeds would be used

The term 'connected' person (see previous page) refers mainly to close relatives. Remember that a transfer to a spouse is not a disposal for CGT purposes.

incidental costs of disposal

Incidental costs are the costs incurred by the taxpayer in selling the asset. Examples include advertising expenses, auction costs, or estate agent's fees for selling a property.

original cost, and incidental costs of acquisition

This relates to the amount paid to acquire the asset in the first place, plus any other costs incurred to buy it. Examples of these costs would include legal fees or auction costs. If the asset was given or bequeathed to the taxpayer, the market value at that time is used. We will examine in the next chapter how to deal with expenditure incurred later to improve the asset.

indexation allowance

This is a deduction that is used to compensate (to some extent) for the impact of inflation on the value of the asset. It works by using figures from the Retail Price Index (RPI) to calculate a factor to multiply by the original cost and any other acquisition costs. This allows for general inflation between the date of acquisition and April 1998 (when indexation for individuals stops). If the asset was acquired in April 1998 or later there will be no indexation allowance since the whole period of ownership occurs too late. The factor is calculated as:

$$\frac{\text{RPI in April 1998} - \text{RPI at the date of acquisition}}{\text{RPI at the date of acquisition}}$$

Remember!

. . . for the indexation allowance to apply, the asset must have been acquired *before* April 1998.

The result of this fraction is rounded to three decimal places before being multiplied by the historical cost figure (eg the cost of acquisition). You should always find that this factor is either less than 1, or just over 1. The highest figure possible is based on the time between March 1982 and April 1998 – which gives a factor of 1.047. If you arrive at a factor greater than this you must have made an error, regardless of the dates!

You will probably be provided with the indexation factor already calculated for you in your examination.

Note that the indexation allowance cannot either

- turn an unindexed gain into a loss, or

- increase the amount of an unindexed loss.

This means that the indexation allowance cannot be a larger amount than the unindexed gain that it follows in the computation. If the figure before indexation is applied is a loss then there can be no indexation allowance at all.

Let's now see how the computation works by using a Case Study. The RPI figures are set out in the Tax Data section at the beginning of this book. However, the figures that we need in this Case Study are repeated here for convenience.

Case Study

HOLLY DAY:
COMPUTATION OF GAIN BEFORE TAPER RELIEF

Holly bought a cottage in Cornwall in August 1990 to use for her holidays. She paid £59,000 for the cottage, and also paid legal fees of £1,000 at the same time to arrange the purchase.

Let us assume three different scenarios:

(a)   In September 2007 Holly sold the cottage for £240,000. The estate agent's fees for the sale were £3,000, and she incurred further legal fees of £2,000.

(b)   In September 2007 Holly sold the cottage for £75,000.

   The estate agent's fees for the sale were £3,000, and she incurred further legal fees of £2,000.

(c)   In September 2007 Holly sold the cottage for £58,000.

   The estate agent's fees for the sale were £3,000, and she incurred further legal fees of £2,000.

required

Using the RPI figures of 128.1 for August 1990 and 162.6 for April 1998, calculate the gain before taper relief (to the nearest £) for each of the situations (a), (b), and (c).

solution to scenario (a)

	£
Proceeds on disposal	240,000
less	
Incidental costs of disposal	(5,000)
Net proceeds	235,000
less	
Original cost	(59,000)
Incidental costs of acquisition	(1,000)
Unindexed gain	175,000
less	
Indexation allowance	(16,140)
Gain before taper relief	158,860

Working for indexation allowance

The factor is calculated as:

$$\frac{(162.6 - 128.1)}{128.1} = 0.269 \text{ (rounded to 3 decimal places)}$$

This is multiplied by the costs incurred in August 1990 of £59,000 + £1,000 = £60,000

0.269 x £60,000   = £16,140

solution to scenario (b)

	£
Proceeds on disposal	75,000
less	
Incidental costs of disposal	(5,000)
Net proceeds	70,000
less	
Original cost	(59,000)
Incidental costs of acquisition	(1,000)
Unindexed gain	10,000
less	
Restricted indexation allowance	(10,000)
Gain before taper relief	Nil

Here the indexation allowance that would be calculated as £16,140 (as in scenario [a]) is restricted to the amount of the unindexed gain of £10,000, so that it won't turn an unindexed gain into a loss.

solution to scenario (c)

	£
Proceeds on disposal	58,000
less	
Incidental costs of disposal	(5,000)
Net proceeds	53,000
less	
Original cost	(59,000)
Incidental costs of acquisition	(1,000)
Unindexed loss	(7,000)
less	
Indexation allowance	Nil
Loss before taper relief	(7,000)

Here there is no indexation allowance since there is an unindexed loss that cannot be increased through indexation.

TAPER RELIEF

Taper relief was introduced to replace indexation and allows for the reduction of some gains that take place after April 1998. It is quite a crude mechanism in comparison to indexation allowance, and works by multiplying the gain before taper relief by a percentage. The percentage depends on how long (after 6th April 1998) the asset was owned before it was disposed of. There are also different percentage rates for business and non-business assets, but we will only need to use the non-business figures for this unit.

The percentages that follow are for non-business assets, and are based on the number of complete years of ownership of the asset that occur after 6th April 1998. There is no allowance for partial years.

For non-business assets acquired before 17th March 1998 an extra 'bonus year' is added to the actual number of years.

Number of whole years of ownership after 6/4/98	Percentage of gain chargeable
2 or fewer	100%
3	95%
4	90%
5	85%
6	80%
7	75%
8	70%
9	65%
10 or more	60%

Taper relief can be confusing, so let us look at some worked examples.

example 1

An asset bought in May 1997, and disposed of in May 2007.

This asset has been owned for 9 complete years after 6/4/98. Any personal asset acquired before 17/3/98 will qualify for the one bonus year, so this makes 10 years. Therefore 60% of the gain before taper relief will be chargeable.

example 2

An asset bought in May 1997, and disposed of in March 2008.

This asset has also been owned for 9 complete years after 6/4/98. Note that the last 11 months is less than a complete year, and so does not count. This asset will also qualify for the one bonus year, so this makes 10 years. Therefore 60% of the gain before taper relief will be chargeable.

example 3

An asset bought in August 1999, and disposed of in February 2008.

There are 8 complete years of ownership here, all occurring after April 1998. There is no bonus year, so 70% of the gain is chargeable.

example 4

An asset bought in February 2004, and disposed of in March 2008.

There are 4 complete years of ownership, and again no bonus year applies. The percentage gain chargeable is 90%.

grouping gains together

It is often convenient to group together gains made in one tax year according to the taper relief percentage that applies. This makes the calculation a little simpler, and also allows us to deal accurately with any losses, as we will see in the next section.

example

Kulvinder is a taxpayer who pays income tax at 40% and had the following four gains in 2007/08, before applying taper relief.

Disposal No.	Acquisition Date	Disposal Date	Gain (before taper)
1	1/1/1990	30/6/2007	£10,000
2	1/3/1997	30/9/2007	£30,000
3	1/1/1998	31/12/2007	£25,000
4	1/1/2000	31/1/2008	£15,000

The first three disposals will all have 60% of the gain chargeable, based on 10 years (including the bonus year).

The last disposal will have 70% of the gain chargeable, since the asset was owned for 8 years.

The calculation will be as follows:	£	£
Gains with 60% chargeable:	10,000	
	30,000	
	25,000	
	65,000 x 60% =	39,000
Gain with 70% chargeable:	15,000 x 70% =	10,500
		49,500
less exempt amount for 2007/08		9,200
Taxable amount		40,300

Capital Gains Tax at 40% = £16,120

DEALING WITH LOSSES

Capital losses arise from disposals in the same way as gains. We also saw in the earlier Case Study (page 6.9) that when an unindexed loss arises there can be no indexation allowance.

When losses have been calculated they are dealt with as follows:

- they are firstly set against gains (before taper relief) arising in the same tax year, until these are reduced to zero, then
- any unused loss is carried forward to set against the next gains (before taper relief) that arise in future tax years – at this stage the annual exempt amount can be safeguarded to some extent

The key to offsetting losses is to remember that the order of calculation is:

- firstly offset **losses**, then deduct
- **taper** relief, then deduct
- **annual** exempt amount.

You will then arrive at the amount subject to capital gains tax.

You may like to form the initial letters LTA into a personal phrase to help you to remember this order. Examples include Large Tangerine Aeroplane or Liverpool Trashes Arsenal!

We will now look in more detail at how the process works.

offsetting losses against gains arising in the same tax year

Any losses that arise during a tax year are offset against capital gains arising from disposals in the same tax year, before taper relief is applied to the resultant figure. There may be several gains in the tax year with different taper relief percentages applying. In these circumstances it makes best use of the loss to set it first against the gain(s) with the highest percentage chargeable (ideally 100%), then against gains with the next highest percentage chargeable and so on until all the loss is set off. This means that the maximum amount of gain is cancelled out by the loss. If there are sufficient losses the gains will be reduced to zero and any balance of loss carried forward. In this case the exempt amount is wasted.

We will see how the system works by using data from the last example, and assuming a loss during 2007/08 of £25,000.

example 1

Kulvinder, a 40% taxpayer, has the following gains with 60% chargeable: £10,000, £30,000, and £25,000. There is also a gain of £15,000 with 70% chargeable. He incurs a capital loss of £25,000 in 2007/08.

We will offset the £25,000 loss firstly against the 70% chargeable gain, followed by the 60% chargeable gains:

	£		£
Gain with 70% chargeable:	15,000		
less part of £25,000 loss	15,000		
Balance	0	x 70%	0
Gains with 60% chargeable:	10,000		
	30,000		
	25,000		
	65,000		
less remainder of £25,000 loss	10,000		
Balance	55,000	x 60% =	33,000
less exempt amount for 2007/08			9,200
Taxable amount			23,800

Capital Gains Tax £23,800 x 40% = £9,520

By setting as much loss as possible against the gain that was 70% chargeable, (the highest percentage in this example), the loss provides most tax benefit.

example 2

Now let's suppose the loss in 2007/08 had been £75,000 instead of £25,000. This would have been dealt with as follows:

We will offset the £75,000 loss firstly against the 70% chargeable gain, followed by the 60% chargeable gains:

	£		£
Gain with 70% chargeable:	15,000		
less part of loss	15,000		
Balance	0	x 70%	0

continued on next page

Gains with 60% chargeable:	10,000		
	30,000		
	25,000		
	65,000		
less remainder of loss	60,000		
Balance	5,000	x 60% =	3,000
less exempt amount for 2007/08			9,200
Taxable amount			0

Notice here that part of the exempt amount is wasted. This cannot be avoided when setting off a loss against gains in the same tax year.

offsetting against gains in a later tax year

This will only occur when there were insufficient gains in the same tax year to offset the loss (or no gains at all). The loss must be offset as soon as possible, by using any gains that occur in the next tax year. The system is very similar to the one just demonstrated, except that in these circumstances an amount of gain before taper relief equal to the annual exempt amount is not offset, and any loss balance carried on forward again. This provides some protection against wasting the exempt amount.

We will now see how this works, again using some data from the last example.

example 3

We will now assume that there were no capital losses in 2007/08, but that a loss of £75,000 was incurred in 2006/07, a year in which no gains arose.

In 2007/08 there are the following gains with 60% chargeable: £10,000, £30,000, and £25,000. There is also a gain of £15,000 with 70% chargeable. The taxpayer already pays income tax at 40%.

We will bring forward the £75,000 loss and offset it in 2007/08, firstly against the 70% chargeable gain, followed by the 60% chargeable gains:

Gain with 70% chargeable:	15,000		
less part of loss	15,000		
Balance	0	x 70%	0

	£	£
Gains with 60% chargeable:	10,000	
	30,000	
	25,000	
	65,000	
less further amount of loss	55,800	
Balance	9,200 x 60% =	5,520
less exempt amount for 2007/08		9,200
Taxable amount		0

Notice that the amount of the loss used is restricted so that a balance (before taper relief) equal to the exempt amount is retained. Although 40% of the exempt amount is wasted, there is (£75,000 – £15,000 – £55,800) = £4,200 of the loss that will be carried forward to be used in the following year.

Contrast this position (where the loss has been brought forward) to the earlier example using the same figures when we assumed the loss was incurred in the same tax year as the gains.

Now apply what you have learnt about capital gains so far by working through the comprehensive Case Study that follows.

Case Study

IVOR LOTT:
CAPITAL GAINS TAX PRINCIPLES

Ivor Lott has taxable income in 2007/08 of £30,000. He also made the following disposals during the tax year:

- On 15/4/2007 he sold his entire holding of 3,000 shares that he owned in Expo Limited for £6.75 each. He had bought all the shares in August 1998 for £10.00 each.

- On 1/6/2007 he sold an antique table for £15,000 that he had bought in July 1996 for £7,000.

- On 1/12/2007 he gave his daughter a field that was located 3 miles away from his home. He bought the field in April 1985 for £2,000. It was valued at £150,000 at the time of the gift, since it was now a possible housing development site.

- On 3/1/2008 he sold his Jaguar E type car for £25,000. He had owned the car since January 1983 when he had bought it for £5,000.

- On 1/3/2008 he sold his holiday cottage in Cornwall for £200,000. He incurred selling costs of £5,000. He had bought the cottage in April 2002 for £152,000, and incurred buying costs of £8,000.

Indexation Factors are as follows:

January 1983 – April 1998	0.968
April 1985 – April 1998	0.716
July 1996 – April 1998	0.067

These have been calculated from the RPI figures and rounded to 3 decimal places.

required

- Calculate any gain or loss before taper relief on each disposal.
- Calculate the capital gains tax payable by Ivor for 2007/08.

solution

Shares in Expo Limited

	£
Proceeds (3,000 x £6.75)	20,250
less cost (3,000 x £10)	(30,000)
Capital loss	(9,750)

Antique table

Proceeds	15,000
less cost	(7,000)
less indexation: 0.067 x £7,000	(469)
Gain before taper relief	7,531

The table was owned for 9 years after 6/4/98, plus a bonus year gives 10 years for taper relief purposes. 60% of this gain is therefore chargeable.

Field

Market Value	150,000
less cost	(2,000)
less indexation: 0.716 x £2,000	(1,432)
Gain before taper relief	146,568

The field was also owned for 9 years after 6/4/98, plus a bonus year gives 10 years for taper relief purposes. 60% of this gain is therefore chargeable.

Car

This asset is exempt from capital gains tax.

Holiday Cottage

Proceeds on disposal		200,000
less		
Incidental costs of disposal		(5,000)
Net proceeds		195,000
less		
Original cost		(152,000)
Incidental costs of acquisition		(8,000)
Gain before taper relief		35,000

There is no indexation allowance because the entire period of ownership occurs after April 1998.

The holiday cottage was owned for 5 complete years after 6/4/98. 85% of this gain is therefore chargeable.

We can now group the gains according to the amount of taper relief, and offset the loss.

	£	£
Gain with 85% chargeable:		
holiday cottage	35,000	
less loss on shares	9,750	
Balance	25,250 x 85% =	21,462
Gains with 60% chargeable:		
antique table	7,531	
field	146,568	
	154,099 x 60% =	92,459
		113,921
less exempt amount for 2007/08		9,200
Taxable amount		104,721
Capital gains tax:		
£4,600 x 20% (to £34,600 including taxable income)		920.00
£100,121 x 40% (the remainder of £104,721)		40,048.40
		40,968.40

Chapter Summary

- Capital gains tax is assessable on individuals who dispose of chargeable assets during the tax year. A disposal usually takes the form of the sale or gift of the asset. All assets are chargeable unless they are exempt. Exempt assets include principal private residences, cars, government securities (gilts), and certain chattels.

- Each disposal uses a separate computation that compares the proceeds or market value with the original cost of the asset. Indexation allowance is also deductible, based on inflation from the time of acquisition up to April 1998.

- Losses are set off against gains before taper relief is applied where appropriate. The amount of taper relief depends on the whole years that the asset was owned after April 1998, with additional relief for assets owned before March 1998. The amount of taper relief also depends on whether the disposal relates to a business or personal asset.

- An annual exempt amount is deductible from the net gains after taper relief. The balance is treated as if it were an additional amount of income, using the same tax bands as for income tax, and applying CGT rates of 10%, 20% and 40%.

Key Terms

Capital Gains Tax (CGT)	a tax that applies to individuals who dispose of chargeable assets - it is a separate tax from income tax, although it shares the same tax bands, and uses the same rates as savings income
disposal	a disposal for CGT purposes is the sale, gift, loss or destruction of an asset
chargeable asset	this term is used to describe assets whose disposal can result in a CGT liability – all assets are chargeable unless they are exempt
exempt asset	an asset that is not chargeable to CGT: exempt assets include principal private residences, cars, gilts, and some chattels

chattel	a tangible, movable asset – ie the majority of personal possessions
wasting chattel	a chattel with an expected life of fewer than 50 years
annual exempt amount	the amount (also known as the 'annual exemption') that is deductible from an individual's net gains in a tax year before CGT is payable – the amount is £9,200 in 2007/08
net proceeds	the proceeds from the sale of an asset, less any incidental costs of selling the asset
unindexed gain	the net proceeds (or market value in some situations) less the original cost of the asset and any other allowable costs incurred – it is the subtotal of the gain computation before indexation allowance is deducted
indexation allowance	an amount that is deductible in the gain computation that compensates for the effect of inflation on the asset between acquisition and April 1998 – it uses the retail price index (RPI) to calculate a factor that is multiplied by the historical cost of the asset
taper relief	a relief in the form of a percentage of the gain that is chargeable – it varies with the number of whole years for which the asset was owned after April 1998, with additional relief for assets owned before March 1998; the amount of taper relief also depends on whether the disposal relates to a business or personal asset
capital loss	a capital loss results when the allowable costs of an asset exceed the sale proceeds (or market value); indexation cannot be used to increase a loss – a loss is used by setting it against a gain in the same year, or if this is not possible, by carrying the loss forward to set against gains in the next available tax year

Student Activities

NOTE: an asterisk (*) after the activity number means that the solution to the question is given at the back of this book.

6.1* Analyse the following list of assets into those that are chargeable to CGT and those that are exempt.

(a) an antique painting sold for £10,000

(b) an individual's second home, used for weekends away

(c) Shares in CIC plc

(d) an individual's only home

(e) a small yacht

(f) an antique bed, bought for £500, and sold for £2,000

(g) a car

(h) Government securities

6.2* Josie had a capital gain on her only disposal in 2007/08 of £15,000 after indexation and taper relief. Her taxable income for the same year was £25,000 (after deducting her personal allowance).

Calculate the amount of Josie's Capital Gains Tax liability for the tax year.

6.3* Tariq had a capital gain on his only disposal in 2007/08 of £26,000 after indexation and taper relief. His income for the same year was £28,000 (before deducting his personal allowance).

Calculate the amount of Tariq's Capital Gains Tax liability for the tax year.

6.4 April bought a holiday cottage in May 1995 for £60,000 and sold it in June 2006 for £130,000. She had no other disposals in 2007/08. Her taxable income for that year was £38,000.

RPI figures were as follows:

May 1995   149.6

April 1998   162.6

June 2007   205.00 (estimated)

Calculate April's CGT liability for the tax year.

6.5 Cliff bought a holiday flat in August 1998 for £50,000 and sold it in January 2008 for £145,000. He had no other disposals in 2007/08. His taxable income for that year (after deducting his personal allowance) was £28,000.

Calculate Cliff's CGT liability for the tax year.

6.6   Ivan Asset had taxable income in 2007/08 of £40,000. He has capital losses brought forward from 2006/07 of £15,000. He made the following disposals during 2007/08:

On 18/5/2007 he sold his entire holding of 5,000 shares that he owned in Astro plc for £12.00 each. He had bought all the shares in June 1998 for £8.00 each.

On 3/1/2008 he sold his Morgan car for £15,000. He had owned the car since January 1999 when he had bought it for £29,000.

On 1/6/2007 he sold an antique dresser for £14,000 that he had bought in July 1996 for £9,000.

On 1/12/2007 he gave his son 4,000 shares in Expo Ltd. He bought all the shares in January 1995 for £2.00 each. The shares were valued at £5 each at the time of the gift.

Indexation factors are as follows:

January 1995 - April 1998	0.114
July 1996 - April 1998	0.067

Required:

(a)   Calculate any gain or loss arising from each of the disposals.

(b)   Calculate the amount of Capital Gains Tax payable for the tax year.

6.7   Justin Shaw had taxable income in 2007/08 of £36,000. He has capital losses brought forward from 2006/07 of £18,000. He made the following disposals during 2007/08:

On 3/1/2008 he sold his yacht for £12,000. He had owned it since January 2001 when he had bought it for £23,000.

On 18/5/2007 he sold his entire holding of 1,000 shares that he owned in Captain plc for £15.00 each. He had bought all the shares in June 1997 for £9.00 each.

On 1/6/2007 he sold an antique painting of a ship for £14,000 that he had bought in July 1984 for £10,000.

On 1/12/2007 he gave his daughter 3,000 shares in Boater Ltd. He bought all the shares in January 1996 for £3.00 each. The shares were valued at £7 each at the time of the gift.

Indexation factors are as follows:

July 1984 - April 1998	0.825
January 1996 - April 1998	0.083
June 1997 - April 1998	0.032

Required:

(a)   Calculate any gain or loss arising from each of the disposals.

(b)   Calculate the amount of Capital Gains Tax payable for the tax year.

7 Capital gains tax – some special rules

this chapter covers . . .

In this chapter we examine the topics of:
- dealing with part disposals
- improvement expenditure
- the principal private residence exemption
- special rules for chattels
- matching rules for shares
- dealing with bonus and rights issues of shares
- paying Capital Gains Tax
- completing the CGT section of the tax return
- keeping records

PERFORMANCE CRITERIA COVERED

unit 19: PREPARING PERSONAL TAXATION COMPUTATIONS

element 19.4 prepare capital gains tax computations

A   identify and value disposed-of chargeable personal assets

B   identify shares disposed of by individuals

C   calculate chargeable gains and allowable losses

D   apply reliefs and exemptions correctly

E   calculate Capital Gains Tax payable

F   record relevant details of gains and the Capital Gains Tax payable legibly and accurately in the tax return

G   make computations and submissions in accordance with current tax law and take account of current Inland Revenue practice

I   give timely and constructive advice to clients on the recording of information relevant to tax returns

DEALING WITH PART DISPOSALS

We saw in the last chapter that a disposal for Capital Gains Tax (CGT) purposes can relate to all or part of an asset. Although part disposal will not apply to many assets that are not divisible, it could apply (for example) to a piece of land.

If an asset was acquired as a whole, and then part of it is sold while the rest is retained, we need to compute the gain (or loss) on the part that was disposed of. The difficulty is that although we know how much the proceeds are for that part of the asset, we probably don't know how much of the original cost of the whole asset relates to that portion.

The way that this issue is tackled is to value the remaining part of the asset at the time of the part disposal. The original cost can then be apportioned by using these figures.

The cost applicable to the part disposed of is:

$$\text{Original cost of whole asset} \quad \times \quad \frac{A}{(A + B)}$$

where   A = Proceeds (or market value) of part disposed of, and

B = Market value of part retained

The following example will illustrate the calculation.

example

Heather bought a large field for £4,000 in January 1991 to keep her horses. In January 2008 she sold a part of the field for £3,000. At the same time the remainder of the field was valued at £9,000.

RPI figures are:

January 1991	130.2
April 1998	162.6

The portion of the original cost relating to the part of the field that was sold would be calculated as:

$$£4,000 \quad \times \quad \frac{£3,000}{(£3,000 + £9,000)}$$

This gives the cost as $£4,000 \times \dfrac{3,000}{12,000} = £1,000.$

The computation would then be carried out in the normal way:

	£
Proceeds	3,000
less cost (as calculated)	(1,000)
indexation allowance	
(162.6 – 130.2) /130.2 = 0.249 x £1,000	(249)
Gain before taper relief	1,751

60% of this gain would then be chargeable, based on (9+1) years.

IMPROVEMENT EXPENDITURE

Where expenditure after acquisition is incurred to enhance an asset, and it is then disposed of in this improved condition, the improvement expenditure forms an allowable cost in the computation.

The expenditure must be of a 'capital' nature, and examples of this could include extending a building or having an antique professionally restored. The improvement expenditure will also attract indexation allowance if it occurred before April 1998. This would run from the date the improvement expenditure was incurred until April 1998. A situation would therefore arise where two (or more) indexation allowances were deducted in the computation, each with different start dates, but all with the same end date, as shown in the diagram below.

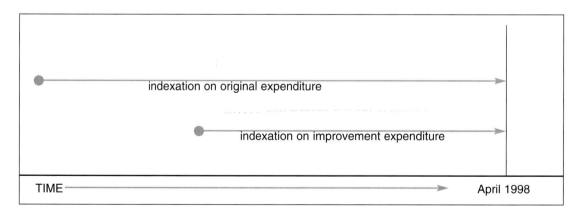

Any taper relief that is calculated on the disposal is based entirely on the original acquisition date, and does not take account of the date of any improvement expenditure.

The following example illustrates the situation:

Sonny Daze bought a holiday cottage for £60,000 in September 1984. In January 1990 he spent £40,000 extending the property. He sold the cottage in May 2007 for £300,000. *proceeds*

Indexation factors are:

September 1984 - April 1998	0.804 *Cost 60,000*
January 1990 - April 1998	0.361 *extendy 40,000*

	£	
Proceeds	300,000	*Sale*
less original cost	(60,000)	*Sep 1984*
improvement expenditure	(40,000)	*Jan 1990*
unindexed gain	200,000	
less indexation allowance on original cost		
0.804 x £60,000	(48,240)	
indexation allowance on extension		
0.361 x £40,000	(14,440)	
Gain before taper relief	137,320	

60% of this gain would then be chargeable, based on (9+1) years.

PRINCIPAL PRIVATE RESIDENCES

We saw in the last chapter that a taxpayer's only or main residence – known as a principal private residence (PPR) – is exempt from Capital Gains Tax. Properties that have never been used as a main residence (for example holiday homes) are fully chargeable.

Where a taxpayer has two properties, and uses them both as main residences, only one can be treated as a PPR, and the taxpayer can elect as to which one it is. This could occur, for example, if a taxpayer used a property near his workplace during the week and another property situated elsewhere at weekends.

A property's status may change if it is occupied as a PPR for only part of its period of ownership. If this happens and the property is subsequently disposed of a gain can arise. In these circumstances the gain is worked out initially based on the whole period of ownership, and then apportioned to arrive at the exempt gain by multiplying the total gain by:

period of occupation (as a PPR)

---

period of ownership

Provided a property has been a PPR for some time during its ownership then the last 3 years of ownership are always regarded as part of the PPR occupation period. This is the case even if there is another PPR in use during that time.

We will now illustrate this using an example:

example

James bought a cottage in the Lake District for £50,000 on 1st January 1985 to use as a holiday home. He retired on 1st January 1995, and decided to sell his PPR and move into the cottage. On 1st January 2000 he bought a house in the Cotswolds as his PPR, moved there and went back to using the Lake District cottage as a holiday home.

On 1st January 2008 he sold the cottage in the Lake District for £250,000.

The indexation factor from January 1985 to April 1998 is 0.783.

We first calculate the gain (before taper relief) based on the whole period of ownership.   £

Proceeds	250,000
less cost	(50,000)
less indexation 0.783 x £50,000	(39,150)
Gain for whole period before taper relief	160,850

We then time apportion the gain, counting the last three years of ownership as occupation, regardless of whether it actually was.

Owned: 1/1/85 – 1/1/08 = 23 years

Occupied as PPR: (1/1/95 – 1/1/00) + (1/1/05 – 1/1/08) = 8 years

Exempt gain: £160,850 x 8/23 = £55,948

Chargeable gain: £160,850 x 15/23 = £104,902

The gain of £104,902 would then be 60% chargeable based on the normal taper relief of (9 + 1) years.

Although in our example we have used periods in whole years, it would also be possible to carry out the apportionment in months.

In addition to the above rule, there are other periods of absence that will count as being occupied as a PPR, provided:

- the property was actually occupied as a PPR at some time both before and after the period, and
- no other property is being treated as a PPR during the period of absence

These additional periods of 'deemed occupation' are:

- three years in total for any reason,
- up to four years when the taxpayer is absent due to UK employment,
- any period when the taxpayer is living abroad due to employment

SPECIAL RULES FOR CHATTELS

Chattels are tangible, moveable items such as furniture, jewellery, works of art and vehicles. As we saw in the last chapter, certain chattels are entirely exempt from Capital Gains Tax. These exempt chattels are:

- wasting chattels (those with an expected life of less than 50 years)
- cars
- chattels that are both bought and sold for £6,000 or less

There are also some special rules about the amount of gain or loss that can occur when chattels are disposed of. Although these rules are not particularly complicated, they do need to be remembered.

chattels sold at a gain for over £6,000

In this situation the gain (before taper relief) is limited to an amount of:

5/3 (Proceeds – £6,000)

Suppose gains (after any indexation, but before taper relief) had been calculated on disposals as follows:

Disposal A

Proceeds   £9,000

Gain   £7,500

The gain would be restricted to 5/3 (£9,000 – £6,000)   = £5,000

£5,000 would therefore be used as the gain figure, and taper relief calculated on this amount as normal.

Disposal B

Proceeds   £9,000

Gain   £2,500

Here the gain would also be restricted to £5,000, but since the calculated gain is only £2,500 the restriction would have no effect. The gain of £2,500 would then be subject to taper relief as normal.

chattels sold at a loss for less than £6,000

If the chattel had also been bought for less than £6,000 the transaction would be exempt from CGT. If the chattel had been acquired for over £6,000 then the loss would be limited by substituting £6,000 for the actual proceeds in the calculation.

For example a chattel bought for £8,000 and sold for £3,000 would have a loss calculated as:

	£
Deemed proceeds	6,000
less actual cost	(8,000)
Loss	(2,000)

Make sure that you understand this process, and remember that it is the proceeds that are deemed to be £6,000. This is an area where it is easy to get confused if you are not careful.

We will now use a Case Study to help consolidate our understanding of the main issues that we have covered in this chapter so far.

Case Study

JUSTIN CREASE:
USING SPECIAL RULES

Justin has taxable income of £40,000 for 2007/08. During that year he made the following disposals.

- He sold an antique lamp in July 2007 for £7,500. The lamp had cost £4,200 when he bought it in January 1999.

- He sold part of a large field for £10,000 in August 2007. He had bought the whole field in January 1990 for £8,000. In August 2007 the market value of the remaining part of the field was £30,000.

- He sold a house in September 2007 for £325,000. He had bought the house in January 1996 for £160,000, and immediately used it as his main residence. He bought a new house in December 2004, and nominated that as his PPR. He rented out the original house from December 2004 until it was sold.

- He sold his gold cufflinks in December 2007 for £5,000. They had been left to him in his Uncle's will in September 1995. The value of the cufflinks at that time was £7,800.

- He bought an antique painting in January 1990 for £25,000. In September 1995 he paid £15,000 to have it professionally restored. The restored painting was sold in January 2008 for £90,000.

The indexation factors have been calculated as follows:

January 1990 – April 1998	0.361
September 1995 – April 1998	0.080
January 1996 – April 1998	0.083

required

- Calculate the gain or loss on each applicable disposal.

- Calculate the amount of Capital Gains Tax that Justin will have to pay in respect of 2007/08.

solution

$\times 5 \div 3$

Antique Lamp   £

Proceeds	7,500
less cost	(4,200)
gain (no indexation)	3,300
but gain restricted to:	
5/3 (£7,500 - £6,000) = £2,500	

(handwritten) Proceeds Deemed

(handwritten) $7500 - 6000 \times 5 \div 3 = 2500$

The gain of £2,500 will be chargeable at 70%, based on 8 years.

Field

Proceeds	10,000
less apportioned cost:	
£8,000 x £10,000 / £40,000	(2,000)
less indexation:	
£2,000 x 0.361	(722)
gain before taper relief	7,278

The gain of £7,278 will be chargeable at 60%, based on (9 + 1) years.

House

The house is entirely exempt. The period when it was rented out still counts as being occupied, as it is less than 3 years, and occurs at the end of the ownership period.

Cufflinks	£
Deemed proceeds	6,000
less value at acquisition	(7,800)
Loss	(1,800)

Antique painting	
Proceeds	90,000
less: cost	(25,000)
improvement expenditure	(15,000)
less:	
indexation on cost	
£25,000 x 0.361	(9,025)
indexation on improvement	
£15,000 x 0.080	(1,200)
Gain before taper relief	39,775

The gain of £39,775 will be chargeable at 60%, based on (9 + 1) years.

We can now group the gains according to the taper relief level, and set off the loss.

	£		£
Chargeable at 70%:			
Antique Lamp	2,500		
less Loss on Cufflinks	(1,800)		
Balance chargeable at 70%	700	x 70%	490
Chargeable at 60%:			
Field	7,278		
Painting	39,775		
Total chargeable at 60%	47,053	x 60%	28,232
			28,722
Less Annual Exempt Amount 2007/08			(9,200)
Subject to CGT			19,522

CGT at 40% = £7,808.80

MATCHING RULES FOR SHARES

We saw in the last chapter that shares are chargeable assets, and that the computation for the acquisition and subsequent disposal of a block of shares is the same as for other assets.

The complication that can arise is when various quantities of the same type of share in the same company are bought and sold. The problem faced is similar to that in any stock valuation situation – how to determine which of the shares that were bought are deemed to be the same ones that were sold. The dilemma is solved in this situation by the application of strict **matching rules**.

When some shares are sold the matching process is carried out by working down the following categories of acquisition, skipping any that do not apply, until all the shares sold have been matched. A separate CGT computation is then used for each separate match.

1 Firstly, any shares bought on the **same day** that the disposal occurs are matched with that disposal.

2 Secondly, any shares bought in the **30 days after** the disposal are matched with those disposed of, (matching the earliest first if more than one acquisition). This probably seems illogical – selling something before it is bought!

3 Thirdly, any shares bought between **6/4/1998 and the disposal date** can be matched. This time you work backwards in time, matching the latest purchases first (ie the 'last in first out' [LIFO] principle).

4 Finally any remaining shares not yet matched are deemed to have come from the 'FA 1985 pool' of shares. This is a device for merging and indexing any shares bought before 6/4/1998 (see page 7.12)

This process is complicated, but forms a likely examination task. The above order of matching is illustrated in the diagram below. The numbers in the diagram relate to the numbered stages described above.

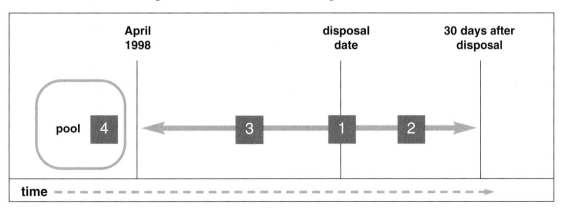

Remember that this matching process only applies where there have been several purchases of the same type of shares in the same company. It does not apply to a mixture of different company's shares, nor is it needed where a shareholding is bought and sold intact.

The following Case Study illustrates how the matching process works.

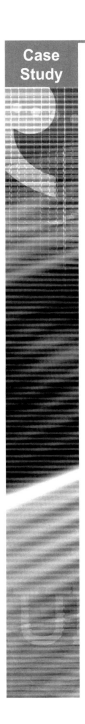

Case Study

MARK THYME:
MATCHING RULES

Mark bought the following ordinary shares in ABC Ltd:

1/5/1998	3,500 shares at £3.00 each	£10,500
1/9/2000	1,000 shares at £3.20 each	£3,200
1/12/2001	1,800 shares at £3.10 each	£5,580
1/6/2007	2,200 shares at £3.50 each	£7,700

On 15/5/2007 he sold 5,500 ordinary shares in ABC Ltd for £4.00 each.

5500 × 4·00   22050

required

- Show how the disposal of shares will be matched against the purchases.
- Calculate the total gain arising from the sale.

solution

The matching is carried out as follows:

There are no shares bought on the 15/5/2007 (the disposal date), so the first possible matching category is skipped.

The 2,200 shares bought on 1/6/2007 were bought in the 30 days after disposal. These are therefore matched against the disposal of 5,500 shares, leaving 3,300 yet to match.

Now, working backwards in time towards 6/4/1998, we match:

- the acquisition of 1,800 shares bought on 1/12/2001
- the acquisition of 1,000 shares bought on 1/9/2000
- the final 500 shares left are matched with some of the 3,500 shares bought on 1/5/1998

We will now have to carry out four separate computations, one for each match. None of these will involve indexation, since they all relate to dates after 5/4/1998.

Computation 1

	£
2,200 shares bought 1/6/2007	
Proceeds (2,200 x £4)	8,800
less cost	(7,700)
Gain before taper relief	1,100
100% will be chargeable (0 years)	

Computation 2

1,800 shares bought 1/12/2001	
Proceeds (1,800 x £4)	7,200
less cost	(5,580)
Gain before taper relief	1,620
85% will be chargeable (5 years)	

Computation 3

1,000 shares bought 1/9/2000	
Proceeds (1,000 x £4)	4,000
less cost	(3,200)
Gain before taper relief	800
80% will be chargeable (6 years)	

Computation 4

500 of the 3,500 shares bought 1/5/1998	
Proceeds (500 x £4)	2,000
less cost (500 x £3)	(1,500)
Gain before taper relief	500
65% will be chargeable (9 years)	

Total Gains

Computation (1) (100%)	1,100
Computation (2) £1,620 x 85%	1,377
Computation (3) £800 x 80%	640
Computation (4) £500 x 65%	325
Total gains after taper relief	3,442

USING THE 'FA 1985 POOL'

This device was introduced in the 1985 Finance Act, and merges (or 'pools') shares in the same company and of the same type together, and applies indexation allowance at the same time. As we just saw, it occurs as the last of the matching rules, and is used to calculate the cost of shares acquired before 6/4/1998.

Although it may seem complicated at first, it is similar to the calculation of weighted average stock valuations (as you have probably studied in Costing), but with the additional complication of indexation allowance.

The pool needs to keep data relating to:

- numbers of shares
- actual costs, and
- indexed costs

These form the three main columns of the pool working.

The pool commences with the first shares bought. The cost of these is then indexed up to the time when other shares are bought (or sold). These are added in, and the cumulative indexed cost is then re-indexed up to the date of the next share transaction. This process is repeated as often as necessary, and the pool is finally indexed up to 5/4/1998. The indexed balance in the pool is then used to calculate the cost of shares from the pool that are sold, by apportionment based on the number of shares. Strictly speaking the indexation is carried out in the pool *without* the normal three decimal place rounding, although if (as in the next example) you are given the rounded indexation factor, simply use it.

We will now demonstrate how the process works using a numerical example.

example

On 1/1/2008 Julie sold 10,000 ordinary shares in WyeCo Ltd for £10 each, from her shareholding of 25,000. Her shareholding had been built up as follows:

1/1/1988 bought 17,000 shares for £5.00 each

1/1/1993 bought 8,000 shares for £7.00 each.

Indexation factors are:

January 1988 - January 1993	0.335
January 1993 - April 1998	0.179

Since there are no acquisitions after April 1998, the whole of the disposal of 10,000 shares will be matched with the pool. The pool will be built up as follows, with the disposal deducted as the latest transaction:

	Number	Cost	Indexed Cost
	£	£	£
1/1/1988 Purchase	17,000	85,000	85,000
Indexation to Jan 1993:			
£85,000 x 0.335			28,475
			113,475
1/1/1993 Purchase	8,000	56,000	56,000
			169,475
Indexation to April 1998:			
£169,475 x 0.179			30,336
Pool Totals	25,000	141,000	199,811
Less Disposal	(10,000)	(56,400)	(79,924)
Pool Balance after disposal	15,000	84,600	119,887

(handwritten annotations: "Sold" next to Less Disposal, "?" above Pool Totals)

You should examine these workings carefully, and note the following:

*   indexation is applied to consecutive periods based on transaction dates; here the periods were:

    January 1988 – January 1993

    January 1993 – April 1998

*   purchases at cost are added to the cumulative indexed cost figure, and the combined amount is then re-indexed to the date of the next transaction

*   the cost figures for the disposal are a proportional amount of the pool costs before disposal, based on the number of shares (e.g. £199,811 x 10,000 / 25,000 = £79,924)

The computation for the disposal will now appear as follows: *(handwritten: "Pool total", "Sold no")*

	£	
Proceeds (10,000 x £10)	100,000	
Less cost	(56,400)	
Less indexation (79,924 – 56,400)	(23,524)	
Gain before taper relief	20,076	

(handwritten: 141,000 x 10,000 / 25,000 = 56400)

The indexation is shown separately in case it needs to be reduced to avoid generating a loss.

This gain will be 60% chargeable, based on 9 + 1 years.

If at some future date there was another disposal of shares from the pool then the pool balances remaining (as above) would be used to determine the cost of the shares in the further disposal.

BONUS AND RIGHTS ISSUES

dealing with bonus shares

Bonus shares are additional shares given free to shareholders based on their current shareholding. This is sometimes called a 'scrip issue' and may be carried out as part of a capital restructuring of the company.

For CGT purposes the bonus shares are treated as if they were acquired at the same time as the original shares that generated the issue. For example a shareholder who owned 1,000 shares that were bought in January 2001 would be entitled to a further 200 shares if there were a bonus issue of 'one for five' shares. The total of 1,200 shares would be treated as bought in January 2001 for the amount paid for the 1,000 shares.

If bonus shares are acquired before April 1998, they are added to the pool when they are received. Since no payment is made, there is no adjustment to the cost or indexed cost figures, and the bonus share transaction date is not relevant for indexation purposes.

The following summary table shows the approach that needs to be taken depending on when the bonus shares and original shares that led to the bonus were acquired.

Bonus Shares		
When bonus shares issued	**When original shares issued**	**Approach to be taken**
Up to and including April 1998	Up to and including April 1998	Add *number only* of bonus shares into pool at time they were acquired. Do not alter cost or indexed cost data.
After April 1998	Up to and including April 1998	Add *number only* of bonus shares into pool after all other acquisitions. Do not alter cost or indexed cost data.
After April 1998	After April 1998	Add *number only* of bonus shares to original shares. Treat each acquisition of original shares separately if there is more than one acquisition. Use new number of shares to apply matching rules.

If the bonus shares are received based on several acquisitions of original shares, the bonus shares will have to be split and then linked separately to each set of original shares. The above rules can then be applied to each share grouping.

For example, suppose 5,000 shares were bought in 1990, and a further 2,000 were bought in 1999. If a bonus issue of 1 for 2 were made after these acquisitions, the 3,500 bonus shares would link as follows:

- 2,500 linked to the 5,000 shares and added to the pool, and

- 1,000 linked to the 2,000 shares bought in 1999.

If a disposal were then made of 4,000 shares these would be matched to the revised number of 3,000 shares acquired in 1999, followed by 1,000 matched with the pool which contains 7,500 shares.

dealing with rights issues

A **rights issue** is the situation where additional shares are sold to existing shareholders, usually at a special price. For matching purposes, the shares that are bought in this way are treated as if they were bought with the original shares. However, any indexation that applies to rights issue shares will only apply from the date that they were paid for.

If rights issue shares were bought before April 1998 they will join the pool and be treated like any other share purchase. Their cost will be added into the pool, and the date they were bought will be treated as a date to index to and from as usual.

If rights issue shares were bought in or after April 1998 they will be added to the original shares (both numbers and costs). The computation will then be carried out in the normal way, with taper relief based on the purchase date of the *original* shares. There would be no indexation available.

The summary table on the next page summarises the approach that needs to be taken depending on when the rights issue was taken up, and when the original shares that led to the rights issue were acquired.

Rights Issue		
When rights issue shares acquired	**When original shares issued**	**Approach to be taken**
Up to and including April 1998	Up to and including April 1998	Treat as normal acquisition - index the pool to the date of acquisition then add *number and cost* of rights issue shares into pool.
After April 1998	Up to and including April 1998	Add *number and cost* of rights issue shares into pool after all other acquisitions. Since the relevant date of this acquisition is after April 1998 there will be no further indexing of the pool value.
After April 1998	After April 1998	Add *number and cost* of rights issue shares to original shares. Treat each acquisition of original shares separately if there is more than one acquisition. Use new number of shares to apply matching rules.

Like bonus shares, if the rights issue has been acquired due to several acquisitions of original shares, the rights issue shares will have to be split and then linked separately to each set of original shares. The above rules can then be applied to each share grouping.

Dealing with share transactions is probably the most complicated area of study in this unit, yet it is a likely examination task. We will therefore use a further Case Study to consolidate understanding.

Case Study

CHER BYERS:
GAINS INCLUDING SHARES AND POOLING

Cher had acquired the following quoted ordinary shares in AbCo Plc.

1/5/1985	1,000 shares at £4.00 each	£4,000
1/1/1990	Bonus issue of 1 for 4 *1,000 ÷ 4 = 250*	
1/1/1992	1,750 shares at £4.20 each	£7,350
1/1/1995	1,500 shares at £4.10 each	£6,150 (Rights issue)
1/12/2001	1,800 shares at £5.10 each	£9,180

On 15/11/2001 she had sold 1,000 of her shareholding.

On 15/5/2007 she sold a further 2,500 ordinary shares in AbCo Plc for £10.00 each.

Cher also made the following disposals during 2007/08:

- On 30/6/2007 she sold a plot of land for £20,000. This originally formed part of a larger field that she bought for £15,000 in January 1992. In June 2007 the remaining portion of land was valued at £40,000.

- On 30/11/2007 she sold an antique ring for £6,600. She had bought it on 1st January 1999 for £3,500.

- On 31/1/2008 she sold an antique painting for £10,000. She had bought it in December 1996 for £14,000.

Cher has taxable income in 2007/08 of £38,000.

required

1   Identify which shares would have already been matched against the disposal that took place on 15/11/2001.

2   Show how the disposal of shares on 15/5/2007 will be matched against the acquisitions, and

3   Calculate the total gain arising from the sale of shares that took place on 15/5/2007.

4   Calculate any gains or losses arising from the disposal of the other assets.

5   Calculate the total Capital Gains Tax payable in respect of 2007/08.

Indexation factors are:

May 1985 - January 1992	0.424
January 1992 - January 1995	0.077
January 1995 - April 1998	0.114
January 1992 - April 1998	0.199

solution

TASK 1

The disposal of 1,000 shares on 15/11/2001 would have been matched with 1,000 of the 1,800 shares that were bought on 1/12/2001 for £5.10 each. This leaves 800 of that purchase at the time of the disposal on 15/5/2007.

TASK 2

Matching of the 15/5/2007 disposal of 2,500 shares will be against:

- 800 shares remaining from the 1/12/2001 purchase

- 1,700 of the shares in the FA 1985 pool

TASK 3

There will therefore be two separate computations:

computation 1 – Shares bought 1/12/2001

	£
Proceeds (800 x £10.00)	8,000
less cost (800 x £5.10)	(4,080)
Gain before taper relief	3,920

85% of this will be chargeable (5 years)

computation 2 – Shares in the FA 1985 pool

To carry out the second computation we must first build up the FA 1985 pool:

	Number	Cost	Indexed Cost
		£	£
1/5/1985 Purchase	1,000	4,000	4,000
1/1/1990 Bonus Issue	250		
Indexation to Jan 1992:			
£4,000 x 0.424			1,696
	1,250	4,000	5,696
1/1/1992 Purchase	1,750	7,350	7,350
	3,000	11,350	13,046
Indexation to Jan 1995			
£13,046 x 0.077			1,005
1/1/1995 Purchase (Rights)	1,500	6,150	6,150
	4,500	17,500	20,201
Indexation to April 1998:			
£20,201 x 0.114			2,303
Pool Totals	4,500	17,500	22,504

continued on next page

Less Disposal	(1,700)	(6,611)	(8,502)
Pool Balance after disposal	2,800	10,889	14,002

We must now calculate the gain on the shares from the pool:

	£
Proceeds (1,700 x £10)	17,000
less cost	(6,611)
less indexation (8,502 – 6,611)	(1,891)
Gain before taper relief	8,498

This gain will be 60% chargeable, based on 9 + 1 years.

Summary of Gains on Shares

Computation 1	£3,920 (85% to be chargeable)
Computation 2	£8,498 (60% to be chargeable)

TASK 4

This task involves the computations on other asset disposals.

Land

	£
Proceeds	20,000
less apportioned cost:	
£15,000 x £20,000 / £60,000	(5,000)
less indexation £5,000 x 0.199	(995)
Gain before taper relief	14,005

60% of this gain will be chargeable (9 + 1 years)

Antique Ring

	£
Proceeds	6,600
less cost	(3,500)
Provisional gain	3,100

Gain is limited to 5/3 (£6,600 - £6,000) = £1,000

There is no indexation, since bought after April 1998.

70% of the gain is chargeable (8 years)

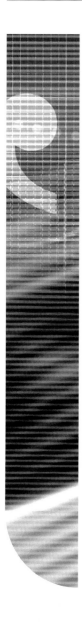

Antique Painting

	£
Proceeds	10,000
less cost	(14,000)
Loss	(4,000)

There is no indexation on a loss.

TASK 5

This is a summary of gains and offset of loss.

	£		£
Gains chargeable at 85%			
Shares – computation (1)	3,920		
less part of loss on painting	(3,920)		
			0
Gains chargeable at 70%			
Antique ring	1,000		
less balance of loss on painting	(80)		
	920	x 70%	644
Gains chargeable at 60%			
Shares – computation (2)	8,498		
Land	14,005		
Balance chargeable at 60%	22,503	x 60%	13,502
			14,146
less annual exempt amount for 2007/08			(9,200)
Amount subject to CGT			4,946

Capital Gains Tax at 40% = £1,978.40

PAYMENT OF CAPITAL GAINS TAX

Capital Gains Tax is payable by individuals by the 31st January following the tax year in which the gains took place. It is payable at the same time (using a combined payment slip) as the balancing Income Tax payment for the same tax year. There is no system of payments on account for CGT.

completing the CGT section of the tax return

The Capital Gains Tax pages of the tax return are a supplementary section, consisting of pages CG1 to CG8.

You may like to note that although the recording of capital gains in the tax return is a requirement of the unit 19 standards, the current AAT examiner has stated that she will not be examining this section of the tax return.

Page CG1 is only used if all the disposals are for quoted shares, and there is no taper relief available.

Pages CG2 and CG3 are completed together, with each disposal being entered along one line across both pages. The best way to explain the completion of the form is to present it in a Case Study. We will therefore use the data from the last Case Study to show how it works.

Case Study

CHER BYERS: COMPLETING THE CGT PAGES

Cher Byers had various disposals in 2007/08 and has a CGT liability of £1,978.40 (see previous page).

required

Using the data from the Case Study, complete pages CG2, CG3, and CG8 from the tax return.

solution

The completed pages are shown on the next pages. You should examine them carefully in conjunction with the Case Study solution shown earlier. The following notes should help you to follow the completion of the form.

(Note also that because the 2007/08 form was not available at the time of going to press, the 2006/07 form has been used, with an amendment to take account of the 2007/08 annual exempt amount.)

One line across pages CG2 and CG3 is used for each disposal, and it is easiest to list the disposals in descending order of chargeable percentages, just as we did when summarising the gains earlier. The sale of shares is therefore treated as two disposals, just as we did in the computations, with each one attracting a different rate of taper relief.

The loss generated in the year is shown in line 13, and totalled into box 8.2. Because this loss was offset entirely against gains in the year, the offset is shown gain by gain in column K1. This column also totals the £4,000 loss.

Note that column L shows the net gain less loss before taper relief for each disposal. This is then multiplied by the taper rate % from column J to arrive at the gain after taper in column M.

explanatory notes continued on page 7.23

A Brief description of asset	AA* Type of disposal. Enter Q, U, L, T or O	B Tick box if estimate or valuation used	C Tick box if asset held at 31 March 1982	D Enter the later of date of acquisition and 16 March 1998	E Enter the date of disposal	F Disposal proceeds	G Enter details of any elections made, reliefs claimed or due and state amount (£)
Gains on assets which are either wholly business or wholly non-business							
1 800 ABCO PLC ORDINARY SHARES	Q			1/12/01	15/5/07	£ 8,000	
2 ANTIQUE RING	O			1/1/99	30/11/07	£ 6,600	
3 1700 ABCO PLC ORDINARY SHARES	Q			16/3/98	15/5/07	£ 17,000	
4 LAND	L			16/3/98	30/6/07	£ 20,000	
5				/ /	/ /	£	
6				/ /	/ /	£	
7				/ /	/ /	£	
8				/ /	/ /	£	
Gains on assets which are partly business and partly non-business (see the notes on page CGN4)							
9				/ /	/ /	£	
10				/ /	/ /	£	

* Column AA for:
- quoted shares or other securities, (see the definition on page CGN3 of the Notes) enter Q
- other shares or securities, enter U
- land and property, enter L
- amounts attributable to settlor (see page CGN4) enter T
- other assets (for example, goodwill), enter O

Complete Pages CG4 to CG6 for all U, L and O transactions

Losses

Brief description of asset	Type of * disposal. Enter Q, U, L or O	Tick box if estimate or valuation used	Tick box if asset held at 31 March 1982	Enter the later of date of acquisition and 16 March 1998	Enter the date of disposal	Disposal proceeds	Enter details of any elections made, reliefs claimed or due and state amount (£)
13 ANTIQUE PAINTING	O			16/3/98	31/1/08	£ 10,000	
14				/ /	/ /	£	
15				/ /	/ /	£	
16				/ /	/ /	£	

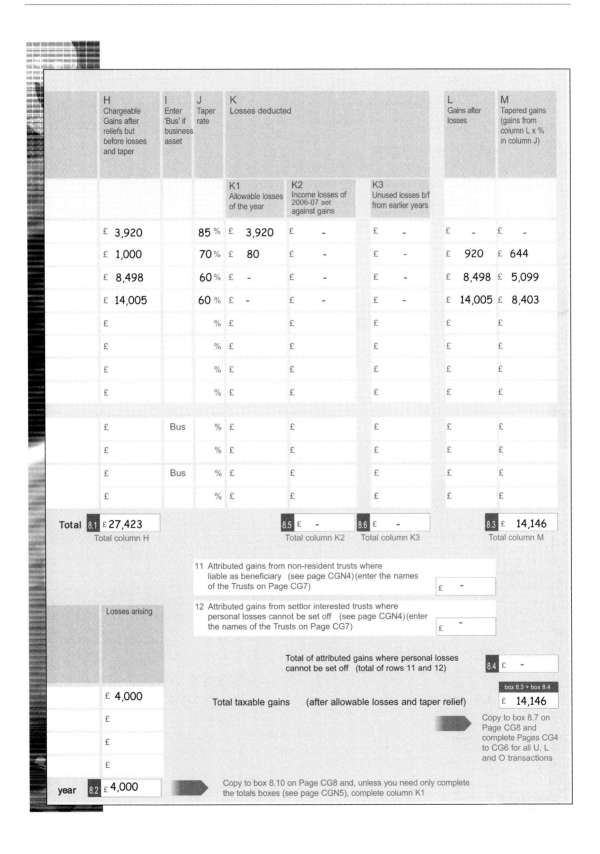

H Chargeable Gains after reliefs but before losses and taper	I Enter 'Bus' if business asset	J Taper rate	K Losses deducted			L Gains after losses	M Tapered gains (gains from column L x % in column J)
			K1 Allowable losses of the year	K2 Income losses of 2006-07 set against gains	K3 Unused losses b/f from earlier years		
£ 3,920		85 %	£ 3,920	£ -	£ -	£ -	£ -
£ 1,000		70 %	£ 80	£ -	£ -	£ 920	£ 644
£ 8,498		60 %	£ -	£ -	£ -	£ 8,498	£ 5,099
£ 14,005		60 %	£ -	£ -	£ -	£ 14,005	£ 8,403
£		%	£	£	£	£	£
£		%	£	£	£	£	£
£		%	£	£	£	£	£
£		%	£	£	£	£	£
£	Bus	%	£	£	£	£	£
£		%	£	£	£	£	£
£	Bus	%	£	£	£	£	£
£		%	£	£	£	£	£

Total 8.1 £ 27,423
Total column H

8.5 £ -   8.6 £ -
Total column K2   Total column K3

8.3 £ 14,146
Total column M

11 Attributed gains from non-resident trusts where liable as beneficiary (see page CGN4)(enter the names of the Trusts on Page CG7)   £ -

12 Attributed gains from settlor interested trusts where personal losses cannot be set off (see page CGN4)(enter the names of the Trusts on Page CG7)   £ -

Total of attributed gains where personal losses cannot be set off (total of rows 11 and 12)   8.4 £ -

Losses arising

£ 4,000

£

£

£

box 8.3 + box 8.4
£ 14,146

Total taxable gains (after allowable losses and taper relief)

Copy to box 8.7 on Page CG8 and complete Pages CG4 to CG6 for all U, L and O transactions

year 8.2 £ 4,000

Copy to box 8.10 on Page CG8 and, unless you need only complete the totals boxes (see page CGN5), complete column K1

Chargeable gains and allowable losses

Once you have completed Page CG1, or Pages CG2 to CG6, fill in this Page.

Have you 'ticked' any row in Column B, 'Tick box if estimate or valuation used' on Pages CG1 or CG2 or in Column C on Page CG2 'Tick box if asset held at 31 March 1982'? **YES**

Have you given details in Column G on Pages CG2 and CG3 of any Capital Gains reliefs claimed or due? **YES**

Are you claiming, and/or using, any clogged losses (see Notes, page CGN11)? **YES**

Enter from Page CG1 or column AA on Page CG2:

- the number of transactions in quoted shares or other securities | box Q | 2 |

- the number of transactions in other shares or securities | box U | 0 |

- the number of transactions in land and property | box L | 1 |

- the number of gains attributed to settlor | box T | 0 |

- the number of other transactions | box O | 2 |

Total taxable gains (from box F7 on page CG1, or boxes 8.3 + 8.4 on page CG3) | 8.7 | £ 14,146 |

Your taxable gains minus the annual exempt amount c (leave blank if '0' or negative) | 8.8 | £ 4,946 |

author's note: the annual exempt amount in 2007/08 is £9,200

Additional liability in respect of non-resident or dual resident trusts (see Notes, page CGN7) | 8.9 | £ |

Capital losses

(If your loss arose on a transaction with a connected person, see page CGN14, you can only set that loss against gains you make on disposals to that same connected person. See the notes on clogged losses on page CGN11.)

■ This year's losses

- Total (normally from box 8.2 on Page CG3 or box F2 on Page CG1. But, if you have clogged losses, see Notes, page CGN11) | 8.10 | £ 4,000 |

- Used against gains (total of column K1 on Page CG3, or the smaller of boxes F1 and F2 on Page CG1) | 8.11 | £ 4,000 |

- Used against earlier years' gains (generally only available to personal representatives, see Notes, page CGN11) | 8.12 | £ - |

- Used against income (only losses of the type described on page CGN10 can be used against income) | 8.13A | £ - | amount claimed against income of 2006-07
  | 8.13B | £ - | amount claimed against income of 2005-06
  box 8.13A + box 8.13B | 8.13 | £ |

  box 8.10 minus (boxes 8.11 + 8.12 + 8.13)
- This year's unused losses | 8.14 | £ |

■ Summary of earlier years' losses

- Unused losses of 1996-97 and later years | 8.15 | £ - |

- Used this year (losses from box 8.15 are used in priority to losses from box 8.18) (column K3 on Page CG3 or box F6 on Page CG1) | 8.16 | £ - |

  box 8.15 minus box 8.16
- Remaining unused losses of 1996-97 and later years | 8.17 | £ |

- Unused losses of 1995-96 and earlier years | 8.18 | £ - |

  box 8.6 minus box 8.16 (or box F6 minus box 8.16)
- Used this year (losses from box 8.15 are used in priority to losses from box 8.18) (column K3 on Page CG3 or box F6 on Page CG1) | 8.19 | £ |

■ Total of unused losses to carry forward

  box 8.14 + box 8.17
- Carried forward losses of 1996-97 and later years | 8.20 | £ - |

  box 8.18 minus box 8.19
- Carried forward losses of 1995-96 and earlier years | 8.21 | £ - |

continued from page 7.19

The total of the taxable gains is taken over to page CG8 box 8.7. The annual exempt amount is then deducted to arrive at the figure in box 8.8. The figure here must agree with the result of the computations – otherwise an error has been made.

Note that boxes Q to O require numbers of transactions in each category, not amounts.

The losses are summarised in boxes 8.10 to 8.21. Make sure that you can follow the logic – the boxes are accounting for the set off of this year's losses and any brought forward to arrive at any losses to be carried on to the next year.

There may well be boxes with descriptions that you are not familiar with, but don't panic. If the issues have not been covered in this book then you can assume that the box will not need to be completed.

KEEPING RECORDS

Since capital gains occur when assets that may have been held for a considerable time are disposed of, this has implications for record keeping. Taxpayers need to plan ahead, and retain records relating to the acquisition of assets that will be chargeable if disposed of.

Typical records that should be kept include:

- contracts, invoices or other purchase documentation relating to the acquisition of assets,
- schedules of purchase and disposal of shares and securities,
- details of any valuations (eg for assets acquired from a deceased's estate, and valuations relating to part disposals)
- documentation relating to the sale of assets

Records for CGT purposes should be retained for the same period of time as those relating to Income Tax. This is one year after the date that the online return must be submitted (eg for 2007/08 records should be kept until 31/01/10). Where records will also relate to later disposals, for example share pool data and information relating to part disposals, they will need to be retained until all the relevant assets have been disposed of.

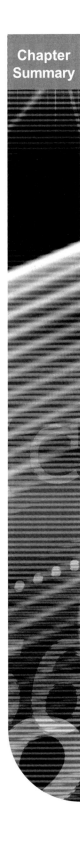

Chapter Summary

- This chapter deals with separate special rules for various circumstances.

- The cost of a part disposal is calculated by apportioning the cost of the whole asset. This is carried out by using the proceeds of the part disposed of as a proportion of the value of the whole asset at the time of disposal.

- Improvement expenditure that is reflected in the asset when disposed of is an allowable cost. It also attracts indexation allowance from the date of expenditure up to April 1998 where appropriate.

- Principal private residences are exempt assets provided they are occupied as such during the whole ownership. Certain periods of absence are treated as deemed periods of occupation. Where there are periods of absence that do not fall under these special rules, the exempt part of the gain on the property is calculated as a proportion of the whole gain, based on the period of occupation as a fraction of the period of ownership.

- Chattels that are acquired and sold for under £6,000 are exempt. Where they are sold at a gain for over £6,000 the gain is restricted to 5/3 of the proceeds minus £6,000. Where sold at a loss for under £6,000, the loss is restricted by substituting £6,000 for the actual proceeds in the computation.

- When shares of the same type in the same company are bought and sold at different times matching rules are used to identify the shares disposed of. Firstly shares bought on the day of disposal are matched. Secondly those bought in the 30 days after disposal are matched. Thirdly shares bought since April 1998 are matched, working backwards in time. Fourthly pre-April 1998 acquisitions are pooled (including indexation) and matched. This is known as the FA 1985 pool.

- Bonus and rights issues are treated as acquired at the time of the shares that they are derived from for matching purposes. They can both appear as part of the FA 1985 pool, or be linked to later purchases.

- Capital Gains Tax is payable by 31st January following the end of the tax year. The gains section of the tax return summarises the computations by using one line for each disposal, and showing the total gains.

- Records must be kept relating to both the acquisition and disposal of chargeable assets. Due to the nature of the assets this may involve retaining documentation for a considerable time.

Key Terms		
	part disposal	occurs when part of an asset is disposed of, but the remainder is retained
	improvement expenditure	capital expenditure that enhances an asset – if the enhancement is still evident at disposal, then the improvement expenditure is an allowable cost
	deemed occupation	periods of absence from a Principal Private Residence that are treated as periods of occupation for CGT purposes
	chattels	tangible, moveable assets
	wasting chattels	chattels with an expected life of less than fifty years
	matching rules for shares	rules which determine which acquisitions of shares are identified with each disposal
	bonus shares	extra shares given to shareholders in proportion to their current shareholding
	rights issue	shares sold to existing shareholders at a special preferential price

Student Activities

NOTE: an asterisk (*) after the activity number means that the solution to the question is given at the back of this book.

7.1*   Alice made the following disposals in 2007/08.

She sold part of a piece of land for £30,000 that she had bought in January 1992. The whole piece of land had cost her £50,000 at that time. At the time of the sale the remaining land was valued at £120,000.

She sold her holiday cottage for £300,000 that she had bought for £60,000 in September 1985. She had also spent £50,000 in January 1992 extending the cottage.

Indexation factors are:
September 1985 - April 1998   0.704
January 1992 - April 1998   0.199

Required:

Calculate the total gains in the tax year for Alice after taper relief.

7.2* Bertie made the following disposals in 2007/08.

He sold an antique painting in April 2007 for £20,000 that he had bought for £5,000 in January 1992. He had the painting professionally restored in January 1995, and this cost £6,000.

He sold an antique table in August 2007 for £7,800. The table had been bought in January 1990 for £1,500.

Indexation factors are:

January 1990 - April 1998	0.361
January 1992 - April 1998	0.199
January 1995 - April 1998	0.114

Required:

Calculate the total gains in the tax year for Bertie after taper relief.

7.3* Christine made the following disposals in 2007/08.

On 15/4/2007 she gave her sister an antique necklace that she had bought in August 1990 for £5,000. The necklace was valued at £8,000 at the time of the gift.

On 15/6/2007 she sold her Jaguar E type car for £18,000. She had bought the car for £6,000 in January 1984, and spent £10,000 in June 1995 having it professionally restored.

On 31/12/2007 she sold her house in Dorking for £450,000. The house had been bought for £80,000 on 1/1/1984. Her use of the house was as follows:

1/1/1984 – 31/12/1993	occupied as Christine's PPR
1/1/1994 – 31/12/1995	rented out as Christine went on a world holiday
1/1/1996 – 31/12/2004	occupied as Christine's PPR
1/1/2005 – 31/12/2007	rented out as Christine moved to a new PPR.

The indexation factor from August 1990 to April 1998 is 0.269.

Required:

Calculate the total gains in the tax year for Christine after taper relief.

7.4 David made the following disposals in 2007/08.

He sold 14,400 of his ordinary shares in Zydeco Ltd on 30/04/2007 for £72,000 in total. His shareholding in this company had been built up as follows:

1/1/1992   Bought 3,000 shares for £3.00 each.

1/1/1999   Bought 12,000 shares for £3.50 each.

1/1/2000   Bought rights issue shares on the basis of 1 for 5 at the price of £2.00 each.

David sold an antique dresser for £6,900 on 30/06/2007. The dresser was bought for £3,000 in January 2000.

David's taxable income in 2007/08 was £25,000 (after personal allowances).

Required:

Calculate any gain made on

- the disposal of shares in April 2007, and
- the disposal of the dresser in June 2007

Calculate the amount of any CGT that will be payable.

7.5 Edward had acquired the following quoted ordinary shares in Exray Plc:

1/5/1985	1,000 shares	£ 8,000
1/1/1992	1,750 shares	£15,750
1/1/1995	1,500 shares	£10,650 (Rights issue)
1/12/2001	1,800 shares	£18,360

On 15/11/2001 he sold 2,000 of his shareholding.

On 15/5/2007 he sold a further 2,500 ordinary shares in Exray Plc for £12.00 each.

Edward also made the following disposals during 2007/08:

- On 30/6/2007 he sold a plot of land for £20,000. This originally formed part of a larger field that he bought for £5,000 in January 1988. In June 2007 the remaining portion of land was valued at £80,000.

- On 30/11/2007 he sold an antique brooch for £9,600. He had bought it on 1 January 1999 for £5,500.

- On 31/1/2008 he sold an antique table for £12,000. He had bought it on 1 December 1999 for £13,500.

Indexation factors are:

May 1985 - January 1992	0.424
January 1992 - January 1995	0.077
January 1995 - April 1998	0.114
January 1998 - April 1998	0.574

Edward has taxable income (after deducting personal allowances) in the tax year of £28,000.

Required:

1 Identify which shares would have already been matched against the disposal that took place on 15/11/2001.

2 Show how the disposal of shares on 15/5/2007 will be matched against the acquisitions, and

3 Calculate the total gain arising from the sale of shares that took place on 15/5/2007.

4 Calculate any gains or losses arising from the disposal of the other assets.

5 Calculate the total Capital Gains Tax payable in respect of the tax year.

6 Complete pages CG2, CG3 and CG8 of the tax return for Edward (see next three pages).

A Brief description of asset	AA* Type of disposal. Enter Q, U, L, T or O	B Tick box if estimate or valuation used	C Tick box if asset held at 31 March 1982	D Enter the later of date of acquisition and 16 March 1998	E Enter the date of disposal	F Disposal proceeds	G Enter details of any elections made, reliefs claimed or due and state amount (£)
Gains on assets which are either wholly business or wholly non-business							
1				/ /	/ /	£	
2				/ /	/ /	£	
3				/ /	/ /	£	
4				/ /	/ /	£	
5				/ /	/ /	£	
6				/ /	/ /	£	
7				/ /	/ /	£	
8				/ /	/ /	£	
Gains on assets which are partly business and partly non-business (see the notes on page CGN4)							
9				/ /	/ /	£	
10				/ /	/ /	£	

* Column AA for:
- quoted shares or other securities, (see the definition on page CGN3 of the Notes) enter Q
- other shares or securities, enter U
- land and property, enter L
- amounts attributable to settlor (see page CGN4) enter T
- other assets (for example, goodwill), enter O   Complete Pages CG4 to CG6 for all U, L and O transactions

Losses

Brief description of asset	Type of * disposal. Enter Q, U, L or O	Tick box if estimate or valuation used	Tick box if asset held at 31 March 1982	Enter the later of date of acquisition and 16 March 1998	Enter the date of disposal	Disposal proceeds	Enter details of any elections made, reliefs claimed or due and state amount (£)
13				/ /	/ /	£	
14				/ /	/ /	£	
15				/ /	/ /	£	
16				/ /	/ /	£	
							Total losses of

H Chargeable Gains after reliefs but before losses and taper	I Enter 'Bus' if business asset	J Taper rate	K Losses deducted			L Gains after losses	M Tapered gains (gains from column L x % in column J)
			K1 Allowable losses of the year	K2 Income losses of 2006-07 set against gains	K3 Unused losses b/f from earlier years		
£		%	£	£	£	£	£
£		%	£	£	£	£	£
£		%	£	£	£	£	£
£		%	£	£	£	£	£
£		%	£	£	£	£	£
£		%	£	£	£	£	£
£		%	£	£	£	£	£
£		%	£	£	£	£	£
£	Bus	%	£	£	£	£	£
£		%	£	£	£	£	£
£	Bus	%	£	£	£	£	£
£		%	£	£	£	£	£

Total 8.1 £

Total column H

8.5 £   8.6 £

Total column K2   Total column K3

8.3 £

Total column M

11 Attributed gains from non-resident trusts where liable as beneficiary (see page CGN4)(enter the names of the Trusts on Page CG7) £

12 Attributed gains from settlor interested trusts where personal losses cannot be set off (see page CGN4)(enter the names of the Trusts on Page CG7) £

Losses arising

Total of attributed gains where personal losses cannot be set off (total of rows 11 and 12)   8.4 £

box 8.3 + box 8.4
£

Total taxable gains (after allowable losses and taper relief)

Copy to box 8.7 on Page CG8 and complete Pages CG4 to CG6 for all U, L and O transactions

£

£

£

£

year 8.2 £

Copy to box 8.10 on Page CG8 and, unless you need only complete the totals boxes (see page CGN5), complete column K1

Chargeable gains and allowable losses

Once you have completed Page CG1, or Pages CG2 to CG6, fill in this Page.

Have you 'ticked' any row in Column B, 'Tick box if estimate or valuation used' on Pages CG1 or CG2 or in Column C on Page CG2 'Tick box if asset held at 31 March 1982'? **YES**

Have you given details in Column G on Pages CG2 and CG3 of any Capital Gains reliefs claimed or due? **YES**

Are you claiming, and/or using, any clogged losses (see Notes, page CGN11)? **YES**

Enter from Page CG1 or column AA on Page CG2:

- the number of transactions in quoted shares or other securities   box Q

- the number of transactions in other shares or securities   box U

- the number of transactions in land and property   box L

- the number of gains attributed to settlor   box T

- the number of other transactions   box O

Total taxable gains (from box F7 on page CG1, or boxes 8.3 + 8.4 on page CG3)   8.7 £

Your taxable gains minus the annual exempt amount c (leave blank if '0' or negative)   8.8 £

Additional liability in respect of non-resident or dual resident trusts (see Notes, page CGN7)   8.9 £

author's note: the annual exempt amount in 2007/08 is £9,200

Capital losses

(If your loss arose on a transaction with a connected person, see page CGN14, you can only set that loss against gains you make on disposals to that same connected person. See the notes on clogged losses on page CGN11.)

■ *This year's losses*

- Total (normally from box 8.2 on Page CG3 or box F2 on Page CG1. But, if you have clogged losses, see Notes, page CGN11)   8.10 £

- Used against gains (total of column K1 on Page CG3, or the smaller of boxes F1 and F2 on Page CG1)   8.11 £

- Used against earlier years' gains (generally only available to personal representatives, see Notes, page CGN11)   8.12 £

- Used against income (only losses of the type described on page CGN10 can be used against income)   8.13A £   amount claimed against income of 2006-07
    8.13B £   amount claimed against income of 2005-06   box 8.13A + box 8.13B   8.13 £

- This year's unused losses   box 8.10 minus (boxes 8.11 + 8.12 + 8.13)   8.14 £

■ *Summary of earlier years' losses*

- Unused losses of 1996-97 and later years   8.15 £

- Used this year (losses from box 8.15 are used in priority to losses from box 8.18) (column K3 on Page CG3 or box F6 on Page CG1)   8.16 £

- Remaining unused losses of 1996-97 and later years   box 8.15 minus box 8.16   8.17 £

- Unused losses of 1995-96 and earlier years   8.18 £

- Used this year (losses from box 8.15 are used in priority to losses from box 8.18) (column K3 on Page CG3 or box F6 on Page CG1)   box 8.6 minus box 8.16 (or box F6 minus box 8.16)   8.19 £

■ *Total of unused losses to carry forward*

- Carried forward losses of 1996-97 and later years   box 8.14 + box 8.17   8.20 £

- Carried forward losses of 1995-96 and earlier years   box 8.18 minus box 8.19   8.21 £

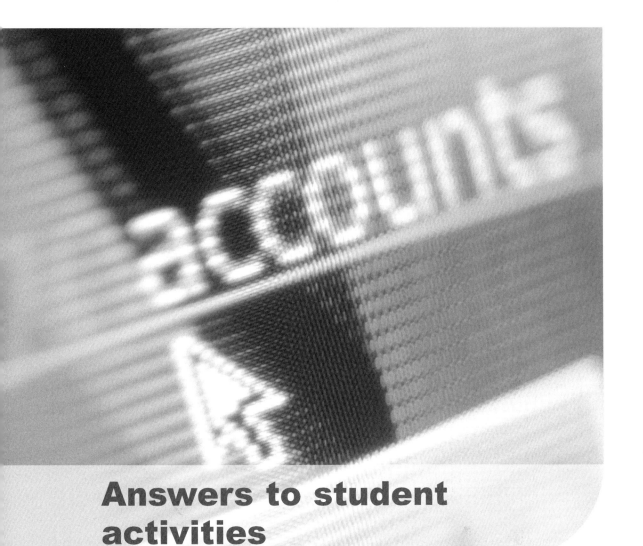

Answers to student activities

The answers in this section relate to the asterisked Student Activities at the end of each chapter.

The answers to the remaining Student Activities (and also to the Practice Examinations) are contained in the *Personal Taxation Tutor Pack*, which is available to tutors and to students who have the permission of their tutor to have access to the answers.

Please call Osborne Books Customer Services on 01905 748071 or visit our website on www.osbornebooks.co.uk for details of this publication.

CHAPTER 1: INTRODUCTION TO INCOME TAX

1.1 The following statements are true: (a), (e), (f). The other statements are false.

1.2 Income Tax Computation for Mary

	£	£
		Tax Paid
Trading Income	2,800	-
Employment Income	12,300	1,289
Property Income	4,500	-
Total Income	19,600	1,289
Less Personal Allowance	5,225	
Taxable Income	14,375	

Income Tax Calculation:

		£
£2,230 x 10%		223.00
£12,145 x 22%		2,671.90
£14,375	Income Tax Liability	2,894.90
	Less already paid	1,289.00
	Income tax to pay	1,605.90

Note

The trading income is based on the accounting year to 30/9/07, because it ends in the tax year 2007/08.

The employment income is based on the amount received in the tax year, irrespective of the period that it relates to.

1.3 (a) Dividend Income, part of Savings and Investment Income

(b) Employment Income – full title Employment, Pensions and Social Security Income

(c) Exempt

(d) Savings Income, part of Savings and Investment Income

(e) Exempt

(f) Property Income

1.4 Income Tax Computation for John

	£	£
		Tax Paid
Employment Income	7,920	325
Property Income	3,000	-
Total Income	10,920	325
Less Personal Allowance	5,225	
Taxable Income	5,695	

Income Tax Calculation:

£2,230 x 10%	223.00
£3,465 x 22%	762.30
£5,695 Income Tax Liability	985.30
Less already paid	325.00
Income tax to pay	660.30

Note:

The property income includes the March rent since it operates on an accruals basis.

The interest on an ISA is exempt.

1.5 Income Tax Computation for Megan

	£	£
		Tax Paid
Trading Income	4,700	-
Employment Income	22,400	3,511
Total Income	27,100	3,511
Less Personal Allowance	5,225	
Taxable Income	21,875	

Income Tax Calculation:

£2,230 x 10%	223.00
£19,645 x 22%	4,321.90
£21,875 Income Tax Liability	4,544.90
Less already paid	3,511.00
Income tax to pay	1,033.90

Note

The trading income is based on the accounting year to 31/12/07, because it ends in the tax year 2007/08.

The employment income is based on the amount received in the tax year, irrespective of the period that it relates to.

CHAPTER 2: INCOME FROM PROPERTY

2.1

		£
Rental Income for period 6/7/07 – 5/4/08	(£5,000 x 9/12)	3,750
Less		
Insurance (9 months at £25)		225
Repairs		200
Assessable property income for 2007/08		3,325

2.2

		£
Rental Income for period 6/11/07 – 5/4/08	(£400 x 5)	2,000
Less		
Mortgage Interest (5 months at £150)		750
Insurance (5 months at £30)		150
Agent's Fees (£1,200 x 5/12)		500
Assessable property income for 2007/08		600

The legal fees relating to the purchase of the property are a capital cost.

2.3

	£	£
Rental Income Receivable		10,000
less allowable expenditure:		
Council Tax	700	
Water Rates	300	
Insurance	400	
Managing Agent's Charges	1,000	
Wear & Tear Allowance		
(£10,000 - £700 - £300) x 10%	900	
		3,300
Assessable property income		6,700

CHAPTER 3: INCOME FROM SAVINGS AND INVESTMENTS

3.1

Savings Income:

Details	Amount Rec'd	Tax Ded'd	Assessable Amount
Nat East Int	£1,600	£400	£2,000
NS&I E.A. Savings a/c	£30	-	£30
NS&I Inv a/c	£300	-	£300
	£1,930	£400	£2,330

Dividend Income:

Details	Amount Rec'd	Tax Credit	Assessable Amount
Osborne plc	£2,700	£300	£3,000

3.2   (a)

Savings Income:

Details	Amount Rec'd	Tax Ded'd	Assessable Amount
Oldport Int	£1,680	£420	£2,100
PCR Deb Int	£2,000	£500	£2,500
NS&I Inv a/c	£100	-	£100
Exchequer Stock	£6,500	-	£6,500
	£10,280	£920	£11,200

Dividend Income:

Details	Amount Rec'd	Tax Credit	Assessable Amount
PCR plc div	£1,440	£160	£1,600

Note that the premium bond prize is exempt from income tax.

(b) see next page

Note: the debenture interest plus the Exchequer Stock interest are recorded in total in boxes 10.12 – 10.14.

3.2 (b)

Q10	Did you receive any income from UK savings and investments?		YES ✔	If yes , tick this box and then fill in boxes 10.1 to 10.26 as appropriate. Include only your share of any joint savings and investments. If not applicable, go to Question 11.

■ *Interest and alternative finance receipts*

- Interest and alternative finance receipts from UK banks or building societies including UK Internet accounts.
If you have more than one bank or building society account enter totals in the boxes.

- enter any bank or building society interest and alternative finance receipts that have not had tax taken off . (Interest and alternative finance receipts are usually taxed before you receive them so make sure you should be filling in box 10.1, rather than boxes 10.2 to 10.4.) Enter other types of interest and alternative finance receipts in boxes 10.5 to 10.14, as appropriate.

Taxable amount
10.1 £

- enter details of taxed bank or building society interest and taxed alternative finance receipts. The Working Sheet on page 11 of your Tax Return Guide will help you fill in boxes 10.2 to 10.4.

	Amount after tax taken off	Tax taken off	Gross amount before tax
	10.2 £ 1,680	10.3 £ 420	10.4 £ 2,100

- Interest distributions from UK authorised unit trusts and open-ended investment companies (dividend distributions go below)

	Amount after tax taken off	Tax taken off	Gross amount before tax
	10.5 £	10.6 £	10.7 £

- National Savings & Investments (other than First Option Bonds and Fixed Rate Savings Bonds)

Taxable amount
10.8 £ 100

- National Savings & Investments First Option Bonds and Fixed Rate Savings Bonds

	Amount after tax taken off	Tax taken off	Gross amount before tax
	10.9 £	10.10 £	10.11 £

- Other income from UK savings and investments (except dividends)

	Amount after tax taken off	Tax taken off	Gross amount before tax
	10.12 £ 8,500	10.13 £ 500	10.14 £ 9,000

■ *Dividends*

- Dividends and other qualifying distributions from UK companies (enter distributions from the tax exempt profits of a Real Estate Investment Trust at Q13)

	Dividend/distribution	Tax credit	Dividend/distribution plus credit
	10.15 £ 1,440	10.16 £ 160	10.17 £ 1,600

- Dividend distributions from UK authorised unit trusts and open-ended investment companies

	Dividend/distribution	Tax credit	Dividend/distribution plus credit
	10.18 £	10.19 £	10.20 £

- Stock dividends from UK companies

	Dividend	Notional tax	Dividend plus notional tax
	10.21 £	10.22 £	10.23 £

- Non-qualifying distributions and loans written off

	Distribution/loan	Notional tax	Taxable amount
	10.24 £	10.25 £	10.26 £

3.3   Income Tax Computation

	Income	Tax Paid
	£	£
Employment Income	28,500	4,853
Property Income	1,900	-
B/S Int	1,500	300
Dividends	4,000	400
Total Income	35,900	5,553
Less Personal Allowance	5,225	
Taxable Income	30,675	

Analysis of Taxable Income:

General Income	(£28,500 + £1,900 - £5,225)	£25,175
Savings Income		£1,500
Dividend Income		£4,000
		£30,675

Income Tax Calculation:

General Income:

£2,230 x 10%		223.00	
£22,945 x 22%	(the rest of £25,175)	5,047.90	
£25,175			5,270.90

Savings Income:

£1,500 x 20% (all in this band)	300.00	
		300.00

Dividend Income:

£4,000 x 10% (all in this band)	400.00	
		400.00
Income Tax Liability		5,970.90
Less Paid		5,553.00
Income Tax to Pay		417.90

CHAPTER 4: INCOME FROM EMPLOYMENT

4.1

		£
Basic salary		18,000
Commission rec'd	30/4/07	1,200
	31/7/07	1,450
	31/10/07	1,080
	31/1/08	1,250
Employment income assessable amount 2007/08		22,980

4.2 Assessable (b), (c), (e), (f – exemption now withdrawn), (g – home to work is private mileage)

Tax-Free (a), (d – interest rate higher than official rate)

4.3

		£
Basic salary		20,000
Company car	(£11,500 x 21%)	2,415
Fuel for car	(£14,400 x 21%)	3,024
Credit card – private expenditure		100
(fuel covered by scale charge)		
Healthcare insurance		730
Employment income assessable amount		26,269

CHAPTER 5: PREPARING INCOME TAX COMPUTATIONS

5.1 (a) Gross equivalent amounts:

Gift Aid £1,950 x 100/78 = £2,500

Pension £2,964 x 100/78 = £3,800

(b) Jo will get tax relief at her highest rate (40%) on her gross payments (22% when the payments are made and the other 18% in calculating her tax). The cost of her payments after tax relief will therefore be:

Gift Aid £2,500 less 40% = £1,500.

Pension £3,800 less 40% = £2,280.

5.2 (a)   **Income Tax Computation**

	£	£ Tax Paid
Property Income	8,400	-
Employment Income	16,500	2,213
Interest rec'd	5,000	1,000
Dividend income	12,000	1,200
Total Income	41,900	4,413
Less Personal Allowance	5,225	
Taxable Income	36,675	

Analysis of Taxable Income:

General Income (£8,400 + £16,500 - £5,225)	£19,675
Savings Income	£5,000
Dividend Income	£12,000
	£36,675

The basic rate band will be increased by the gross equivalent of the pension payment (£2,340 x 100/78 = £3,000). This makes the new top of the band £34,600 + £3,000 = £37,600.

Income Tax Calculation:

General Income:	£	£
£2,230 x 10%	223.00	
£17,445 x 22% (to £19,675)	3,837.90	
		4,060.90
Savings Income		
£5,000 x 20% (all in this band)		1,000.00
Dividend Income		
£12,000 x 10% (all in this band)		1,200.00
Income tax liability		6,260.90
Less paid		4,413.00
Balance to pay		1,847.90

(b)   Payments will need to be made on account for 2008/09 (unless a claim is made that 2008/09 income will be lower).

Each payment on account will be 50% of £1,847.90 = £923 (rounded down), payable on 31/1/09 (along with the 2007/08 balance) and 31/7/09.

CHAPTER 6: CAPITAL GAINS TAX – THE MAIN PRINCIPLES

6.1   Chargeable Assets: (a), (b), (c).

Exempt Assets: (d), (e – wasting chattel), (f – chattel sold for a gain for under £6,000), (g), (h).

6.2

	£	£
Gain after taper relief	15,000	
less annual exempt amount	(9,200)	
Amount subject to CGT	5,800	
Capital Gains Tax:		
£5,800 x 20% (under cumulative total of £34,600, including £25,000 taxable income)		1,160.00

6.3

	£	
Gain after taper relief	26,000	
less annual exempt amount	(9,200)	
Amount subject to CGT	16,800	

Amount of basic rate band remaining after income tax is calculated:
(£34,600 – (£28,000 - £5,225)) = £11,825.

Capital Gains Tax:	
£11,825 x 20% (as above)	2,365.00
£4,975 x 40% (rest of £16,800)	1,990.00
	4,355.00

CHAPTER 7: CAPITAL GAINS TAX – SOME SPECIAL RULES

7.1   £

Land

Proceeds	30,000
less apportioned cost:	
£50,000 x £30,000 / £150,000	(10,000)
less indexation allowance	
£10,000 x 0.199	(1,990)
Gain before taper	18,010

60% will be chargeable (9 + 1 years)

Cottage

Proceeds	300,000
less cost	(60,000)
extension	(50,000)
less indexation allowances	
(1) £60,000 x 0.704	(42,240)
(2) £50,000 x 0.199	(9,950)
Gain before taper	137,810

60% will be chargeable (9 + 1 years)

Total gains:	Land	18,010			
	Cottage	137,810			
Total gains		155,820	x 60%	=	£93,492

7.2

	£
Painting	
Proceeds	20,000
less cost	(5,000)
less restoration	(6,000)
less indexation allowances	
(1) £5,000 x 0.199	(995)
(2) £6,000 x 0.114	(684)
Gain before taper	7,321

60% will be chargeable (9 + 1 years)

	£
Table	
Proceeds	7,800
less cost:	(1,500)
less indexation allowance	
£1,500 x 0.361	(542)
Gain before taper	5,758

But gain limited to 5/3 (£7,800 - £6,000) = £3,000.

60% will be chargeable (9 + 1 years)

		£			
Total gains:	Painting	7,321			
	Table	3,000			
Total gains:		10,321	x 60%	=	£6,193

7.3   Necklace   £

Deemed Proceeds   8,000

less cost: (5,000)

less indexation allowance

£5,000 x 0.269   (1,345)

Gain before taper   1,655

Gain limited to 5/3 (£8,000 - £6,000) = £3,333 - limit does not apply.

60% will be chargeable (9 + 1 years)

Car is an exempt asset

House is also entirely exempt:

World holiday period counts as deemed occupation under the 'absence for any reason' rule since it is for less than 3 years and is between periods of actual occupation.

The final period counts as deemed occupation since it is the last 3 years of ownership, and was a PPR before this.

Total gains are therefore £1,655 x 60% = £993.

Practice examination tasks

There are two types of practice examination in this section:

Half papers (for Section 1 or Section 2 of the examination)
There are four half papers for Section 1 and four half papers for Section 2 of the examination. Tax forms are not provided within the tasks for these half papers, but are readily available (please see 'tax forms and tax years' below).

Full papers
There are three full practice papers provided here. The third paper is reproduced by kind permission of AAT. Tax forms *are* provided within these papers.

Tax forms and tax years
Tax forms for use in these tasks are those available at the time of going to press (June 2007) and therefore cover the 2006-07 tax year rather than the 2007-08 tax year. The forms will still 'work' in the various tasks. These forms may be photocopied from the Appendix, or downloaded from the Student or Tutor Resources section on www.osbornebooks.co.uk or from www.hmrc.gov.uk
If you are using this book in 2008 you will find more up-to-date forms on www.hmrc.gov.uk

Answers to practice examinations
The answers to all the Practice Examinations and larger size photocopiable tax forms are contained in the *Personal Taxation Tutor Pack*. Please call Osborne Books Customer Services on 01905 748071 or visit our website on www.osbornebooks.co.uk for details of this publication.

LIST OF PRACTICE EXAMINATIONS – TAX YEAR 2007/08

'Half' papers - Section 1

'Half' papers - Section 2

Full papers

Tax rates and other data

Tax rates and other data needed for carrying out tax calculations are detailed in the 'Tax Data' section at the beginning of this book.

Exam Section 1, tax year 2007/08

You should spend about 90 minutes on this practice half-paper.

DATA

It is November 2008. You work for a small firm of accountants, Baldwin and Benson. Your senior has just brought you some papers relating to a new client, Sylvia Summers. Sylvia has some income from renting out property, and investments, and is also employed as a Solicitor by a local practice. You have been asked to work out some tax figures for the client, and to help complete her tax return for 2007/08.

Rental Income

You are initially given some information regarding Sylvia Summer's rental income. She has provided the following profit statement, which gives details of this in the tax year.

	£	£
Rental Income		15,500
less expenditure:		
Insurance	500	
Redecoration	950	
Depreciation of Furniture	300	
Installation of Central Heating	2,500	
Letting Agent's Fees	1,550	
		5,800
Profit		9,700

Your senior also gives you the following information:

* The rent relates to one property. There is a property income loss of £3,000 that has been brought forward from the previous tax year in relation to the property.

* The tenants have occupied the property throughout the current period, and are responsible for paying their own Council Tax and Water Rates.

* The property is rented out on a fully furnished basis, and wear and tear allowance is claimable.

Employment

Sylvia's P60 showed gross pay of £40,000, and tax deducted of £10,000. She is entitled to the following benefits:

* A petrol engine car, with a list price when new of £18,000, and emission rating of 190 g/km.

* Petrol for both business and private mileage, paid for by her employer.

* Vouchers to spend on an annual holiday. The vouchers that she received in the summer of 2007 had a face value of £1,000, and cost her employer £850.

Investment Income

Sylvia received the following amounts during the tax year:
- dividend cheques for £1,800 from her shareholding
- bank deposit account interest of £4,000 net
- building society interest from her cash ISA account of £200

Task 1.1

Using the data on rental income, calculate the assessable property income for Sylvia Summer for the tax year.

Task 1.2

Calculate the total assessable employment income for the tax year for Sylvia, including benefits in kind.

Task 1.3

Calculate the assessable amounts of (a) savings and (b) dividend income for the tax year, and the amounts of tax that have already been paid out of these amounts.

Task 1.4

Calculate Sylvia's total taxable income for the tax year, after deducting her personal allowance. Also calculate the tax that has been deducted from this income.

Task 1.5

Analyse Sylvia's total taxable income into 'general income', 'savings income', and 'dividend income'. Use this information to calculate how much income tax Sylvia owes for the tax year, after accounting for the amounts that have been deducted at source.

Task 1.6

Complete the sections of the tax return for Sylvia relating to 'Land and Property', and 'Employment'. If the 2007/08 forms are not yet available, you should adapt and use the 2006/07 forms.

You may copy the appropriate form pages from the Appendix in this book or download them, either from the Student Resources Section of www.osbornebooks.co.uk or from www.hmrc.gov.uk

Task 1.7

State the latest dates that Sylvia must

(a)   submit the 2007/08 return if paper-based format used.

(b)   submit the 2007/08 return if online submission used.

(c)   pay the balance of income tax for 2007/08.

(a)

(b)

(c)

'half' paper 2   Exam Section 1, tax year 2007/08

You should spend about 90 minutes on this practice half-paper.

DATA

It is November 2008. You are an accounting technician, working in the small clients division of a firm of accountants, Cuthbert and Caldicott. One of your clients, Arthur Ambrose has brought in some data relating to his affairs for the tax year 2007/08. Arthur has considerable income from investments, and is also employed as an administrator by a national company. The job involves Arthur in some extensive travel. Your job is to carry out some tax work for the client, and to complete parts of his tax return for 2007/08.

General Information

Arthur is 35 years old. He paid a net amount of £1,560 into a personal pension plan during the tax year.

Investment Income

The following is a summary of the amounts *received* during the tax year.

	£
Bank Interest	8,000
Dividends	10,800
Interest on Government Securities (rec'd gross)	6,400
Interest from National Savings & Investments Accounts:	
Easy Access Savings Account	30
Investment Account	4,900

Employment Details

Arthur had a gross basic pay of £23,000 per year throughout the tax year. He also received bonuses in respect of calendar years as follows:

£3,500 received in May 2007 relating to 2006

£4,200 received in May 2008 relating to 2007

He paid £4,800 Income Tax during the year through PAYE.

Arthur used his own car for business trips, and received 60p per mile from the company for this. He claimed and received the agreed amount for all the 12,000 business miles that he undertook.

Arthur personally paid out the following amounts, and reclaimed them all from his employer.

	£
Hotel costs (whilst on business trips)	1,800
Entertaining business clients	500
Membership of the Association of Commercial Administrators (an approved body)	150

Task 1.1

Calculate separately the assessable amounts of savings and dividend income for the tax year, together with the amounts of tax deducted at source.

Task 1.2

Calculate the assessable amount of employment income for the tax year, clearly showing any benefits in kind and deductible expenditure.

Task 1.3

Calculate Arthur's total tax liability for the tax year, and the amount of tax that he has yet to pay.

Task 1.4

Write brief notes advising Arthur on the typical records that he should keep relating to his income tax affairs, and how long they should be kept. You should suggest at least four types of document.

Task 1.5

Arthur has heard that he may be offered a company car in future. Private fuel would also be paid for by his employer. Write a memo to Arthur that explains briefly:

- how the assessable benefit for use of the car is calculated

- how the assessable benefit for the provision of fuel for private use is calculated.

You do not need to calculate the benefit that would apply to any specific car. Assume 2007/08 rules will apply.

Task 1.6

Complete the employment pages of Arthur's tax return for 2007/08. If the 2007/08 forms are not yet available you should adapt and use the 2006/07 forms.

You may copy the appropriate form pages from the Appendix in this book or download them, either from the Student Resources Section of www.osbornebooks.co.uk or from www.hmrc.gov.uk

'half' paper **3** Exam Section 1, tax year 2007/08

You should spend about 90 minutes on this practice half-paper.

DATA

It is June 2008. You work for a small firm of accountants, Dunster & Company. Your senior has just brought you some papers relating to a new client, Mervyn Mellor. Mervyn has some income from renting out property and from investments, and is also employed as an estate agent by a local partnership. You have been asked to work out some tax figures for the client, and to help complete his tax return for 2007/08.

Rental Income

You are initially given some information regarding Mervyn Mellor's rental income. He has provided the following details relating to the tax year.

	£
Rental Income	12,500
Related Expenditure:	
Insurance & General Expenses	750
Installation of Double Glazing	3,000
Maintenance	1,200
Letting Agent's Fees	1,250

Your senior also gives you the following information:

- The rent relates to one property.

- The tenant had occupied the property through the current period until 31st March 2008, when he left owing rent of £500. The £12,500 rental income is shown after deducting this amount as irrecoverable.

- The property is rented out on an unfurnished basis.

Employment

Mervyn's P60 showed gross pay of £20,000, and tax deducted of £3,800. The gross pay includes commission on house sales of £6,000. He is entitled to the following benefits:

- A 1400cc petrol engine car, with a list price when new of £13,000, and emission rating of 173 g/km.

- Petrol for both business and private mileage, paid for by his employer.

- A loan to fund home improvements. The partnership lent Mervyn £12,000 in March 2007 at an interest rate of 2%. He has paid interest only on the loan so far.

Investment Income

Mervyn received the following amounts during the tax year:

• dividend cheques for £2,700 from his shareholding

• bank deposit account interest of £6,000 net

• building society interest of £160 net

Task 1.1

Using the data on rental income, calculate the assessable property income for Mervyn Mellor for the tax year.

Task 1.2

Calculate the total assessable employment income for the tax year for Mervyn, including benefits in kind.

Task 1.3

Calculate the assessable amounts of (a) savings and (b) dividend income for the tax year, and the amounts of tax that have already been paid out of these amounts.

Task 1.4

Calculate Mervyn's total taxable income for the tax year, after deducting his personal allowance. Also calculate the amount of tax that has been deducted at source.

Task 1.5

Analyse Mervyn's total taxable income into 'general income', 'savings income', and 'dividend income'. Use this information to calculate how much income tax Mervyn owes for the tax year, after accounting for the amounts that have been deducted at source.

Task 1.6

Mervyn's wife, Audrey has left a message requesting details of her husband's tax liability so that she can help plan their finances.

Write brief notes that will form the basis of your reply to her.

Task 1.7

Complete the sections of the tax return for Mervyn relating to 'Land and Property', and 'Employment'. If the 2007/08 forms are not yet available, you should adapt and use the 2006/07 forms.

You may copy the appropriate form pages from the Appendix in this book or download them, either from the Student Resources Section of www.osbornebooks.co.uk or from www.hmrc.gov.uk

'half' paper **4** Exam Section 1, tax year 2007/08

You should spend about 90 minutes on this practice half-paper.

DATA

It is May 2008. You are an accounting technician, working in the taxation division of a firm of accountants, Delwyn and Dawson. One of your clients, Thomas Wilson has brought in some data relating to his affairs for the tax year 2007/08. Thomas has some income from investments, and is also employed as a travel agent by a local company. The job involves Thomas in some business travel. Your job is to carry out some tax work for the client, and to complete parts of his tax return for 2007/08.

General Information

Thomas is 45 years old. He paid a net amount of £624 to charity through the gift aid scheme during the tax year.

Investment Income

The following is a summary of the amounts *received* during the tax year.

	£
Bank Interest	1,000
Dividends	1,080
Interest on Government Securities (rec'd gross)	6,400
Prizes from his holding of Premium Bonds	1,500

Employment Details

Thomas had a gross basic pay of £18,000 per year throughout the tax year.

Thomas used his own car for business trips, and received 50p per mile from the company for this. He claimed and received the agreed amount for all the 2,500 business miles that he undertook.

Thomas was allowed to take a holiday at a special price due to his employment as a travel agent. The holiday had a retail value of £2,000, and Thomas just paid the company the cost price of the holiday of £1,200.

He personally paid out the following amounts, and reclaimed them all from his employer:

	£
Subsistence costs (whilst on business trips)	800
Membership of the English Association of Travel Staff (an approved HMRC body)	80

Task 1.1

Calculate separately the assessable amounts of savings and dividend income for the tax year, together with the amounts of tax deducted at source.

Task 1.2

Calculate the assessable amount of employment income for the tax year, clearly showing any benefits in kind and deductible expenditure.

Task 1.3

Calculate Thomas' total tax liability for the tax year, before deducting PAYE.

Task 1.4

Thomas is worried that one year he may forget to both submit his online tax return and to pay any income tax due. If he did not submit the return nor pay the outstanding tax for 2007/08 until 31/3/2009, explain in outline any financial implications for Thomas.

Task 1.5

Complete the employment pages of Thomas' tax return. If the 2007/08 forms are not yet available, you should adapt and use the 2006/07 forms.

You may copy the appropriate form pages from the Appendix in this book or download them, either from the Student Resources Section of www.osbornebooks.co.uk or from www.hmrc.gov.uk

Exam Section 2, tax year 2007/08

You should spend about 90 minutes on this practice half-paper.

DATA

It is November 2008. You work for a small firm of accountants, Gambol and Grace. Your senior has just brought you some papers relating to a new client, Susan Sylvester.

Susan has the following income for 2007/08:

- Income from self-employment as a script editor of £17,000 (agreed amount)

- Interest from a bank account of £3,200 (amount received)

- Dividends received of £1,800 (amount received)

- Rental income of £4,000 (agreed amount)

Susan paid £1,950 (net) into a personal pension plan during the year. She has made no payments of tax except where it was deducted at source.

Susan also disposed of some of her assets during the tax year as follows:

- On 30/6/2007 she sold 2,000 of the ordinary shares that she owned in Deluxe plc (a quoted company), receiving £18,000. The shareholding had been built up as follows:

    1,000 shares bought 1/1/99 for £3,500

    2,000 shares bought 1/1/00 for £8,100

    1,500 shares bought 1/1/01 for £6,000

- On 30/9/2007 she gave her daughter a ring that she had bought for £3,000 on 1st January 1990. The ring was valued at £8,000 when she gave it to her daughter.

- On 31/12/2007 she sold her sailing dinghy for £1,000. She had bought it on 1st December 2000 for £1,800.

The following indexation factor is available:

January 1990 – April 1998   0.361

Task 2.1

Using a tax computation, calculate Susan's income tax liability for the tax year, and the amount of tax that has not been paid.

Task 2.1 continued

Task 2.2

Calculate the capital gain or loss on the disposal of each chargeable asset during the tax year.

Task 2.3

Calculate the amount of capital gains tax that Susan should pay for the tax year.

Task 2.4

State the latest dates by which the outstanding income tax and capital gains tax for the tax year should be paid.

Task 2.5

Susan has asked for some advice on the records that she should keep in connection with her capital assets and capital gains tax. Outline briefly the sort of records that she should keep, and how long they should normally be retained.

'half'
paper **6** **Exam Section 2, tax year 2007/08**

You should spend about 90 minutes on this practice half-paper.

DATA

It is November 2008. You work for a small firm of accountants, Edgar & Company. Your senior has just brought you some papers relating to a new client, Vikram Singh.

Vikram's total assessable income (before deducting his personal allowance) has already been calculated as £27,500.

Vikram has a capital loss of £3,800 brought forward from the last tax year.

Vikram disposed of some of his assets during 2007/08, as follows:

- On 31/1/08 he sold 4,000 of the ordinary shares that he owned in Sooper plc (a quoted company), receiving £32,000. The shareholding had been built up as follows;

    1,000 shares bought 1/1/95 for £5,500

    Bonus issue of 1 for 4 on 1/1/97

    750 shares bought 1/3/98 for £8,100

    1,500 shares bought 1/1/01 for £6,000

    1,000 shares bought 1/1/08 for £6,500

- On 30/6/2007 he sold an antique watch for £6,900 that he had bought for £3,000 on January 1st 1990.

- On 1/8/07 he sold his car for £2,500. He had bought it in December 2003 for £4,800.

- On 30/9/07 he sold his holiday cottage for £295,000, less estate agent's charges of 3%. He had bought it on 1/5/1990 for £40,000. In January 1995 he had spent £25,000 on an extension, and £2,000 on general house maintenance.

- On 1/12/98 he was left an antique painting in his grandfather's will. The painting was valued at that time at £5,000. He sold the painting on 31/1/2008 for £9,000.

The following indexation factors are available:

January 1995 – March 1998	0.101
March 1998 – April 1998	0.011
January 1990 – April 1998	0.361
May 1990 – April 1998	0.288
January 1995 – April 1998	0.114

Task 2.1

Show how the shares in Sooper plc that were sold should be matched against the acquisitions.

Task 2.2

Calculate the gains or losses on each matching of shares, before taper relief.

Task 2.3

Calculate the gain or loss on each of the other disposals that are chargeable, before taper relief.

Task 2.4

Show how the capital loss brought forward is relieved against the gains, and calculate the amount of capital gains tax to be paid for the tax year.

Task 2.5

Vikram has told you that he has been offered the chance to buy shares in Sooper plc through a 'one for five rights issue', at a price of £5.00 each. Vikram is unsure about what a rights issue is and how these shares will be treated when they are ultimately sold. He has had no transactions in the shares of Sooper plc since 31/1/08.

Respond to Vikram's query in the form of an email that explains what a rights issue is and how a subsequent disposal of shares in Sooper plc would be treated for CGT purposes.

'half' paper 7 — Exam Section 2, tax year 2007/08

You should spend about 90 minutes on this practice half-paper.

DATA

It is June 2008. You work in the taxation section of a firm of accountants, Mamouth and Company. Your senior has just brought you some papers relating to a client, Maxwell Roberts.

Maxwell has the following income for 2007/08:

* Income from employment as a chef of £23,000 (per P60)

* Interest from a building society account of £1,600 (amount received)

* Dividends received of £5,400 (amount received)

* Rental income of £6,000 (agreed amount)

Maxwell paid £2,184 (net) into a personal pension plan during the year. He paid £3,500 under PAYE.

Maxwell also disposed of some of his assets as follows:

* On 31/5/07 he sold 3,000 of the ordinary shares that he owned in Grande plc (a quoted company), receiving £30,000. The shareholding had been built up as follows;

    2,000 shares bought 1/1/99 for £6,500

    2,000 shares bought 1/1/00 for £8,100

    1,500 shares bought 1/1/01 for £4,500 through a '3 for 8' rights issue

* On 31/7/07 he sold part of a plot of land for £25,000. The land was part of a larger plot that had been bought on 1st January 1989 for £30,000. The remaining part of the land was valued at £100,000 at the time of the sale.

* On 1/3/08 he sold a gold tie-pin for £4,000. He had bought it in December 2000 for £2,800.

The following indexation factor is available:

January 1989 – April 1998   0.465

Task 2.1

Using a tax computation, calculate Maxwell's income tax liability for the tax year, and the amount of tax that has not been paid.

Task 2.2

Calculate the capital gain or loss on each chargeable disposal during the tax year.

Task 2.3

Calculate the amount of capital gains tax that Maxwell should pay for the tax year.

Task 2.4

Maxwell has been given the opportunity to work abroad for his current employer for two years. He would let out his UK house that he owns and live in rented accommodation while he was away. He is concerned about any capital gains tax implications on his UK house when he comes to sell it.

Explain the likely CGT position regarding Maxwell's house, based on the details given.

'half' paper 8 Exam Section 2, tax year 2007/08

You should spend about 90 minutes on this practice half-paper.

DATA

It is June 2008. You work in the tax department of a firm of accountants, Elgar & Company. Your senior has just brought you some papers relating to a new client, Sonita Patel.

Sonita's total assessable income (before deducting her personal allowance) has already been calculated as £28,150.

Sonita disposed of some of her assets, as follows:

- On 31/10/07 she sold 5,500 of the ordinary shares that she owned in Cooper plc (a quoted company), receiving £60,500. The shareholding had been built up as follows:

  1,200 shares bought 1/1/90 for £7,200

  Bonus issue of 1 for 6 on 1/1/97

  1,600 shares bought 1/3/98 for £11,200

  1,500 shares bought 1/1/01 for £12,000

  3,000 shares bought 1/1/03 for £21,000

- On 30/6/2007 she sold a gold necklace for £7,200 that she had bought for £4,000 on January 1st 1994.

- On 31/12/07 she disposed of a leather armchair by taking it to the local recycling centre, as it was worn out. She had bought it in December 2000 for £1,800.

- On 30/1/08 she sold her holiday cottage for £215,000. She had bought it on 1/5/1992 for £60,000. In January 1999 she had spent £55,000 on an extension, and £3,000 on redecoration.

- On 1/1/99 her uncle gave her an antique grandfather clock. It was valued at that time at £3,500. She sold the clock on 31/1/08 for £7,600.

- On 28/2/2008 she sold 4,000 shares in Xantia plc (a quoted company), for £3.50 each. The shares had all been bought for £5.00 each on 15/4/02.

The following indexation factors are available:

January 1990 – March 1998   0.346
March 1998 – April 1998   0.011
January 1994 – April 1998   0.151
May 1992 – April 1998   0.167

Task 2.1

Show how the shares in Cooper plc that were sold should be matched against the acquisitions.

Task 2.2

Calculate the gains or losses on each matching of Cooper plc shares, before taper relief.

Task 2.3

Calculate the gain or loss on each of the other disposals that are chargeable, before taper relief.

Task 2.4

Show how any loss is relieved against the gains, and calculate the amount of capital gains tax to be paid for the tax year.

Task 2.5

Sonita is aware that some taxpayers need to make income tax payments on account. She is concerned that because of the large amount of Capital Gains Tax that is due relating to 2007/08 she will be required to pay amounts of CGT on account for 2008/09.

Write a brief note explaining whether she will need to make such payments on account for 2008/09.

'full'
paper **1** Practice exam, tax year 2007/08

This examination paper is in TWO SECTIONS.

You have to show competence in BOTH sections.

You should therefore attempt and aim to complete EVERY task in EACH section.

You should spend about 90 minutes on Section 1 and 90 minutes on Section 2.

15 minutes reading time will be allowed.

Today's date is 30 November 2008. You are a part-qualified accounting technician working in the tax department of a firm of accountants, Penny & Co.

SECTION 1

DATA

You have been supplied with the following information for the year ended 5 April 2008 in respect of Mr Albert Worth, a client of the firm for many years.

1 Albert has been employed as manager of a computer company since 1 April 2007. His salary is £27,000pa. He was awarded a bonus for the year of £2,000, which was paid on 12 May 2008.

2 He received the following benefits throughout the year:

- use of a new motor car with a list price of £22,400 and emissions of 202g/km from its 1998cc diesel engine

- all diesel fuel for business and private mileage

- a laptop computer for private use at home which cost £2,000

- an interest free loan of £3,000 for personal use

- payment of his annual subscription of £90 to the Institute of Computer Practitioners (an approved body)

3 He received the following income from letting a furnished property, 27 Long Drive:

	£	£
Rental income receivable		6,000
less: Council tax	400	
Annual revenue expenses	1,200	
Cost of building front porch	2,400	
		4,000
Surplus for year		2,000

4   He received the following income from investments:

	£
Interest on HSBC Bank account (amount credited)	800
Interest on National Savings and Investments – Investment account	500
Interest on National Savings Certificates	300
Dividends on shares (cheques received)	1,800

5   Albert buys and sells antiques. HM Revenue & Customs have agreed that this income is assessable as trading income and for this tax year his assessable income has been agreed at £2,800.

6   Albert made a cheque payment of £780 into his personal pension fund.

Task 1.1

Calculate Albert's total assessable income from employment for the year.

Task 1.2

Calculate Albert's assessable property income for the year.

Task 1.3

Calculate Albert's assessable savings and dividend income for the year.

Task 1.4

Complete the employment pages of Albert's Tax Return for the year (see next 2 pages). Note that the tax return form here relates to the 2006/07 tax year as the 2007/08 form was unavailable at the time of going to press.

Task 1.5

Prepare an income tax computation for Albert for the year showing the balance of tax payable before taking account of PAYE.

Name

Tax reference

Fill in these boxes first

If you want help, look up the box numbers in the Notes.

Details of employer

Employer's PAYE reference - the 'HM Revenue & Customs office number and reference' on your P60 or 'PAYE reference' on your P45

1.1

Employer's name

1.2

Date employment started
(only if between 6 April 2006 and 5 April 2007)

1.3   /   /

Date employment finished
(only if between 6 April 2006 and 5 April 2007)

1.4   /   /

Employer's address

1.5

Tick box 1.6 if you were a director of the company

1.6

and, if so, tick box 1.7 if it was a close company

1.7

Postcode

Income from employment

■ **Money** - see Notes, page EN3.

	Before tax
• Payments from P60 (or P45)	1.8 £
• Payments not on P60, etc. - tips	1.9 £
- other payments (excluding expenses entered below and lump sums and compensation payments or benefits entered overleaf)	1.10 £

Tax taken off

• UK tax taken off payments in boxes 1.8 to 1.10   1.11 £

■ **Benefits and expenses** - see Notes, pages EN3 to EN6. If any benefits connected with termination of employment were received, or enjoyed, after that termination and were from a   former employer you need Help Sheet IR204, available from the Orderline. Do not enter such benefits here.

	Amount			Amount
• Assets transferred/ payments made for you	1.12 £		• Vans	1.18 £
• Vouchers, credit cards and tokens	1.13 £		• Interest-free and low-interest loans see Notes, page EN5.	1.19 £
• Living accommodation	1.14 £		box 1.20 is not used.	
• Excess mileage allowance and passenger payments	1.15 £		• Private medical or dental insurance	1.21 £
• Company cars	1.16 £		• Other benefits	1.22 £
• Fuel for company cars	1.17 £		• Expenses payments received and balancing charges	1.23 £

Income from employment continued

■ *Lump sums and compensation payments or benefits including such payments and benefits from a former employer*

You must read pages EN6 and EN7 of the Notes **before** filling in boxes 1.24 to 1.30.

Reliefs

- £30,000 exception — 1.24 £
- Foreign service and disability — 1.25 £
- Retirement and death lump sums — 1.26 £
- Exempt employer's contributions to an overseas pension scheme — 1.26A £

Taxable lump sums

- From box B of Help Sheet IR204 — 1.27 £
- From box K of Help Sheet IR204 — 1.28 £
- From box L of Help Sheet IR204 — 1.29 £

- Tax taken off payments in boxes 1.27 to 1.29 - leave blank if this tax is included in the box 1.11 figure but tick box 1.30A. — Tax taken off 1.30 £

- Tick this box if you have left box 1.30 blank because the tax is included in the box 1.11 figure — 1.30A

■ *Foreign earnings not taxable in the UK in the year ended 5 April 2007* — 1.31 £
 - see Notes, page EN7.

■ *Expenses you incurred in doing your job* - see Notes, pages EN7 and EN8.

- Travel and subsistence costs — 1.32 £
- Fixed deductions for expenses — 1.33 £
- Professional fees and subscriptions — 1.34 £
- Other expenses and capital allowances — 1.35 £
- Tick box 1.36 if the figure in box 1.32 includes travel between your home and a permanent workplace — 1.36

■ *Seafarers' Earnings Deduction* — 1.37 £
 - enter the amount of the earnings that attract the deduction, not the tax
 - enter ship names in box 1.40 (see Notes, page EN8 and Help Sheet IR205)

■ *Foreign tax for which tax credit relief not claimed* — 1.38 £

Student Loans

■ *Student Loans repaid by deduction by employer* - see Notes, page EN8. — 1.39 £

- Tick box 1.39A if your income is under Repayment of Teachers' Loans Scheme — 1.39A

1.40 *Additional information*

Now fill in any other supplementar y Pages that apply to you.
Otherwise, go back to page 2 in your Tax Return and finish filling it in.

Task 1.6

Draft a memo explaining to Albert

- the alternative ways, and dates by which his tax return must be submitted

- the dates of payment of income tax not deducted from income and the consequence of late payment

---

MEMORANDUM

To

From   A Student   **Date** today

Subject

SECTION 2

DATA

Albert disposed of the following capital assets during the year:

			£

1	Holly Cottage	sale proceeds on 2 July 2007	156,000
		purchase price on 12 May 1994	40,000
		cost of extension on 3 June 2000	10,000
		The cottage had been used by Albert's family for holidays throughout its ownership.	

2	Shares in Mixco plc	sale proceeds of 8,000 shares on 15 May 2007	64,000
		cost of 10,000 shares bought on 1 May 1994	22,500
		cost of 5,000 shares on 3 July 2006	25,000
		bonus issue of 1 for 2 on 1 August 2006	

| 3 | Gold necklace | sale proceeds on 3 May 2007 | 6,300 |
| | | cost on 21 June 2005 | 1,000 |

Albert had unrelieved capital losses of £8,000 at 6 April 2007.

The following indexation factor is available:

May 1994 – April 1998   0.124

Task 2.1

Calculate the capital gains on the disposal of the above capital assets by Albert during the year.

Task 2.2

Calculate the capital gains tax payable by Albert for the year.

This examination paper is in TWO SECTIONS.

You have to show competence in BOTH sections.

You should therefore attempt and aim to complete EVERY task in EACH section.

You should spend about 90 minutes on Section 1 and 90 minutes on Section 2.

15 minutes reading time will be allowed.

SECTION 1

DATA

It is June 2008. You work for Maddison and Menthol, a medium sized firm of accountants, in their tax department. Your senior has just brought you some papers relating to a client, Trevor Thomas. Trevor has some income from renting out property and investments, and is also employed as an Administrator by a local company. You have been asked to work out some tax figures for the client, and to help complete his tax return for 2007/08.

Rental Income

You are initially given some information regarding Trevor Thomas' rental income. He has provided the following profit statement, which gives details of this in the tax year.

	£	£
Rental Income		13,500
less expenditure		
Insurance	350	
Redecoration	750	
Depreciation of Furniture	300	
Repairs to roof	500	
Letting Agent's Fees	1,350	
Building new garage	2,800	
		6,050
Profit		7,450

Your senior also gives you the following information:

- The rent relates to one property. There is a property income loss of £1,500 that has been brought forward from the previous tax year in relation to the property.

- The tenants have occupied the property throughout the current period, and are responsible for paying their own Council Tax and Water Rates.

- The roof repairs relate to replacing dislodged tiles.

- The property is rented out on a fully furnished basis, and wear and tear allowance is claimable.

Employment

Trevor's P60 showed gross pay of £20,000, and tax deducted of £4,500. He is entitled to the following benefits:

- A 2,100cc diesel engine car, with a list price when new of £19,000, and emission rating of 184 g/km.

- Diesel fuel for both business and private mileage, paid for by his employer.

- Trevor lives rent-free in a flat owned by the company. The flat was bought for £100,000 in 2001. Its annual value is £900. Trevor is responsible for all the expenses relating to the flat, and has provided all his own furniture.

Investment Income

Trevor received the following amounts during the tax year:

- dividend cheques for £2,250 from his shareholding

- bank deposit account interest of £1,200 net

- building society interest from his cash ISA account of £200

- gross interest from his Government securities of £2,400

Task 1.1

Using the data on rental income, calculate the assessable property income for Trevor Thomas for the tax year.

Task 1.2

Calculate the total assessable employment income for the tax year for Trevor, including benefits in kind.

Task 1.3

Calculate the assessable amounts of (a) savings and (b) dividend income for the tax year, and the amounts of tax that have already been paid out of these amounts.

Task 1.4

Calculate Trevor's total taxable income for the tax year, after deducting his personal allowance, and analyse it into general income, savings income, and dividend income.

Task 1.5

Calculate how much income tax Trevor owes for the tax year, after accounting for the amounts that have been deducted at source.

Task 1.6

Complete the sections of the tax return for Trevor relating to 'Land and Property', and 'Employment' (shown on the four pages that follow). Please complete the forms illustrated as appropriate. Note that the tax return form here relates to the 2006/07 tax year as the 2007/08 form was unavailable at the time of going to press.

Task 1.7

Estimate the amount of tax that Trevor should pay on account for 2008/09 on 31/1/09. Assume that Trevor does not believe that his income in 2008/09 will be lower than that for 2007/08.

Name	Tax reference

Fill in these boxes first

If you want help, look up the box numbers in the Notes.

Are you claiming Rent a Room relief for gross rents of £4,250 or less?
(Or £2,125 if the claim is shared?)
Read the Notes on page LN2 to find out:
- whether you can claim Rent a Room relief; and
- how to claim relief for gross rents over £4,250.

Yes

If 'Yes', tick box. If this is your only income from UK property, you have finished these Pages

Is your income from furnished holiday lettings?
If not applicable, please turn over and fill in Page L2 to give details of your property income

Yes

If 'Yes', tick box and fill in boxes 5.1 to 5.18 before completing Page L2

Furnished holiday lettings in the UK

- Income from furnished holiday lettings — 5.1 £

- **Expenses** (furnished holiday lettings only)

- Rent, rates, insurance, ground rents etc. — 5.2 £

- Repairs, maintenance and renewals — 5.3 £

- Finance charges, including interest — 5.4 £

- Legal and professional costs — 5.5 £

- Costs of services provided, including wages — 5.6 £

- Other expenses — 5.7 £

total of boxes 5.2 to 5.7
5.8 £

Net profit (put figures in brackets if a loss)

box 5.1 minus box 5.8
5.9 £

- **Tax adjustments**

- Private use — 5.10 £

- Balancing charges — 5.11 £

box 5.10 + box 5.11
5.12 £

- Capital allowances — 5.13 £

- Tick box 5.13A if box 5.13 includes enhanced capital allowances for designated environmentally beneficial plant and machinery — 5.13A

Profit for the year (copy to box 5.19). If a loss, enter '0' in box 5.14 and put the loss in box 5.15

boxes 5.9 + 5.12 minus box 5.13
5.14 £

Loss for the year (if you have entered '0' in box 5.14)

boxes 5.9 + 5.12 minus box 5.13
5.15 £

- **Losses**

- Loss offset against 2006–07 total income — 5.16 £

- Loss - relief to be calculated by reference to earlier years

see Notes, page LN4
5.17 £

- Loss offset against other income from property (copy to box 5.38)

see Notes, page LN4
5.18 £

Other property income (not including dividends from a UK Real Estate Investment Trust - go to box 13.1 - 13.3 on page 5 of the Tax Return)

■ Income

● Furnished holiday lettings profits	*copy from box 5.14* 5.19 £	
● Rents and other income from land and property	5.20 £	*Tax taken off* 5.21 £
● Chargeable premiums	5.22 £	
● Reverse premiums	5.22A £	*boxes 5.19 + 5.20 + 5.22 + 5.22A* 5.23 £

■ Expenses (do not include figures you have already put in boxes 5.2 to 5.7 on Page L1)

● Rent, rates, insurance, ground rents etc.	5.24 £	
● Repairs, maintenance and renewals	5.25 £	
● Finance charges, including interest	5.26 £	
● Legal and professional costs	5.27 £	
● Costs of services provided, including wages	5.28 £	
● Other expenses	5.29 £	*total of boxes 5.24 to 5.29* 5.30 £

Net profit (put figures in brackets if a loss)   *box 5.23 minus box 5.30*   5.31 £

■ Tax adjustments

● Private use	5.32 £	
● Balancing charges - including those arising under Business Premises Renovation Allowance which should also be included in box 23.8	5.33 £	*box 5.32 + box 5.33* 5.34 £
● Rent a Room exempt amount	5.35 £	
● Capital allowances - including those arising under Business Premises Renovation Allowance which should also be included in box 23.7	5.36 £	
● Tick box 5.36A if box 5.36 includes a claim for 100% capital allowances for flats over shops	5.36A	
● Tick box 5.36B if box 5.36 includes enhanced capital allowances for designated environmentally beneficial plant and machinery	5.36B	
● Landlord's Energy Saving Allowance	5.36C £	
● 10% wear and tear	5.37 £	
● Furnished holiday lettings losses	*copy from box 5.18* 5.38 £	*total of boxes 5.35 to 5.38* 5.39 £

Adjusted profit (if a loss, enter '0' in box 5.40 and put the loss in box 5.41)   *boxes 5.31 + 5.34 minus box 5.39*   5.40 £

Adjusted loss (if you have entered '0' in box 5.40)   *boxes 5.31 + 5.34 minus box 5.39*   5.41 £

● Loss brought forward from previous year   5.42 £

Profit for the year   *box 5.40 minus box 5.42*   5.43 £

■ Losses etc.

● Loss offset against total income - read the note on page LN8	5.44 £
● Loss to carry forward to following year	5.45 £
● Tick box 5.46 if these Pages include details of property let jointly	5.46
● Tick box 5.47 if all property income ceased in the year to 5 April 2007 and you do not expect to receive such income again, in the year to 5 April 2008	5.47

Now fill in any other supplementary Pages that apply to you.
Otherwise, go back to page 2 of your Tax Return and finish filling it in.

Fill in these boxes first

Name

Tax reference

If you want help, look up the box numbers in the Notes.

Details of employer

Employer's PAYE reference - the 'HM Revenue & Customs office number and reference' on your P60 or 'PAYE reference' on your P45

1.1

Employer's name

1.2

Date employment started
(only if between 6 April 2006 and 5 April 2007)

1.3   /   /

Date employment finished
(only if between 6 April 2006 and 5 April 2007)

1.4   /   /

Employer's address

1.5

Postcode

Tick box 1.6 if you were a director of the company

1.6

and, if so, tick box 1.7 if it was a close company

1.7

Income from employment

■ *Money* - see Notes, page EN3.

Before tax

● Payments from P60 (or P45)   **1.8** £

● Payments not on P60, etc.   - tips   **1.9** £

   - other payments (excluding expenses entered below and lump sums and compensation payments or benefits entered overleaf)   **1.10** £

Tax taken off

● UK tax taken off payments in boxes 1.8 to 1.10   **1.11** £

■ *Benefits and expenses* - see Notes, pages EN3 to EN6. If any benefits connected with termination of employment were received, or enjoyed, after that termination and were from a former employer you need Help Sheet IR204, available from the Orderline. Do not enter such benefits here.

● Assets transferred/ payments made for you   Amount   **1.12** £

● Vouchers, credit cards and tokens   Amount   **1.13** £

● Living accommodation   Amount   **1.14** £

● Excess mileage allowance and passenger payments   Amount   **1.15** £

● Company cars   Amount   **1.16** £

● Fuel for company cars   Amount   **1.17** £

● Vans   Amount   **1.18** £

● Interest-free and low-interest loans see Notes, page EN5.   Amount   **1.19** £

box 1.20 is not used.

● Private medical or dental insurance   Amount   **1.21** £

● Other benefits   Amount   **1.22** £

● Expenses payments received and balancing charges   Amount   **1.23** £

■ *Lump sums and compensation payments or benefits including such payments and benefits from a former employer*

You must read pages EN6 and EN7 of the Notes **before** filling in boxes 1.24 to 1.30.

Reliefs

- £30,000 exception — **1.24** £
- Foreign service and disability — **1.25** £
- Retirement and death lump sums — **1.26** £
- Exempt employer's contributions to an overseas pension scheme — **1.26A** £

Taxable lump sums

- From box B of Help Sheet IR204 — **1.27** £
- From box K of Help Sheet IR204 — **1.28** £
- From box L of Help Sheet IR204 — **1.29** £

- Tax taken off payments in boxes 1.27 to 1.29 - leave blank if this tax is included in the box 1.11 figure but tick box 1.30A. — Tax taken off **1.30** £

- Tick this box if you have left box 1.30 blank because the tax is included in the box 1.11 figure — **1.30A**

■ *Foreign earnings not taxable in the UK in the year ended 5 April 2007* — **1.31** £
  - see Notes, page EN7.

■ *Expenses you incurred in doing your job* - see Notes, pages EN7 and EN8.

- Travel and subsistence costs — **1.32** £
- Fixed deductions for expenses — **1.33** £
- Professional fees and subscriptions — **1.34** £
- Other expenses and capital allowances — **1.35** £
- Tick box 1.36 if the figure in box 1.32 includes travel between your home and a permanent workplace — **1.36**

■ *Seafarers' Earnings Deduction* — **1.37** £
  - enter the amount of the earnings that attract the deduction, not the tax
  - enter ship names in box 1.40 (see Notes, page EN8 and Help Sheet IR205)

■ *Foreign tax for which tax credit relief not claimed* — **1.38** £

Student Loans

■ *Student Loans repaid by deduction by employer* - see Notes, page EN8. — **1.39** £

- Tick box 1.39A if your income is under Repayment of Teachers' Loans Scheme — **1.39A**

1.40 *Additional information*

Now fill in any other supplementar y Pages that apply to you.
Otherwise, go back to page 2 in your Tax Return and finish filling it in.

SECTION 2

DATA

Trevor Thomas had £5,000 capital loss brought forward from the previous tax year.

Trevor disposed of some of his assets during the tax year as follows:

- On 31/1/08 he sold his government securities for £5,000 when they matured. He had bought them in one block in August 1997 for £4,500.

- On 30/6/07 he sold 4,500 of the ordinary shares that he owned in TA plc, receiving £42,750. The shareholding had been built up as follows;

  2,000 shares bought 1/1/96 for £8,500

  1 for 4 bonus shares received 1/1/97

  2,000 shares bought 1/2/98 for £9,100

  1,500 shares bought 1/1/01 for £7,200

- On 31/7/07 he sold part of a plot of land for £35,000. The land was part of a larger plot that had been bought on 1st January 1987 for £40,000. The remaining part of the land was valued at £140,000 at the time of the sale.

- On 31/8/07 he sold a gold watch for £6,900. He had bought it in December 2000 for £4,800.

The following indexation factors are available:

August 1997 – April 1998	0.026
January 1996 – February 1998	0.067
February 1998 – April 1998	0.014
January 1987 – April 1998	0.626

Task 2.1

Show how the disposal of shares should be matched against the acquisitions, and calculate the gains or losses on disposal for each matching.

Task 2.2

Calculate the capital gain or loss on each of the other disposals of chargeable assets during the tax year.

Task 2.3

Calculate the amount of capital gains tax that Trevor should pay for the tax year.

Task 2.4

Suggest typical records that Trevor should maintain in respect of

(a)   his savings and investment income

(b)   his property income

(c)   his capital gains

Task 2.4 continued

'full' **3** **Practice exam, tax year 2007/08,**
paper **updated sample material courtesy AAT**

This examination paper is in TWO SECTIONS.

You have to show competence in BOTH sections.

You should therefore attempt and aim to complete EVERY task in EACH section.

You should spend about 70 minutes on Section 1 and 110 minutes on Section 2.

15 minutes reading time will be allowed.

SECTION 1

DATA

The date is May 2008. You work for Autumn Jewels Ltd in its payroll department. One of the employees, Phil Bright, has asked if you could help him complete his 2007/08 tax return.

From the company records, you determine that his employment income comprises:

1   Annual salary of £18,500.

2   Throughout the year, he was provided with a 2,500cc petrol engine company car that had a list price of £28,600 when new. It has an emission rating of 202g/km. The company pays all running costs.

3   In July 2004 he was provided with a company loan of £20,000 on which he pays interest at 2.5% per annum. No capital repayment of the loan has been made.

4   He pays pension contributions to the employer pension scheme at 5% of his salary.

Phil Bright gives you the following additional information:

1   He is 42 years old.

2   He received dividend cheques of £5,400 during the tax year.

3   He also received building society interest of £4,160, net.

4   He paid an annual subscription to his professional organisation of £250.

Task 1.1

Calculate the total assessable employment benefits in kind for the tax year.

Task 1.2

Prepare a schedule of income for the tax year, clearly showing the distinction between general, savings and dividend income. Phil Bright's personal allowances should be deducted, as appropriate.

Task 1.3

Calculate the net income tax payable for the tax year, before deducting PAYE.

Task 1.4

Another employee, Beryl Simmons, has heard that you are helping Phil Bright sort out his tax. She asks you what you have been doing for Phil, so that she can see if you can also help her.

Discuss how you should reply to this request.

Task 1.5

Complete the attached tax return for employment income of Phil Bright (see next two pages). Note that the tax return form here relates to the 2006/07 tax year as the 2007/08 form was unavailable at the time of going to press.

Name

Tax reference

Fill in these boxes first

If you want help, look up the box numbers in the Notes.

Details of employer

Employer's PAYE reference - the 'HM Revenue & Customs office number and reference' on your P60 or 'PAYE reference' on your P45

1.1

Employer's name

1.2

Date employment started
(only if between 6 April 2006 and 5 April 2007)

1.3   /   /

Date employment finished
(only if between 6 April 2006 and 5 April 2007)

1.4   /   /

Employer's address

1.5

Tick box 1.6 if you were a director of the company

1.6

and, if so, tick box 1.7 if it was a close company

1.7

Postcode

Income from employment

■ *Money* - see Notes, page EN3.

Before tax

- Payments from P60 (or P45) 1.8 £

- Payments not on P60, etc. - tips 1.9 £

  - other payments (excluding expenses entered below and lump sums and compensation payments or benefits entered overleaf) 1.10 £

Tax taken off

- UK tax taken off payments in boxes 1.8 to 1.10 1.11 £

■ *Benefits and expenses* - see Notes, pages EN3 to EN6. If any benefits connected with termination of employment were received, or enjoyed, after that termination and were from a former employer you need Help Sheet IR204, available from the Orderline. Do not enter such benefits here.

Amount

- Assets transferred/ payments made for you 1.12 £

- Vouchers, credit cards and tokens 1.13 £

- Living accommodation 1.14 £

- Excess mileage allowance and passenger payments 1.15 £

- Company cars 1.16 £

- Fuel for company cars 1.17 £

Amount

- Vans 1.18 £

- Interest-free and low-interest loans see Notes, page EN5. 1.19 £

box 1.20 is not used.

- Private medical or dental insurance 1.21 £

- Other benefits 1.22 £

- Expenses payments received and balancing charges 1.23 £

■ *Lump sums and compensation payments or benefits including such payments and benefits from a former employer*

You must read pages EN6 and EN7 of the Notes **before** filling in boxes 1.24 to 1.30.

Reliefs

- £30,000 exception   **1.24** £

- Foreign service and disability   **1.25** £

- Retirement and death lump sums   **1.26** £

- Exempt employer's contributions to an overseas pension scheme **1.26A** £

Taxable lump sums

- From box B of Help Sheet IR204   **1.27** £

- From box K of Help Sheet IR204   **1.28** £

- From box L of Help Sheet IR204   **1.29** £

- Tax taken off payments in boxes 1.27 to 1.29 - leave blank
  if this tax is included in the box 1.11 figure but tick box 1.30A.   Tax taken off **1.30** £

- Tick this box if you have left box 1.30 blank because the tax is
  included in the box 1.11 figure   **1.30A**

■ *Foreign earnings not taxable in the UK in the year ended 5 April 2007*   **1.31** £
  - see Notes, page EN7.

■ *Expenses you incurred in doing your job* - see Notes, pages EN7 and EN8.

- Travel and subsistence costs   **1.32** £

- Fixed deductions for expenses   **1.33** £

- Professional fees and subscriptions   **1.34** £

- Other expenses and capital allowances   **1.35** £

- Tick box 1.36 if the figure in box 1.32 includes travel between your home and a permanent workplace   **1.36**

■ *Seafarers' Earnings Deduction*   **1.37** £
  - enter the amount of the earnings that attract the deduction, not the tax
  - enter ship names in box 1.40 (see Notes, page EN8 and Help Sheet IR205)

■ *Foreign tax for which tax credit relief not claimed*   **1.38** £

■ *Student Loans repaid by deduction by employer* - see Notes, page EN8.   **1.39** £

- Tick box 1.39A if your income is under Repayment of Teachers' Loans Scheme   **1.39A**

1.40 *Additional information*

Now fill in any other supplementar y Pages that apply to you.
Otherwise, go back to page 2 in your Tax Return and finish filling it in.

SECTION 2

DATA

You work for a firm of Chartered Accountants in the tax department. One of your clients, Jeanette Alsop, has had three capital transactions during the year 2007/08.

1 **Shares**

In January 2008, Jeanette sold all her shares in Purple Ltd for £45,000. These shares do not qualify as business assets. Your records show that her transactions in the shares of Purple Ltd were as follows:

Date	Transaction	No of Shares	£
April 1986	Purchased	300	3,000
May 1990	Purchased	500	8,500
June 1992	Bonus issue	1 for 5	
April 1995	Purchased	1,000	16,000
March 1999	Sold	400	7,600

2 **Motor car**

In November 2007, Jeanette sold a twenty-five year old car that she has owned since December 1985. She originally paid £600 for the car, but sold it for £8,500.

3 **Land**

Jeanette bought 10 acres of land as an investment in August 1996 for £80,000. In February 2008, she sold 4 acres of this land to a property developer for £71,000. The remaining 6 acres were valued at £95,000 on the date of sale.

Jeanette Alsop also owns a variety of properties that she rents out. The total rent receivable from these properties totalled £4,800 for 2007/08, of which she had received £4,000 by 5th April 2008. Of the remaining £800, £500 was deemed irrecoverable. She also had property losses brought forward from the previous tax year of £1,600.

The following indexation factors are available:

April 1986 – May 1990	0.292
May 1990 – April 1995	0.181
April 1995 – April 1998	0.091
December 1985 – April 1998	0.693
August 1996 – April 1998	0.062

Task 2.1

Calculate the taxable gain or loss, after any taper relief, made on the disposal of the shares in Purple Ltd, if applicable.

Task 2.2

Calculate the taxable gain or loss, after any taper relief, made on the disposal of the car, if applicable.

Task 2.3

Calculate the taxable gain or loss, after any taper relief, made on the disposal of the land, if applicable.

Task 2.4

Calculate the property income chargeable to tax for the tax year.

Task 2.5

Assuming Jeanette Alsop has no other income, calculate her tax liability for the tax year, assuming that she is only entitled to the basic personal allowance.

Task 2.6

Jeanette Alsop informs you that when she completed her 2006/07 income tax return,

- she failed to declare £800 received from a building society

- all her other income in that tax year was taxed at basic rate, and totalled £300 short of the 40% tax band

- as the building society interest had already suffered tax at source, she thought that she did not need to declare it

She has heard that this was not the right thing to do, and she has sought your advice.

Write a memo to Jeanette Alsop advising her of the best course of action to take with regard to her dealings with HM Revenue & Customs, and the penalties, surcharges and/or interest she may have to pay when her mis-declaration is notified. You do not need to calculate the tax implications of this mistake.

MEMORANDUM

To   Jeanette Alsop

From   A Student   **Date** 1 June 2008

Subject   Late declaration of income

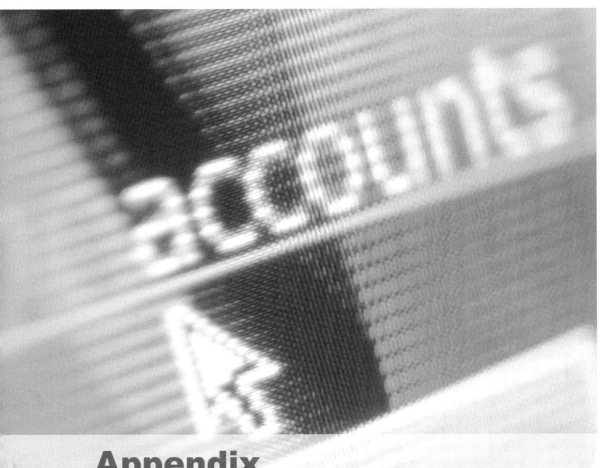

Appendix
Photocopiable tax forms

This Appendix contains Tax forms for use in student activities and practice examinations. The forms may be photocopied from this book, or alternatively downloaded from the Student or Tutor Resources section on www.osbornebooks.co.uk or from www.hmrc.gov.uk

The tax forms were those available at the time of going to press (June 2007) and therefore cover the 2006-07 tax year rather than the 2007-08 tax year. The forms will still 'work' in the various exercises. If you are using this book in 2008 you will find more up-to-date forms at www.hmrc.gov.uk

The forms shown here are:

HM Revenue & Customs

P11D EXPENSES AND BENEFITS 2006–07

Please ensure your entries are clear on both sides of the form.

Employer details

Employer name

Employer PAYE reference

Note to employer
Complete this return for a director, or an employee who earned at a rate of £8,500 a year or more during the year to 5 April 2007.

Note to employee
Your employer has filled in this form, keep it in a safe place. You will need it to complete your 2006–07 Tax Return if you get one.

Employee details

Employee name

If a director tick here ▶

Date of birth *in figures (if known)*

D D M M Y Y Y Y

Works number/department

National Insurance number

Sex **M – Male F – Female**

Employers pay Class 1A National Insurance contributions on most benefits. These are shown in boxes which are brown and have a **1A** indicator

A | Assets transferred (cars, property, goods or other assets)

Description of asset

Cost/Market value £ – Amount made good or from which tax deducted £ = Cash equivalent **1.12** £ **1A**

B | Payments made on behalf of employee

Description of payment **1.12** £

Tax on notional payments not borne by employee within 90 days of receipt of each notional payment **1.12** £

C | Vouchers or credit cards

Value of vouchers and payments made using credit cards or tokens (for qualifying childcare vouchers the excess over £55 a week)

Gross amount £ – Amount made good or from which tax deducted £ = Cash equivalent **1.13** £

D | Living accommodation

Cash equivalent of accommodation provided for employee, or his/her family or household

Cash equivalent **1.14** £ **1A**

E | Mileage allowance and passenger payments

Amount of car and mileage allowances paid to employee for business travel in employee's own vehicle, and passenger payments, in excess of maximum exempt amounts *(See P11D Guide for 2006–07 exempt rates)*

Taxable amount **1.15** £

F | Cars and car fuel *If more than two cars were made available, either at the same time or in succession, please give details on a separate sheet*

	Car 1	Car 2
Make and Model		
Date first registered	/ /	/ /
Approved CO_2 emissions figure for cars registered on or after 1 January 1998 *Tick box if the car does not have an approved CO_2 figure*	g/km *See P11D Guide for details of cars that have no approved CO_2 figure*	g/km *See P11D Guide for details of cars that have no approved CO_2 figure*
Engine size	cc	cc
Type of fuel or power used *Please use the key letter shown in the P11D Guide*		
Dates car was available *Only enter a 'from' or 'to' date if the car was first made available and/or ceased to be available in 2006–07*	From / / to / /	From / / to / /
List price of car *Including car and standard accessories only: if there is no list price, or if it is a classic car, employers see booklet 480*	£	£
Accessories *All non-standard accessories, see P11D Guide*	£	£
Capital contributions (maximum £5,000) the employee made towards the cost of car or accessories	£	£
Amount paid by employee for private use of the car	£	£
Date free fuel was withdrawn *Tick if reinstated in year (see P11D Guide)*	/ /	/ /
Cash equivalent of each car	£	£

Total cash equivalent of all cars available in 2006–07 **1.16** £ **1A**

Cash equivalent of fuel for each car	£	£

Total cash equivalent of fuel for all cars available in 2006–07 **1.17** £ **1A**

G **Vans**

Cash equivalent of all vans made available for private use **1.18** £ _____ 1A

H **Interest-free and low interest loans**
If the total amount outstanding on all loans does not exceed £5,000 at any time in the year, there is no need to complete this section.

	Loan 1	Loan 2
Number of joint borrowers *(if applicable)*		
Amount outstanding at 5 April 2006 or at date loan was made if later	£	£
Amount outstanding at 5 April 2007 or at date loan was discharged if earlier	£	£
Maximum amount outstanding at any time in the year	£	£
Total amount of interest paid by the borrower in 2006–07 – *enter "NIL" if none was paid*	£	£
Date loan was made in 2006–07 if applicable	/ /	/ /
Date loan was discharged in 2006–07 if applicable	/ /	/ /

Cash equivalent of loans after deducting any interest paid by the borrower **1.19** £ _____ 1A **1.19** £ _____ 1A

I **Private medical treatment or insurance**

	Cost to you	Amount made good or from which tax deducted	Cash equivalent
Private medical treatment or insurance	£	− £	= **1.21** £ _____ 1A

J **Qualifying relocation expenses payments and benefits**
Non-qualifying benefits and expenses go in sections M and N below

Excess over £8,000 of all qualifying relocation expenses payments and benefits for each move **1.22** £ _____ 1A

K **Services supplied**

	Cost to you	Amount made good or from which tax deducted	Cash equivalent
Services supplied to the employee	£	− £	= **1.22** £ _____ 1A

L **Assets placed at the employee's disposal**

	Annual value plus expenses incurred	Amount made good or from which tax deducted	Cash equivalent
Description of asset _____	£	− £	= **1.22** £ _____ 1A

M **Other items (including subscriptions and professional fees)**

	Cost to you	Amount made good or from which tax deducted	Cash equivalent
Description of other items _____	£	− £	= **1.22** £ _____ 1A
Description of other items _____	£	− £	= **1.22** £

		Tax paid
Income tax paid but not deducted from director's remuneration		**1.22** £

N **Expenses payments made to, or on behalf of, the employee**

	Cost to you	Amount made good or from which tax deducted	Taxable payment
Travelling and subsistence payments *(except mileage allowance payments for employee's own car - see section E)*	£	− £	= **1.23** £
Entertainment *(trading organisations read P11D Guide and then enter a tick or a cross as appropriate here)* ▢	£	− £	= **1.23** £
General expenses allowance for business travel	£	− £	= **1.23** £
Payments for use of home telephone	£	− £	= **1.23** £
Non-qualifying relocation expenses *(those not shown in sections J or M)*	£	− £	= **1.23** £
Description of other expenses _____	£	− £	= **1.23** £

Tax Return for the year ended 5 April **2007**

UTR
Tax reference
Employer reference

Issue address

Date

HM Revenue & Customs office address

For
Reference

Telephone

Please read this page before you start to fill in your Tax Return.

The green arrows and instructions will guide you through your Tax Return.

This Notice requires you, by law, to send us a Tax Return containing details of your income and capital gains, together with any documents asked for, for the year 6 April 2006 to 5 April 2007.

Time limits

You must get your Tax Return to us by the later of:

- 30 September 2007 and two months after the date this Notice was given, if you want us to calculate your tax, OR

- 31 January 2008 and three months after the date this Notice was given if you calculate your tax yourself. If you miss this date you risk a penalty.

And you must pay any tax due by:

- 31 January 2008 to avoid interest and surcharges.

To do this you can:

- file online – it is safe, quick and your tax calculation is done for you, and an instant online acknowledgement will tell you that your Tax Return has been safely received. Register for the online service at www.hmrc.gov.uk and select Self Assessment under 'do it online'

- fill in this form and any supplementary Pages you may need

- use another HM Revenue & Customs approved paper Tax Return.

If you need help we are here – online and on the phone (your own office or the Helpline when the office is closed).

If you make a false return you risk being charged penalties and interest.

SA100

INCOME AND CAPITAL GAINS *for the year ended 5 April 2007*

Step 1
Answer the Questions below to check if you need supplementary Pages to give details of particular income or capital gains. Pages 6 and 7 of your Tax Return Guide will help you decide. (Ask the Orderline for a copy of the Guide if we have not sent you one with your Tax Return.) If you answer 'Yes' ring the Orderline on 0845 9000 404 (textphone available), or fax 0845 9000 604, for the appropriate supplementary Pages and Notes.

Or you can go to www.hmrc.gov.uk and print copies from our website.

If you live or work abroad you can ring the Orderline using the International Access code followed by (+44) 161 930 8331 , or fax (+44) 161 930 8444 .

The Orderline is closed Christmas Day, Boxing Day and New Year's Day.

If you need supplementary Pages, tick the boxes below when you have got them.

Q1
Were you an employee, or office holder, or director, or agency worker or did you receive payments or benefits from a former employer (excluding a pension) in the year ended 5 April 2007?

If you were a non-resident director of a UK company but received no remuneration, see the Notes to the Employment Pages, page EN2.

YES ☐   EMPLOYMENT

Q2
Did you have any taxable income from securities options, share options, shares or share related benefits in the year?
(This does not include:
- dividends, or
- dividend shares ceasing to be subject to a HM Revenue & Customs approved share incentive plan within three years of acquisition they go in Question 10.)

YES ☐   SHARE SCHEMES

Q3
Were you self-employed (but not in partnership)?
(You should also tick 'Yes' if you were a Name at Lloyd's.)

YES ☐   SELF-EMPLOYMENT

Q4
Were you in partnership?

YES ☐   PARTNERSHIP

Q5
Did you receive any rent or other income from land and property in the UK?

YES ☐   LAND & PROPERTY

Q6
Did you have any taxable income or payments from overseas pensions or benefits, or from foreign companies or savings institutions, offshore funds or trusts abroad, or from land and property abroad or gains on foreign insurance policies?

YES ☐

Have you, or could you have, received or enjoyed directly or indirectly, or benefited in any way from, income or payments of a foreign entity as a result of a transfer of assets made in this or earlier years?

YES ☐

Do you want to claim foreign tax credit relief for foreign tax paid on foreign income, payments or gains?

YES ☐   FOREIGN

Q7
Did you receive, or are you deemed to have received, income from a trust, settlement or the residue of a deceased person's estate?

YES ☐   TRUSTS ETC.

Q8
Capital gains - read the guidance on page 7 of the Tax Return Guide.

- If you have disposed of your only or main residence do you need the Capital Gains Pages?

  YES ☐

- Did you dispose of other chargeable assets worth more than £35,200 in total?

  YES ☐

- Answer 'Yes' if:
  - allowable losses are deducted from your chargeable gains, which total more than £8,800 before deduction and before taper relief, or
  - no allowable losses are deducted from your chargeable gains and after taper relief your taxable gains total more than £8,800, or
  - you want to make a claim or election for the year.

  YES ☐   CAPITAL GAINS

Q9
Do you consider that you were, for all or part of the year, (a) not resident in the UK, and/or (b) not ordinarily resident in the UK, and/or (c) not domiciled in the UK and this was relevant to your Income Tax or Capital Gains Tax liabilities, or (d) dual resident in the UK and another country?

YES ☐   NON-RESIDENCE ETC.

Q25
Pensions - tax charges and taxable lump sums- first read the guidance on page 7 of the Tax Return Guide and if applicable answer 'Yes'.

YES ☐   PENSIONS

Step 2
Fill in any supplementary Pages BEFORE going to Step 3.

Please use blue or black ink to fill in your Tax Return and please do not include pence.   Round down your income and gains. Round up your tax credits and tax deductions. Round to the nearest pound.

When you have filled in all the supplementary Pages you need, tick this box. ☐

Step 3
Fill in Questions 10 to 24. If you answer 'Yes', fill in the relevant boxes. If not applicable, go to the next question.

INCOME *for the year ended 5 April 2007*

Q10 Did you receive any income from UK savings and investments? **YES**

If yes , tick this box and then fill in boxes 10.1 to 10.26 as appropriate. Include only your share of any joint savings and investments. If not applicable, go to Question 11.

■ *Interest and alternative finance receipts*

● Interest and alternative finance receipts from UK banks or building societies including UK Internet accounts.
If you have more than one bank or building society account enter totals in the boxes.

- enter any bank or building society interest and alternative finance receipts that have not had tax taken off . (Interest and alternative finance receipts are usually taxed before you receive them so make sure you should be filling in box 10.1, rather than boxes 10.2 to 10.4.) Enter other types of interest and alternative finance receipts in boxes 10.5 to 10.14, as appropriate.

Taxable amount
10.1 £

- enter details of taxed bank or building society interest and taxed alternative finance receipts. The Working Sheet on page 11 of your Tax Return Guide will help you fill in boxes 10.2 to 10.4.

Amount after tax taken off	Tax taken off	Gross amount before tax
10.2 £	**10.3** £	**10.4** £

● Interest distributions from UK authorised unit trusts and open-ended investment companies (dividend distributions go below)

Amount after tax taken off	Tax taken off	Gross amount before tax
10.5 £	**10.6** £	**10.7** £

● National Savings & Investments (other than First Option Bonds and Fixed Rate Savings Bonds and the first £70 of interest from an Ordinary Account)

Taxable amount
10.8 £

● National Savings & Investments First Option Bonds and Fixed Rate Savings Bonds

Amount after tax taken off	Tax taken off	Gross amount before tax
10.9 £	**10.10** £	**10.11** £

● Other income from UK savings and investments (except dividends)

Amount after tax taken off	Tax taken off	Gross amount before tax
10.12 £	**10.13** £	**10.14** £

■ *Dividends*

● Dividends and other qualifying distributions from UK companies (enter distributions from the tax exempt profits of a Real Estate Investment Trust at Q13)

Dividend/distribution	Tax credit	Dividend/distribution plus credit
10.15 £	**10.16** £	**10.17** £

● Dividend distributions from UK authorised unit trusts and open-ended investment companies

Dividend/distribution	Tax credit	Dividend/distribution plus credit
10.18 £	**10.19** £	**10.20** £

● Stock dividends from UK companies

Dividend	Notional tax	Dividend plus notional tax
10.21 £	**10.22** £	**10.23** £

● Non-qualifying distributions and loans written off

Distribution/loan	Notional tax	Taxable amount
10.24 £	**10.25** £	**10.26** £

INCOME *for the year ended 5 April 2007, continued*

Q11 Did you receive a taxable UK pension, retirement annuity, Social Security benefit or Statutory Payment?
Read the notes on pages 13 to 16 of the Tax Return Guide.

YES

If yes , tick this box and then fill in boxes 11.1 to 11.14 as appropriate.
If not applicable, go to Question 12.

■ *State pensions and benefits*

Taxable amount for 2006–07

- State Pension- enter the total of your entitlements for the year — **11.1** £

	Tax taken off	Gross amount before tax
State Pension Lump Sum	**11.1A** £	**11.1B** £

- Widow's Pension or Bereavement Allowance — **11.2** £

- Widowed Mother's Allowance or Widowed Parent's Allowance — **11.3** £

- Industrial Death Benefit Pension — **11.4** £

- Jobseeker's Allowance — **11.5** £

- Carer's Allowance — **11.6** £

- Statutory Sick, Maternity, Paternity and Adoption Pay paid by HM Revenue & Customs — **11.7** £

	Tax taken off	Gross amount before tax
Taxable Incapacity Benefit	**11.8** £	**11.9** £

■ *Other pensions and retirement annuities*

- Pensions (other than State Pensions), retirement annuities and triviality and wind-up lump sum pension payments - If you have more than one pension or annuity, please add them together and complete boxes 11.10 to 11.12. Provide the name of the pension payer, amount of pension and tax deducted of each one in box 11.14 or box 23.9 if there is insufficient space. Read the notes on page 15 of the Tax Return Guide.

Amount after tax taken off	Tax taken off	Gross amount before tax
11.10 £	**11.11** £	**11.12** £

11.14

- Deduction - see the note for box 11.13 on page 16 of your Tax Return Guide.

Amount of deduction
11.13 £

Q12 Did you make any gains on UK life insurance policies, life annuities or capital redemption policies or receive refunds of surplus funds from additional voluntary contributions?

YES

If yes , tick this box and then fill in boxes 12.1 to 12.12 as appropriate.
If not applicable, go to Question 13.

	Number of years		Amount of gain(s)
Gains on UK annuities and friendly societies' life insurance policies where no tax is treated as paid	**12.1**		**12.2** £

	Number of years	Tax treated as paid	Amount of gain(s)
Gains on UK life insurance policies etc. on which tax is treated as paid - read the notes on pages 16 to 18 of your Tax Return Guide.	**12.3**	**12.4** £	**12.5** £

	Number of years	Tax taken off	Amount of gain(s)
Gains on life insurance policies in ISAs that have been made void	**12.6**	**12.7** £	**12.8** £

	Amount
Deficiency relief	**12.9** £

	Amount received	Notional tax	Amount plus notional tax
Refunds of surplus funds from additional voluntary contributions	**12.10** £	**12.11** £	**12.12** £

INCOME AND RELIEFS *for the year ended 5 April 2007*

Q13 Did you receive any other taxable income or benefit which you have not already entered elsewhere in your Tax Return? Fill in any supplementary Pages before answering Question 13. (Supplementary Pages follow page 10, or are available from the Orderline, or www.hmrc.gov.uk)

YES — If yes , tick this box and then fill in boxes 13.1 to 13.6 as appropriate. If not applicable, go to Question 14.

- Other taxable income (including dividends from the tax-exempt profits of a UK Real Estate Investment Trust that are normally paid under deduction of tax and any benefit arising from a pre-owned asset). Read the notes on pages 18 and 21 of the Tax Return Guide. Also provide details in box 23.9.

Amount after tax taken off	Tax taken off	Amount before tax
13.1 £	13.2 £	13.3 £

- Tick box 13.1A if you have claimed enhanced capital allowances for designated environmentally beneficial plant and machinery to arrive at box 13.1

13.1A

Losses brought forward	Earlier years' losses used in 2006–07
13.4 £	13.5 £

2006–07 losses carried forward

13.6 £

Q14 Do you want to claim relief for your pension contributions?

If your pension contributions are taken off your pay before it is taxed, no more tax relief is due – leave Question 14 blank. If you make any other type of pension contribution read page 21 of the Tax Return Guide and then complete Question 14.

YES — If yes , tick this box and then fill in boxes 14.1 to 14.4 as appropriate. If not applicable, go to Question 15.

- ■ *Contributions you paid with basic rate tax deducted (called relief at source)* – contributions paid to a personal pension or stakeholder pension scheme, or group personal pension; contributions paid to a Free-standing AVC Scheme; contributions paid to other pension schemes after deducting basic rate tax.

- Enter the full amount of the contribution and add back the basic rate tax deducted. Read the notes on page 21 of your Tax Return Guide.

14.1 £

- ■ *Contributions you paid in full* – Enter the amount of contributions you paid. Read the notes on page 21 of the Tax Return Guide.

- Contributions under a retirement annuity contract paid in full without deducting basic rate tax

14.2 £

- Contributions paid to your employer's occupational pension scheme which were not deducted from your pay before tax

14.3 £

- Contributions paid to a non-UK registered overseas pension scheme which are eligible for tax relief, and were not deducted from your pay before tax

14.4 £

Q15 Do you want to claim any of the following reliefs?

If you have made any annual payments, after basic rate tax, answer 'Yes' to Question 15 and fill in box 15.9. If you have made any gifts to charity go to Question 15A.

YES — If yes , tick this box and then fill in boxes 15.1 to 15.12, as appropriate. If not applicable, go to Question 15A.

- Interest and alternative finance payments eligible for relief on qualifying loans and arrangements

Amount of payment

15.1 £

- Maintenance or alimony payments you have made under a court order, Child Support Agency assessment or other legally binding order or agreement

Amount claimed, up to £2,350

15.2 £

To claim this relief, either you, your former spouse or former civil partner must have been 65 or over on 5 April 2000. So, if your date of birth, which is to be entered in box 22.6, is after 5 April 1935, enter your former spouse's or former civil partner's date of birth in box 15.2A - see page 23 of your Tax Return Guide.

Former spouse's/civil partner's date of birth

15.2A / /

- Subscriptions for Venture Capital Trust shares (up to £200,000)

Amount on which relief is claimed

15.3 £

- Subscriptions under the Enterprise Investment Scheme (up to £400,000) - also provide details in the 'Additional information' box, box 23.9, on page 10 - see page 23 of your Tax Return Guide.

Amount on which relief is claimed

15.4 £

RELIEFS *for the year ended 5 April 2007, continued*

- Community Investment Tax relief - invested amount relating to previous tax year(s) and on which relief is due   **15.5** £

- Community Investment Tax relief - invested amount for 2006-07   **15.6** £

Total amount on which relief is claimed
box 15.5 + box 15.6
15.7 £

- Post-cessation expenses, pre-incorporation losses brought forward and losses on deeply discounted securities, etc. - see page 23 of your Tax Return Guide.

Amount of payment/loss
15.8 £

- Trade annuities and patent royalties

Payments made
15.9 £

- Payments to a trade union or friendly society for death benefits

Half amount of payment
15.10 £

- Payments to your employer's compulsory widow's, widower's, surviving civil partner's or orphan's benefit scheme - available in some circumstances first read the notes on page 24 of your Tax Return Guide

Relief claimed
15.11 £

- Relief claimed on a qualifying distribution on the redemption of bonus shares or securities

Relief claimed
15.12 £

Q15A Have you made any gifts to charity?   YES

If yes , tick this box and then read page 25 of your Tax Return Guide. Fill in boxes 15A.1 to 15A.7 as appropriate.
If not applicable, go to Question 16.

- Gift Aid payments, including covenanted payments to charities, made between 6 April 2006 and 5 April 2007   **15A.1** £

- The total of any 'one-off' payments included in box 15A.1   **15A.2** £

- Gift Aid payments made after 5 April 2006 but treated as if made in the tax year 2005–06   **15A.3** £

- Gift Aid payments made after 5 April 2007 but to be treated as if made in the tax year 2006–07   **15A.4** £

box 15A1 + box 15A.4 minus box 15A.3

- Total relief claimed in 2006–07   **15A.5** £

- Gifts of qualifying investments to charities – shares and securities   **15A.6** £

- Gifts of qualifying investments to charities – real property   **15A.7** £

Q16 Do you want to claim blind person's allowance, or married couple's allowance?   YES
If you are resident in the UK you get your personal allowance of £5,035 automatically.
If you were born before 6 April 1942, enter your date of birth in box 22.6 - you may get a higher age-related personal allowance.

If yes, tick this box and then read pages 26 to 28 of your Tax Return Guide. Fill in boxes 16.1 to 16.17 as appropriate.
If not applicable, go to Question 17.

■ *Blind person's allowance*

If first year of claim, date of registration
16.1   /   /

Local authority (or other register)
16.2

■ *Married couple's allowance*

This allowance can only be claimed if either you or your spouse or civil partner were born before 6 April 1935, and:

- you are a man or woman who married before 5 December 2005, or
- you are a man, woman or civil partner who married or formed a civil partnership on or after 5 December 2005.

The allowance is made up of two amounts - a minimum amount (worth up to £235) and an age-related amount, dependent on the income of the husband (for marriages before 5 December 2005) or the person with the higher income (for marriages and civil partnerships formed on or after 5 December 2005). Special rules apply if you are a married woman or a civil partner who does not have the higher income. Further guidance is given, beginning on page 27 of the Tax Return Guide.

If both you and your spouse or civil partner were born after 5 April 1935 you cannot claim. Do not complete boxes 16.3 to 16.13.

If you can claim, fill in boxes 16.3 and 16.4.

- Enter your date of birth (if born before 6 April 1935)   **16.3**   /   /

- Enter your spouse or civil partner's date of birth (only if born before 6 April 1935 and if older than you)   **16.4**   /   /

ALLOWANCES AND OTHER INFORMATION *for the year ended 5 April 2007*

Then, if you are a married man, who married before 5 December 2005, or you married or formed a civil partnership on or after 5 December 2005 and you have the higher income, fill in boxes 16.5 to 16.9.

If you are a married woman, who married before 5 December 2005, or you married or formed a civil partnership on or after 5 December 2005 but you do not have the higher income, fill in boxes 16.10 to 16.13 to claim half, or all, of the minimum amount of the married couple's allowance.

- Spouse or civil partner's full name **16.5** [   ]
- Date of marriage or formation of civil partnership (if after 5 April 2006) **16.6** [/ /]

- Tick box 16.7 or box 16.8 where half, or all, of the minimum amount of the allowance has been allocated to your wife, husband or civil partner

  Half **16.7** [ ] All **16.8** [ ]

- Enter in box 16.9 the date of birth of any previous wife, husband or former civil partner, with whom you lived at any time during 2006–07. Read 'Special rules if you are married or formed a civil partnership in the year ended 5 April 2007' on page 28 of your Tax Return Guide before completing box 16.9.

  16.9 [/ /]

- Tick box 16.10 or 16.11 where half, or all, of the minimum amount of the allowance has been allocated to you

  Half **16.10** [ ] All **16.11** [ ]

- Spouse or civil partner's full name **16.12** [   ]
- Date of marriage or formation of civil partnership (if after 5 April 2006) **16.13** [/ /]

■ *Transfer of surplus allowances* - read page 28 of your Tax Return Guide before you fill in boxes 16.14 to 16.17.

- Tick box 16.14 if you want your spouse or civil partner to have your unused allowances **16.14** [ ]

- Tick box 16.15 if you want to have your spouse's or civil partner's unused allowances **16.15** [ ]

Please give details in the 'Additional information' box, box 23.9, on page 10

If you want to calculate your tax, enter the amount of the surplus allowances you can have

- Blind person's surplus allowance **16.16** £ [   ]
- Married couple's surplus allowance **16.17** £ [   ]

Q17 Do you have an Income Contingent Student Loan for which you have received notification that repayment commenced before 6 April 2007? You must read the note on page 28 of your Tax Return Guide before ticking the 'Yes' box.

YES [ ] If yes, tick this box. If not applicable, go to Question 18.

If yes, and you are calculating your tax enter, in Question 18, box 18.2A, the amount you work out is repayable in 2006–07.

Q18 Do you want to calculate your tax and, if appropriate, Class 4 National Insurance contributions and Student Loan Repayment?

YES [ ] Use your Tax Calculation Guide then fill in boxes 18.1 to 18.8 as appropriate.

- Underpaid tax for earlier years included in your tax code for 2006-07 **18.1** £ [   ]
- Underpaid tax for 2006–07 included in your tax code for 2007–08 **18.2** £ [   ]
- Student Loan Repayment due **18.2A** £ [   ]
- Class 4 NICs due **18.2B** £ [   ]
- Pension charges due- enter the amount from box 32 of the Pensions supplementary Page **18.2C** £ [   ]
- Total tax, Class 4 NICs and Student Loan Repayment due for 2006–07before you made any payments on account (put the amount in brackets if an overpayment.) **18.3** £ [   ]
- Tax due calculated by reference to earlier years- see the notes on page 10 of your Tax Calculation Guide (SA151W). **18.4** £ [   ]
- Reduction in tax due calculated by reference to earlier years- see the notes on page 10 of your Tax Calculation Guide (SA151W). **18.5** £ [   ]
- Tick box 18.6 if you are claiming to reduce your 2007–08 payments on account. Make sure you enter the reduced amount of your first payment in box 18.7. Then, in the 'Additional information' box, box 23.9 on page 10, say why you are making a claim **18.6** [ ]
- Your first payment on account for 2007–08 (please include the pence.) **18.7** £ [   ]
- Any 2007–08 tax you are reclaiming now **18.8** £ [   ]

OTHER INFORMATION *for the year ended 5 April 2007, continued*

Q19 Do you want to claim a repayment if you have paid too much tax? *(If you do not tick 'Yes' or the tax you have overpaid is below £10, we will use the amount you are owed to reduce your next tax bill.)*

YES

If yes, tick this box. Then, if you want to give all or part of your repayment to a nominated charity, go to Question 19A; if you want to claim a repayment, go to Question 19B.
If not applicable, go to Question 20.

Q19A Do you want to nominate a charity to receive all or part of your repayment? *See page 29 of your Tax Return Guide.*

YES

If yes, tick this box and then read page 29 of your Tax Return Guide. Fill in boxes 19A.1 to 19A.5 as appropriate.
If not applicable, go to Question 19B.

- Tick box 19A.1 if you want to nominate a charity to receive all of your repayment   **19A.1**

- If you want to nominate a charity to receive part of your repayment, enter the amount in box 19A.2
  – if you want the remainder of your repayment to be paid to you or your nominee, you must fill in Question 19B below.   **19A.2** £

- Charity code – to get the Charity code go to www.hmrc.gov.uk , or ring the Helpline, or contact us.   **19A.3** | | | | **G**

- Tick box 19A.4 if you wish Gift Aid to apply and are making the declaration below   **19A.4**

- Tick box 19A.5 if we can provide the charity with your name and address when we notify them of your donation   **19A.5**

Gift Aid declaration – I want my gift to the nominated charity to be treated as a Gift Aid donation. The charity will receive basic rate Income Tax on my gift. I confirm that I will pay at least as much Income or Capital Gains Tax in 2007–08 as the charity will receive on my donation.

Q19B Do you want your repayment to be paid to you, or to your nominee?

YES

If yes, tick this box and then fill in boxes 19B.1 to 19B.14 as appropriate.
If not applicable, go to Question 20.

Repayments will be sent direct to your bank or building society account. This is the safest and quickest method of payment. If you do not have an account, tick box 19B.8. If you would like repayment made to your nominee, tick box 19B.2 or 19B.9.

Should the repayment be sent:

- to your bank or building society account? Tick box 19B.1 and fill in boxes 19B.3 to 19B.7.   **19B.1**

OR

- to your nominee's bank or building society account? Tick box 19B.2 and fill in boxes 19B.3 to 19B.7 and 19B.11 to 19B.14.   **19B.2**

- If you do not have a bank or building society account, read the notes on page 29 of your Tax Return Guide, and tick box 19B.8.   **19B.8**

- If you would like a cheque to be sent to your nominee, tick box 19B.9 and fill in boxes 19B.11 to 19B.14.   **19B.9**

- If your nominee is your adviser, tick box 19B.10.   **19B.10**

Name of bank or building society
19B.3

Name of account holder
19B.4

Branch sort code
19B.5

Account number
19B.6

Building society reference
19B.7

Adviser's reference for you (if your nominee is your adviser)
19B.11

I authorise
My nominee/adviser name
19B.12
to receive the amount due on my behalf.

Nominee/adviser address
19B.13

Postcode

19B.14 This authority must be signed by you. A photocopy of your signature will not do.

Signature

OTHER INFORMATION *for the year ended 5 April 2007, continued*

Q20 Have you already had any 2006–07 tax refunded or set off by your HM Revenue & Customs office or by Jobcentre Plus? Read the notes on page 29 of your Tax Return Guide.

YES

If yes, tick this box and then enter the amount of the refund in box 20.1.

20.1 £

Q21 Is your name or address on the front of the Tax Return wrong? If you are filling in an approved substitute Tax Return, see the notes on page 29 of the Tax Return Guide.

YES

If yes, please tick this box and make any corrections on the front of the form.

Q22 Please give other personal details in boxes 22.1 to 22.7.

This information helps us to be more efficient and effective.

Your daytime telephone number (including the area code)

22.1

Your adviser's telephone number (including the area code)

22.2

and their name and address

22.3

Postcode

Your first two forenames

22.4

Say if you are single, married/in a civil partnership, widowed/a surviving civil partner, divorced/civil partnership dissolved or separated

22.5

Your date of birth (If you were born before 6 April 1942, you may get a higher age-related personal allowance.)

22.6 / /

Your National Insurance number (if known and not on page 1 of your Tax Return)

22.7

Q23 If they apply, please tick boxes 23.1 to 23.4, and complete boxes 23.5 to 23.8. Provide any additional information in box 23.9, on page 10.

- If you owe tax for 2006–07 and have a PAYE tax code, we will try and collect the tax due (if it is less than £2,000) through your tax code for 2008–09. Tick box 23.1 if you do not want the tax collected through your PAYE tax code read Key Dates on page 3 of your Tax Return Guide before completing this box.

23.1

- Tick box 23.1A if you are likely to owe tax for 2007–08 on income other than employed earnings or pensions and you do not want us to use your 2007–08 PAYE tax code to collect that tax during the year

23.1A

- Tick box 23.2 if this Tax Return contains figures that are provisional because you do not yet have final figures. Page 30 of the Tax Return Guide explains the circumstances in which provisional figures may be used and asks for some additional information to be provided in box 23.9, on page 10

23.2

- Tick box 23.3 if you are claiming relief now for 2007–08 trading, or certain capital, losses. Enter in box 23.9 the amount and year

23.3

- Tick box 23.4 if you are claiming to have post-cessation or other business receipts taxed as income of an earlier year. Enter in box 23.9 the amount and year

23.4

- Disclosure of tax avoidance schemes - if you are a party to one or more disclosable tax avoidance schemes you must complete boxes 23.5 and 23.6. Give details of each scheme on a separate line. If you are party to more than 3 schemes give further details in the 'Additional information' box, box 23.9, on page 10

Scheme reference number

23.5

Tax year in which the expected advantage arises - year ended 5 April

23.6

- Business Premises Renovation Allowance (BPRA) - Read page 31 of the Guide and enter the amounts of BPRA included in the capital allowances and balancing charges boxes on the Self-employment and Land and Property Pages

Capital allowance

23.7 £

Balancing charge

23.8 £

OTHER INFORMATION *for the year ended 5 April 2007, continued*

23.9 *Additional information*

Q24 Declaration

I have filled in and am sending back to you the following Pages:

In the second box enter the number of complete sets of supplementary Pages enclosed.

	Tick	Number of sets			Tick	Number of sets			Tick
1 TO 10 OF THIS FORM				PARTNERSHIP				CAPITAL GAINS	
EMPLOYMENT				LAND & PROPERTY				NON-RESIDENCE ETC	
SHARE SCHEMES		Number of sets		FOREIGN				PENSIONS	
SELF-EMPLOYMENT				TRUSTS ETC					

Before you send your completed Tax Return, you must sign the statement below.
If you give false information or conceal any part of your income or chargeable gains, you may be liable to financial penalties and/or you may be prosecuted.

24.1 The information I have given in this Tax Return is correct and complete to the best of my knowledge and belief.

Signature   Date

There are very few reasons why we accept a signature from someone who is not the person making this Tax Return but if you are signing for someone else please read the notes on page 31 of your Tax Return Guide, and :

enter the capacity in which you are signing (for example, as executor or receiver)

24.2

enter the name of the person you are signing for

24.3

please PRINT your name and address in box 24.4

24.4

Postcode

Income for the year ended 5 April 2007

HM Revenue & Customs

EMPLOYMENT

Fill in these boxes first

Name

Tax reference

If you want help, look up the box numbers in the Notes.

Details of employer

Employer's PAYE reference - the 'HM Revenue & Customs office number and reference' on your P60 or 'PAYE reference' on your P45

1.1

Employer's name

1.2

Date employment started
(only if between 6 April 2006 and 5 April 2007)

1.3 / /

Date employment finished
(only if between 6 April 2006 and 5 April 2007)

1.4 / /

Employer's address

1.5

Postcode

Tick box 1.6 if you were a director of the company

1.6

and, if so, tick box 1.7 if it was a close company

1.7

Income from employment

■ **Money** - see Notes, page EN3.

Before tax

- Payments from P60 (or P45)   **1.8** £

- Payments not on P60, etc.   - tips   **1.9** £

   - other payments (excluding expenses entered below and lump sums and compensation payments or benefits entered overleaf)   **1.10** £

Tax taken off

- UK tax taken off payments in boxes 1.8 to 1.10   **1.11** £

■ **Benefits and expenses** - see Notes, pages EN3 to EN6. If any benefits connected with termination of employment were received, or enjoyed, after that termination and were from a   former employer you need Help Sheet IR204, available from the Orderline. Do not enter such benefits here.

Assets transferred/ payments made for you	Amount **1.12** £	Vans — Amount **1.18** £
Vouchers, credit cards and tokens	Amount **1.13** £	Interest-free and low-interest loans see Notes, page EN5. — Amount **1.19** £
Living accommodation	Amount **1.14** £	box 1.20 is not used.
Excess mileage allowance and passenger payments	Amount **1.15** £	Private medical or dental insurance — Amount **1.21** £
Company cars	Amount **1.16** £	Other benefits — Amount **1.22** £
Fuel for company cars	Amount **1.17** £	Expenses payments received and balancing charges — Amount **1.23** £

Income from employment continued

■ *Lump sums and compensation payments or benefits including such payments and benefits from a former employer*

You must read pages EN6 and EN7 of the Notes **before** filling in boxes 1.24 to 1.30.

Reliefs

- £30,000 exception — **1.24** £
- Foreign service and disability — **1.25** £
- Retirement and death lump sums — **1.26** £
- Exempt employer's contributions to an overseas pension scheme — **1.26A** £

Taxable lump sums

- From box B of Help Sheet IR204 — **1.27** £
- From box K of Help Sheet IR204 — **1.28** £
- From box L of Help Sheet IR204 — **1.29** £

- Tax taken off payments in boxes 1.27 to 1.29 - leave blank if this tax is included in the box 1.11 figure but tick box 1.30A. Tax taken off **1.30** £

- Tick this box if you have left box 1.30 blank because the tax is included in the box 1.11 figure — **1.30A**

■ *Foreign earnings not taxable in the UK in the year ended 5 April 2007* — **1.31** £
  - see Notes, page EN7.

■ *Expenses you incurred in doing your job* - see Notes, pages EN7 and EN8.

- Travel and subsistence costs — **1.32** £
- Fixed deductions for expenses — **1.33** £
- Professional fees and subscriptions — **1.34** £
- Other expenses and capital allowances — **1.35** £
- Tick box 1.36 if the figure in box 1.32 includes travel between your home and a permanent workplace — **1.36**

■ *Seafarers' Earnings Deduction* — **1.37** £
  - enter the amount of the earnings that attract the deduction, not the tax
  - enter ship names in box 1.40 (see Notes, page EN8 and Help Sheet IR205)

■ *Foreign tax for which tax credit relief not claimed* — **1.38** £

Student Loans

■ *Student Loans repaid by deduction by employer* - see Notes, page EN8. — **1.39** £

- Tick box 1.39A if your income is under Repayment of Teachers' Loans Scheme — **1.39A**

1.40 *Additional information*

Now fill in any other supplementary Pages that apply to you.
Otherwise, go back to page 2 in your Tax Return and finish filling it in.

HM Revenue & Customs

Income for the year ended 5 April 2007

LAND AND PROPERTY

Name

Tax reference

Fill in these boxes first

If you want help, look up the box numbers in the Notes.

Are you claiming Rent a Room relief for gross rents of £4,250 or less?
(Or £2,125 if the claim is shared?)
Read the Notes on page LN2 to find out:
- whether you can claim Rent a Room relief; and
- how to claim relief for gross rents over £4,250.

Yes

If 'Yes', tick box. If this is your only income from UK property, you have finished these Pages

Is your income from furnished holiday lettings?
If not applicable, please turn over and fill in Page L2 to give details of your property income

Yes

If 'Yes', tick box and fill in boxes 5.1 to 5.18 before completing Page L2

Furnished holiday lettings in the UK

- Income from furnished holiday lettings .... **5.1** £

- ■ *Expenses* (furnished holiday lettings only)

- Rent, rates, insurance, ground rents etc. **5.2** £

- Repairs, maintenance and renewals **5.3** £

- Finance charges, including interest **5.4** £

- Legal and professional costs **5.5** £

- Costs of services provided, including wages **5.6** £

- Other expenses **5.7** £

total of boxes 5.2 to 5.7
5.8 £

Net profit   (put figures in brackets if a loss)

box 5.1 minus box 5.8
5.9 £

- ■ *Tax adjustments*

- Private use **5.10** £

- Balancing charges **5.11** £

box 5.10 + box 5.11
5.12 £

- Capital allowances **5.13** £

- Tick box 5.13A if box 5.13 includes enhanced capital allowances for designated environmentally beneficial plant and machinery **5.13A**

Profit for the year   (copy to box 5.19). If a loss, enter '0' in box 5.14 and put the loss in box 5.15

boxes 5.9 + 5.12 minus box 5.13
5.14 £

Loss for the year (if you have entered '0' in box 5.14)

boxes 5.9 + 5.12 minus box 5.13
5.15 £

- ■ *Losses*

- Loss offset against 2006–07 total income **5.16** £

- Loss - relief to be calculated by reference to earlier years

see Notes, page LN4
5.17 £

- Loss offset against other income from property (copy to box 5.38)

see Notes, page LN4
5.18 £

Other property income (not including dividends from a UK Real Estate Investment Trust - go to box 13.1 - 13.3 on page 5 of the Tax Return)

■ Income

	copy from box 5.14	
● Furnished holiday lettings profits	5.19 £	
● Rents and other income from land and property	5.20 £	Tax taken off 5.21 £
● Chargeable premiums	5.22 £	
● Reverse premiums	5.22A £	boxes 5.19 + 5.20 + 5.22 + 5.22A 5.23 £

■ Expenses (do not include figures you have already put in boxes 5.2 to 5.7 on Page L1)

● Rent, rates, insurance, ground rents etc.	5.24 £
● Repairs, maintenance and renewals	5.25 £
● Finance charges, including interest	5.26 £
● Legal and professional costs	5.27 £
● Costs of services provided, including wages	5.28 £
● Other expenses	5.29 £

total of boxes 5.24 to 5.29
5.30 £

box 5.23 minus box 5.30
5.31 £

Net profit (put figures in brackets if a loss)

■ Tax adjustments

● Private use — 5.32 £

● Balancing charges - including those arising under Business Premises Renovation Allowance which should also be included in box 23.8 — 5.33 £

box 5.32 + box 5.33
5.34 £

● Rent a Room exempt amount — 5.35 £

● Capital allowances - including those arising under Business Premises Renovation Allowance which should also be included in box 23.7 — 5.36 £

● Tick box 5.36A if box 5.36 includes a claim for 100% capital allowances for flats over shops — 5.36A

● Tick box 5.36B if box 5.36 includes enhanced capital allowances for designated environmentally beneficial plant and machinery — 5.36B

● Landlord's Energy Saving Allowance — 5.36C £

● 10% wear and tear — 5.37 £

● Furnished holiday lettings losses — copy from box 5.18 — 5.38 £

total of boxes 5.35 to 5.38
5.39 £

Adjusted profit (if a loss, enter '0' in box 5.40 and put the loss in box 5.41)

boxes 5.31 + 5.34 minus box 5.39
5.40 £

Adjusted loss (if you have entered '0' in box 5.40)

boxes 5.31 + 5.34 minus box 5.39
5.41 £

● Loss brought forward from previous year — 5.42 £

Profit for the year

box 5.40 minus box 5.42
5.43 £

■ Losses etc.

● Loss offset against total income - read the note on page LN8 — 5.44 £

● Loss to carry forward to following year — 5.45 £

● Tick box 5.46 if these Pages include details of property let jointly — 5.46

● Tick box 5.47 if all property income ceased in the year to 5 April 2007 and you do not expect to receive such income again, in the year to 5 April 2008 — 5.47

Now fill in any other supplementar y Pages that apply to you.
Otherwise, go back to page 2 of your Tax Return and finish filling it in.

Your 2006-07 Capital Gains Tax liability

A Brief description of asset	AA* Type of disposal. Enter Q, U, L, T or O	B Tick box if estimate or valuation used	C Tick box if asset held at 31March 1982	D Enter the later of date of acquisition and 16 March 1998	E Enter the date of disposal	F Disposal proceeds	G Enter details of any elections made, reliefs claimed or due and state amount (£)
Gains on assets which are either wholly business or wholly non-business							
1				/ /	/ /	£	
2				/ /	/ /	£	
3				/ /	/ /	£	
4				/ /	/ /	£	
5				/ /	/ /	£	
6				/ /	/ /	£	
7				/ /	/ /	£	
8				/ /	/ /	£	
Gains on assets which are partly business and partly non-business (see the notes on page CGN4)							
9				/ /	/ /	£	
10				/ /	/ /	£	

* Column AA for:
- quoted shares or other securities, (see the definition on page CGN3 of the Notes) enter Q
- other shares or securities, enter U
- land and property, enter L
- amounts attributable to settlor (see page CGN4) enter T
- other assets (for example, goodwill), enter O

Complete Pages CG4 to CG6 for all U, L and O transactions

Losses

Brief description of asset	Type of * disposal. Enter Q, U, L or O	Tick box if estimate or valuation used	Tick box if asset held at 31March 1982	Enter the later of date of acquisition and 16 March 1998	Enter the date of disposal	Disposal proceeds	Enter details of any elections made, reliefs claimed or due and state amount (£)
13				/ /	/ /	£	
14				/ /	/ /	£	
15				/ /	/ /	£	
16				/ /	/ /	£	

Total losses of

	H Chargeable Gains after reliefs but before losses and taper	I Enter 'Bus' if business asset	J Taper rate	K Losses deducted			L Gains after losses	M Tapered gains (gains from column L x % in column J)
				K1 Allowable losses of the year	K2 Income losses of 2006-07 set against gains	K3 Unused losses b/f from earlier years		
	£		%	£	£	£	£	£
	£		%	£	£	£	£	£
	£		%	£	£	£	£	£
	£		%	£	£	£	£	£
	£		%	£	£	£	£	£
	£		%	£	£	£	£	£
	£		%	£	£	£	£	£
	£		%	£	£	£	£	£
	£	Bus	%	£	£	£	£	£
	£		%	£	£	£	£	£
	£	Bus	%	£	£	£	£	£
	£		%	£	£	£	£	£

Total 8.1 £ — Total column H

8.5 £ — Total column K2

8.6 £ — Total column K3

8.3 £ — Total column M

11 Attributed gains from non-resident trusts where liable as beneficiary (see page CGN4) (enter the names of the Trusts on Page CG7) £

12 Attributed gains from settlor interested trusts where personal losses cannot be set off (see page CGN4) (enter the names of the Trusts on Page CG7) £

Total of attributed gains where personal losses cannot be set off (total of rows 11 and 12) 8.4 £

box 8.3 + box 8.4

Total taxable gains (after allowable losses and taper relief) £

Copy to box 8.7 on Page CG8 and complete Pages CG4 to CG6 for all U, L and O transactions

Losses arising

£
£
£
£

year 8.2 £

Copy to box 8.10 on Page CG8 and, unless you need only complete the totals boxes (see page CGN5), complete column K1

Chargeable gains and allowable losses

Once you have completed Page CG1, or Pages CG2 to CG6, fill in this Page.

Have you 'ticked' any row in Column B, 'Tick box if estimate or valuation used' on Pages CG1 or CG2 or in Column C on Page CG2 'Tick box if asset held at 31 March 1982'?	YES
Have you given details in Column G on Pages CG2 and CG3 of any Capital Gains reliefs claimed or due?	YES
Are you claiming, and/or using, any clogged losses (see Notes, page CGN11)?	YES

Enter from Page CG1 or column AA on Page CG2:

- the number of transactions in quoted shares or other securities — box Q
- the number of transactions in other shares or securities — box U
- the number of transactions in land and property — box L
- the number of gains attributed to settlor — box T
- the number of other transactions — box O

Total taxable gains (from box F7 on page CG1, or boxes 8.3 + 8.4 on page CG3)	8.7	£
Your taxable gains minus the annual exempt amount c (leave blank if '0' or negative)	8.8	£
Additional liability in respect of non-resident or dual resident trusts (see Notes, page CGN7)	8.9	£

author's note: the annual exempt amount in 2007/08 was £9,200

Capital losses

(If your loss arose on a transaction with a connected person, see page CGN14, you can only set that loss against gains you make on disposals to that same connected person. See the notes on clogged losses on page CGN11.)

■ This year's losses

- Total (normally from box 8.2 on Page CG3 or box F2 on Page CG1. But, if you have clogged losses, see Notes, page CGN11) — 8.10 £
- Used against gains (total of column K1 on Page CG3, or the smaller of boxes F1 and F2 on Page CG1) — 8.11 £
- Used against earlier years' gains (generally only available to personal representatives, see Notes, page CGN11) — 8.12 £
- Used against income (only losses of the type described on page CGN10 can be used against income) — 8.13A £ amount claimed against income of 2006-07 — 8.13B £ amount claimed against income of 2005-06 — box 8.13A + box 8.13B 8.13 £
- This year's unused losses — box 8.10 minus (boxes 8.11 + 8.12 + 8.13) 8.14 £

■ Summary of earlier years' losses

- Unused losses of 1996-97 and later years — 8.15 £
- Used this year (losses from box 8.15 are used in priority to losses from box 8.18) (column K3 on Page CG3 or box F6 on Page CG1) — 8.16 £
- Remaining unused losses of 1996-97 and later years — box 8.15 minus box 8.16 8.17 £
- Unused losses of 1995-96 and earlier years — 8.18 £
- Used this year (losses from box 8.15 are used in priority to losses from box 8.18) (column K3 on Page CG3 or box F6 on Page CG1) — box 8.6 minus box 8.16 (or box F6 minus box 8.16) 8.19 £

■ Total of unused losses to carry forward

- Carried forward losses of 1996-97 and later years — box 8.14 + box 8.17 8.20 £
- Carried forward losses of 1995-96 and earlier years — box 8.18 minus box 8.19 8.21 £

Index

for your notes